MONTGOMERY COLLEGE
TAKOMA PARK CAMPUS LIBRARY
TAKOMA PARK, MARYLAND

DICTIONARY
OF
U.S. GOVERNMENT
STATISTICAL TERMS

Alfred N. Garwood
Senior Editor

Louise L. Hornor
Editor

information
publications

SEP 2 8 1992

ISBN 0-931845-24-6 (paper)
ISBN 0-931845-25-4 (library)

© 1991 Information Publications
printed in the United States of America

All rights reserved. No part of this
book may be reproduced or transmitted in
any form or by any means, electronic or
mechanical, including photocopying and
recording, or by any information storage
and retrieval system without permission
in writing from the publisher.

Information Publications
3790 El Camino Real, Ste. 162
Palo Alto, CA 94306-3389
(415) 965-4449

DICTIONARY
OF
U.S. GOVERNMENT
STATISTICAL TERMS

WITHDRAWN

TABLE OF CONTENTS

INTRODUCTION

The Dictionary of U.S. Government Statistical Terms was conceived as an aid to non-specialist data users: students, researchers, librarians, and businesspeople. When using a statistical publication of the federal government and coming across a term whose meaning is unclear in the context of that table or report, such users can turn to this Dictionary for simple, clear, definitions of the most commonly occurring terms in regular government serial publications. Dictionary of U.S. Government Statistical Terms is meant to serve as a basic guide to the terms found in such diverse government publications as Statistical Abstract, Survey of Current Business, and Census Bureau products.

In preparing to compile the Dictionary, two central distinctions were drawn at the outset. First, there is a difference between providing a definition of a term and summarizing the methodology of how the data that the term defines was collected. The Dictionary's role is to concentrate on providing the definition and includes the methodology only when it is necessary to secure an understanding of the term and how it is used in a specific federal publication.

Second, there is a difference between a dictionary and an encyclopedia. The goal of this work is to provide definitions extensive enough so that the user has an understanding of what is meant by a term, but not so comprehensive that each entry extensively explains the concepts and context surrounding the term. Expanded entries which describe the history and background of the concept are included only to the extent that they are required to provide meaningful basic definitions.

To be included in the Dictionary, a term had to meet one or more of the following criteria. A term is included if it has a specialized meaning in government usage, even though it may have a well understood sense in ordinary English. This specialized meaning clearly determines one's understanding of the data presented. Words such as *household* and *establishment* fall into this category. A term is included if it is used extensively in a wide variety of federal publications. *Personal income* and *megawatt* are examples of such terms.

There are also some very short definitions provided for generally understood concepts such as *government appropriation* and *life expectancy* which are necessary to the understanding of some specialized terms in the Dictionary. These are basically secondary terms, definitions data users would seek after reading a definition of the primary term they were seeking to define.

The Dictionary also contains a number of explanations of federal survey programs, most typically those regular programs conducted by the Bureau of the Census and the Department of Labor Statistics. Although the entry for, say, the Current Population Survey (CPS), is longer that it needs to be for strictly definitional purposes, the inclusion of certain background information is essential for Dictionary users to understand what role the CPS plays and how this role affects terms and concepts.

A few of the most commonly encountered terms from the field of statistics, such as *mean* and *median,* are included. Terms which require more than a basic knowledge of mathematics to understand are left to statistics textbooks.

The following types of terms were, as a rule, excluded from this Dictionary. Where the distinction between the government's use of a term and its common English definition lies primarily in the data-collection methodology, the term is not included. An example of this type of excluded term is *vault cash.* The term is self-explanatory as the cash a bank has on hand in its vaults; further explanation would involve methodological details such as when the cash is counted, whether this is a weekly average, etc. No definition is provided for terms and classifications that appear in standard government classification manuals like the Dictionary of Occupational Titles (DOT), the Standard Industrial Classification Manual (SIC), and the Standard Occupational Classification Manual (SOC). These terms are part of a numbered or otherwise specially ordered classification scheme. Ratios and indexes are usually not defined, except in cases where the meaning of the terms used in the ratio or index title needs definition. Also excluded are specialized terms that appear in studies that have been conducted only once or are conducted less frequently than once every two years, and terms from those surveys done in cooperation with a non-government entity such as a research organization or university which do not appear frequently and are not of general interest. Words and terms in surveys of a highly specialized nature, especially from studies in the sciences, medicine, engineering, and certain aspects of financial accounting, which are not likely to confront ordinary data users are not included here, even though such surveys are done by government agencies and appear regularly.

Even with strict adherence to the above guidelines, and despite all efforts to avoid this fate, the Dictionary may retain a certain eclecticism, reflecting to some extent the interests and biases of the editor. Hopefully such biases of selection are small, and that all important terms are defined fully here. As was stated at the outset, the central purpose of this Dictionary is to provide answers to the first questions a user of government statistical data has about the meaning of government terminology.

Within the constraints outlined above, the Dictionary provides for these needs by answering five basic questions about a term: which government agency defines the term, cited in square brackets; in what way is the federal government's usage special; what is excluded and included by the meaning of this term; how does the methodology of the underlying data collection procedure affect the definition of this term; and what other terms and concepts are closely related to the term, cited after **See** or **See also**.

Readers should pay careful attention to the department credited with the definition. Unfortunately not every government department uses a word in the same way, and even within an agency, definitions can vary from program to program. In looking for a definition in this Dictionary data users should be armed with both the term they seek to define, and the original survey source where it is used (e.g., employment, from the Current Population Survey).

The definitions provided here are based on printed materials published by federal government departments. These publications are listed in the bibliography and the department defining the term is cited in brackets as the first part of each entry. In some cases, the definition was taken verbatim from an agency glossary, particularly Census Bureau terminology and crime terminology from the Bureau of Justice Statistics. In other cases, a definition was constructed from methodological explanations of data collection programs, produced by the government agency. In a few cases, where the department provided no published definition or provided an unclear or self-contradictory definition, the agency itself had to be contacted.

A few definitions are taken from publications of non-government data collection agencies. This is due to the fact that the federal data for these categories of information is reprinted from private-sector publications. Included in this small group of definitions are certain hospital terms based on data collected by the American Hospital Association, and certain business measures from Dun & Bradstreet and McGraw Hill.

In writing the definitions the aim has been to provide users of this volume with as complete and accurate a presentation as is possible of the way a federal agency uses a term. This has been done without editorial comment. As a matter of style, the flavor of the federal departments' prose has been left intact to a good degree, and has been edited only when the original bureaucratese served to obscure rather than clarify the department's meaning. Although much government terminology is shrugged off as silly or self important, often what appears to be wordiness is actually an effective way of drawing important distinctions and clarifying concepts.

In closing, it should be pointed out that this Dictionary was compiled for federal document to Dictionary use; i.e., it presumes the user starts with a term which requires definition, and then turns to this Dictionary. Although it may work to use it the other way around due to the numerous **See** and **See also** references, the Dictionary is not intended for someone who starts with a general question about terminology and wonders what related or specialized words and terms the federal government uses to describe and define that concept.

LIST OF ABBREVIATIONS

ADA	average daily attendance
ADC	average daily census
ADM	average daily membership
AFDC	Aid to Families with Dependent Children
AHA	American Hospital Association
AHS	American Housing Survey
AMA	American Medical Association
ANRC	Alaska Native Regional Corporation
ANVSA	Alaska Native Village Statistical Area
AOA	American Osteopathic Association
ASM	Annual Survey of Manufactures
ASTM	American Society for Testing and Materials
BCD	Business Conditions Digest
BEA	Bureau of Economic Analysis
BHP	Bureau of Health Professionals
BJS	Bureau of Justice Statistics
BLS	Bureau of Labor Statistics
BNA	block numbering area
Btu	British thermal unit
CBD	central business district
CCD	census county division
CD	certificate of deposit *or* Congressional district
CDC	Centers for Disease Control
CDP	census designated place
CES	Current Employment Statistics program
CEX	Consumer Expenditure Survey
CHINS	children in need of supervision
c.i.f.	cost, insurance, and freight
CLF	civilian labor force
CMHC	federally funded community mental health center
CMSA	Consolidated Metropolitan Statistical Area
CPI	Consumer Price Index
CPI-U	Consumer Price Index for urban consumers
CPI-W	Consumer Price Index for urban wage and clerical workers
CPS	Current Population Survey
DIME	dual independent map encoding
DOT	Dictionary of Occupational Titles
DSM-III	Diagnostic and Statistical Manual of Mental Disorders, 3rd Edition
EBS	Employee Benefits Survey
ECI	Employment Cost Index

ED	census enumeration district
ENR	Engineering News-Record
f.a.s.	free alongside ship
FBI	Federal Bureau of Investigation
FHA	Federal Housing Administration
FICA	Federal Insurance Contribution Act
FIPS	Federal Information Processing Standards
FNMA	Federal National Mortgage Association
FTE	full time equivalent
FY	fiscal year
GBF/DIME	geographic base file/dual independent map encoding
GED	General Education Development
GNP	Gross National Product
GPO	Government Printing Office
GW	gigawatt
GWh	gigawatthour
HHS	Department of Health and Human Services
HMO	health maintenance organization
HUD	Housing and Urban Development
ICD	International Classification of Diseases, Ninth Edition
ICD-9-CM	International Classification of Diseases, Ninth Edition, Clinical Modification
ICDA-8	International Classification of Diseases, Ninth Revision, Adapted for Use in the United States
IFR	instrument flight rules
IMF	International Monetary Fund
I-O	input-output accounts
IPA	Individual Practice Association
JINS	juvenile in need of supervision
kW	kilowatt
kWh	kilowatthour
LIFO	last-in, first out
LMA	labor market area
LNA	Leading National Advertisers
LPG	liquified petroleum gas
MA	Metropolitan Area
MCD	minor civil division
MINS	minor in need of supervision
MMDA	money market deposit account
MMMF	money market mutual fund
MMWR	Morbidity and Mortality Weekly Report
MRC	major retail center
MSA	Metropolitan Statistical Area

MW	megawatt
MWh	megawatthour
NAB	Newspaper Advertising Bureau
NAMCS	National Ambulatory Medical Care Survey
NCHS	National Center for Health Statistics
NCS	National Crime Survey
n.e.c.	not elsewhere classified
NECMA	New England County Metropolitan Area
NHANES	National Health and Nutrition Examination Survey
NHDS	National Hospital Discharge Survey
NHES	National Health Examination Survey
NHIS	National Health Interview Survey
NIP	National Income Product Account
NIPA	National Income Product Accounts
NMCUES	National Medical Care Utilization and Expenditure Survey
NMFI	National Master Facility Inventory
NNHS	National Nursing Home Study
NPS	National Prisoner Statistics program
NTIS	National Technical Information Service
OBSCIS	Offender-Based State Corrections Information System
OES	Occupational Employment Statistics survey
OMB	Office of Management and the Budget
OSHA	Occupational Safety and Health Administration
PATC	National Survey of Professional, Administrative, Technical, and Clerical Pay
PHS	Public Health Service
PINS	persons in need of supervision
PMSA	Primary Metropolitan Statistical Area
PPI	Producer Price Index
RP	repurchase agreement
RTC	residential treatment center for emotionally disturbed children
SAT	scholastic aptitude test
SDR	Special Drawing Rights
SEUA	Special Economic Urban Area
SHA	State health agency
SIC	Standard Industrial Classification
SIPP	Survey of Income and Program Participation
SMSA	Standard Metropolitan Statistical Area
SNG	synthetic natural gas
SOC	Standard Occupational Classification
SOP	stage of processing
SSA	Social Security Administration
SSI	Supplemental Security Income
STOL	short takeoff and landing aircraft

TDSA	tribal designated statistical area
TIGER	Topologically Integrated Geographic Encoding and Referencing
TJSA	tribal jurisdiction statistical area
UA	urbanized area
UCFE	Unemployment Compensation for Federal Employees program
UCR	Uniform Crime Reports
UI	unemployment insurance
UPR	Uniform Parole Reports
VFR	visual flight rules
VTD	voting district
W	watt
Wh	watthour
WHO	World Health Organization

DICTIONARY
OF
U.S. GOVERNMENT
STATISTICAL TERMS

A

abortion (legal) [Department of Health and Human Services-Public Health Service; National Center for Health Statistics] A legal abortion is a procedure causing the expulsion of a fetus from the womb, performed by a licensed physician, or someone acting under the supervision of a licensed physician. There are two main sources for data on legal abortions that appear in federal publications. The first source is the Centers for Disease Control (CDC) which collects data from central health agencies, hospitals and other medical facilities, as well as from the National Center for Health Statistics (NCHS). The second is a private organization, the Alan Guttmacher Institute, which conducts an annual survey of abortion providers. The Guttmacher Institute's data are collected from a survey universe of 3,092 hospitals, non-hospital clinics, and physicians identified as providers of abortion services. Over recent years, the number of abortions estimated by the Guttmacher Institute has been about 20% higher than the number reported to the CDC. The Guttmacher figures are perhaps the more widely used, and are published in the Bureau of the Census' Statistical Abstract of the United States. They include totals for the nation as a whole, as well as the 50 States and the District of Columbia. The data originally appears in the Institute's publication, Family Planning Perspectives.

absence (student) [Department of Education-National Center for Education Statistics] An absence is the non-attendance of a student on a day or half-day when school is in session. Absences are frequently counted to the nearest half-day or half-session.

See also **day of absence.**

accreditation (education) [Department of Education-National Center for Education Statistics] Accreditation is an official decision by a State Department of Education or other recognized agency having authority that, in its judgment, a given educational unit has met established standards of quality. These standards may or may not have legal status.

achievement test [Department of Education-Center for Education Statistics] An achievement test is an examination that measures the extent to which a person has acquired certain information or mastered certain skills, usually as a result of specific instruction.

acreage allotment [Department of Agriculture-Office of Governmental and Public Affairs] An acreage allotment is an individual farm's share, based on its previous production, of the national acreage needed to produce sufficient supplies of a particular crop. Allotments apply only to four crops: peanuts, rice, extra long staple cotton, and tobacco.

active aircraft [Department of Transportation-Federal Aviation Administration] All legally registered aircraft which flew one or more hours during a given reporting period are counted as active aircraft. Data for active aircraft are reported by the Federal Aviation Administration on an annual basis.

active physician see **physician.**

acute condition see **condition (health).**

ADA see **average daily attendance (ADA).**

ADC see **average daily census (ADC) (hospital).**

additions (inpatient) [Department of Health and Human Services-Public Health Service; Alcohol, Drug Abuse, and Mental Health Administration] Inpatient additions is a measure of the number of persons admitted or readmitted to inpatient services during a given reporting period. Additions also include those persons returned from long term leave or transferred from non-inpatient components of organizations (e.g. outpatient, or partial care) to inpatient status. Each time a person is admitted, readmitted, or returns from long term leave during a survey year it is counted as an addition.
   See also **admission (hospital).**

additions (non-inpatient) [Department of Health and Human Services-Public Health Service; Alcohol, Drug Abuse, and Mental Health Administration] Non-inpatient additions is a measure of the number of persons admitted or readmitted to outpatient or partial care settings or transferred to one of these settings from another organization or another setting with the same organization during a survey year.

adjusted base period price [Department of Agriculture-Office of Governmental and Public Affairs] The adjusted base period price is the average price received by farmers in the most recent 10 years divided by the index of average prices received by farmers for all farm products in the same ten years. 1910-1914 = 100 in this calculation. The adjusted base period price is used in parity calculations.
   See also **parity index; parity price; parity ratio.**

ADM see **average daily membership (ADM).**

admission (hospital) [American Hospital Association] Admission is a measure of the number of inpatients, excluding newborns, accepted for inpatient service in a hospital. The number of admissions is reported for a given period, usually a calendar year.

adult [Department of Justice-Bureau of Justice Statistics] In criminal justice usage, an adult is a person who is within the original jurisdiction of a criminal, rather than a juvenile, court because his or her age was above a statutorily specified limit at the time of the alleged commission of a criminal act.

advertising cost see **magazine advertising cost; newspaper advertising expenditures.**

advertising index see **help-wanted advertising index.**

AFDC see **Aid to Families with Dependent Children.**

aftercare (corrections) [Department of Justice-Bureau of Justice Statistics] In juvenile justice usage, aftercare is the status or program membership of a juvenile who has been committed to a treatment or confinement facility, conditionally released from the facility, and placed in a supervisory and/or treatment program. Aftercare is also known as *juvenile parole.*

age (persons) [Department of Commerce-Bureau of the Census] For Census Bureau surveys, the age of persons is reported as age at last birthday, i.e. age in completed years. It is often calculated by subtracting the date of birth from the reference date. The reference date is the date of the examination, interview, or other contact with the individual.

age adjustment [Department of Health and Human Services-Public Health Service; National Center for Health Statistics] Age adjustment is a statistical method used to account for differences in a population due to age. Using the direct method, age adjustment is the application of the age specific rates in a population of interest to a standardized age distribution in order to eliminate the differences in observed rates that result from age differences in population composition. This adjustment is usually done when comparing two or more populations at one point in time, or one population at two or more points in time. Death rates are frequently age adjusted.

agency and private trust transaction [Department of Commerce-Bureau of the Census] In state and local financial accounting, an agency and private trust transaction is a transaction which involves the receipt, holding, and disbursement of money by the government as agent or trustee for other governments, or private persons. For example, the collection of local government taxes by a State government agency, or collection of Federal income taxes and social security payments by a State or local government both fall under the category of agency and private trust transactions. The Census Bureau in its reporting of government finance typically excludes agency and private trust transactions from calculations.

agency security [Federal Reserve Bank of New York] An agency security is a bond or note that is an obligation of a federal agency or corporation (e.g., Export-Import Bank; Federal Housing Administration; Federal National Mortgage Association) which involves government sponsorship or guarantee, but is not a direct obligation of the U.S. Treasury.

agents, brokers, and commission merchants see **wholesale trade.**

aggravated assault 1. [Department of Justice-Bureau of Justice Statistics] As used in the Uniform Crime Reports (UCR) to describe post-arrest statistics, aggravated assault is the unlawful intentional causing of bodily injury with or without a deadly weapon, or the unlawful intentional attempting or threatening of serious bodily injury or death with a deadly or dangerous weapon. Attempted murder and assault to commit murder are classified in the UCR as aggravated assault, UCR 4. Assault for the unlawful taking of property is classified as robbery. Assault to commit rape is classified as forcible rape. Assaults where no dangerous or deadly weapon is used and no serious injury is inflicted are classified as UCR 9, other assaults-simple, not aggravated. Aggravated assault is a violent crime, a Part I offense, and a UCR Crime Index offense.

2. The National Crime Survey (NCS) defines aggravated assault as an attack with a weapon resulting in any injury or any attack without a weapon resulting either in serious injury (e.g., broken bones, loss of teeth, internal injuries, loss of consciousness) or in undetermined injury requiring two or more days of hospitalization. Also included in the NCS definition of aggravated assaults are attempted assaults with a weapon. Assaults for the purpose of effecting rape are classified as rape; those for the purpose of effecting robbery as personal robbery.

See also **assault; crime index; National Crime Survey (NCS); Part I offenses; personal crimes; personal robbery; rape; Uniform Crime Reports (UCR).**

aggravating circumstance [Department of Justice-Bureau of Justice Statistics] A circumstance relating to the commission of a crime which causes its gravity to be greater than that of the average instance of the given type of offense is considered an aggravating circumstance. Examples of aggravating circumstances are the causing of serious bodily injury, the use of a deadly or dangerous weapon, or the accidental or intentional commission of one crime in the course of committing another crime, or as a means of committing another crime. Aggravating circumstances may be formally or informally considered by a judge or paroling authority in deciding the sentence for a convicted person within the penalty range provided by statute for a given offense. An aggravating circumstance is the opposite of a mitigating circumstance.

See also **mitigating circumstance.**

aggregate payrolls [Department of Labor-Bureau of Labor Statistics] Aggregate payrolls is a measure of pay to employees in non-agricultural establishments. Aggregate payrolls includes pay before deductions for Social Security, unemployment insurance, group insurance, withholding tax, salary reduction plans, bonds, and union dues. It includes pay for overtime, shift premiums, holidays, vacations, and sick leave, paid directly by the employer to the employee for the pay period surveyed. Excluded are bonuses unless earned and paid regularly each pay period, other pay not earned in the pay period, tips, and the value of free rent, fuel, meals, or other payments in kind. The information used to compile aggregate payrolls is based on data from the Current Employment Statistics (CES) program.

See also **Current Employment Statistics (CES) program.**

agreement corporation [Federal Reserve Bank of New York] An agreement corporation is a state chartered U.S. corporation which engages in international banking and finance and does not accept domestic deposits. In practice, agreement corporations are usually majority owned by a U.S. banking organization.

See also **Edge Act corporation.**

AHS see **American Housing Survey (AHS).**

Aid to Families with Dependent Children (AFDC) [Department of Health and Human Services-Social Security Administration] Aid to Families with Dependent Children (AFDC) is a program administered by the Social Security Administration which provides cash assistance to needy families with children who have been deprived of support and care because of parental death or absence. In some States, families with children who have been deprived of support and care because of parental unemployment are eligible for AFDC assistance.

air carrier [Department of Transportation-Federal Aviation Administration] An air carrier is one of all aircraft operators which, taken as a group, comprise the nation's commercial air transport system. The Federal Aviation Administration collects and publishes data concerning air carriers, which are comprised of five component groups:

A *certified route air carrier* holds a Certificate of Public Convenience and Necessity issued by the Civil Aeronautics Board authorizing the performance of scheduled service over specified routes, and a limited amount of non-scheduled service.

An *air taxi* is a carrier which transports persons, property, and mail using aircraft under 30 seats or with a maximum payload capacity of less than 7,500 pounds. An air taxi does not hold a Certificate of Public Convenience and Necessity nor economic authority as issued by the Civil Aeronautics Board. A commuter air carrier is an air taxi which performs at least five round trip flights per week between two or more points and publishes flight schedules which specify the times, days of the week, and points between which such flights are performed.

A *supplemental air carrier* holds a Certificate of Public Convenience and Necessity issued by the Civil Aeronautics Board, authorizing the performance of passenger and cargo charter services supplementing the scheduled service of the certified route air carriers.

A *commercial operator* is a person who, for compensation or for hire, engages in the carriage of aircraft in air commerce of persons or property other than as a certified route carrier, air taxi, supplemental air carrier, or foreign air carrier. Commercial operators of large aircraft (reported as a separate sub-group by the FAA) are those operating aircraft of more than 12,500 pounds maximum takeoff weight.

An *air travel club* is an operator who engages in the carriage by airplanes of persons who are required to qualify for that carriage by payment of an assessment, dues, membership fee, or similar type of remittance.

See also **aircraft operator**.

air taxi see **air carrier**.

air traffic hub [Department of Transportation-Federal Aviation Administration] An air traffic hub is not an airport, but a city or Metropolitan Area (MA) which requires aviation services. Air traffic hubs are divided into four classes as determined by their percentage of the total enplaned passengers in scheduled service of the fixed-wing operations of domestic certified route air carriers in the United States.

Large air traffic hubs are those with 1% or more of the total enplaned passengers; *medium air traffic hubs* are those enplaning from 0.25% to 0.99% of total enplaned passengers; *small air traffic hubs* are those enplaning from 0.05% to 0.24% of the total enplaned passengers; and *non-hubs* are those enplaning less than 0.05% of the total enplaned passengers.

air travel club see **air carrier**.

aircraft accident [Department of Transportation-Federal Aviation Administration] As defined by the National Transportation Safety Board, an aircraft accident is an occurrence associated with the operation of an aircraft which: takes place between the time any person boards the aircraft with the intention of flight, until the time all such persons have disembarked; and, in which any person suffers death or serious injury as a result of being in or upon the aircraft, or by direct contact with the aircraft or anything attached thereto. Aircraft accidents also include occurrences in which an aircraft receives substantial damage. The Board further defines at length what it means by both serious injury to persons and substantial damage to aircraft.

ircraft operation [Department of Transportation-Federal Aviation Administration] An aircraft operation is the takeoff or landing of an aircraft. Operations are classified into two types, local operations and itinerant operations. *Local operations* are those which: operate either in the local traffic pattern or within sight of the airport; or, are known to be departing for, or arriving from, flight in local practice areas within a 20-mile radius of the airport; or, execute simulated instrument approaches or low passes at the airport. *Itinerant operations* are all non-local operations.

rcraft operator [Department of Transportation-Federal Aviation Administration] An aircraft operator is any person or legal person who causes or authorizes the operation of an aircraft, such as the owner, lessee, or bailee of an aircraft. An aircraft operator may or may not be a pilot.

rcraft type [Department of Transportation-Federal Aviation Administration] Aircraft are classified into five major types: *fixed-wing aircraft, rotorcraft, gliders, dirigibles,* and *balloons.*

rman [Department of Transportation-Federal Aviation Administration] An airman is a pilot, mechanic, or other licensed aviation technician.

rport [Department of Transportation-Federal Aviation Administration] An airport is an area of land or water that is used or intended to be used for the landing and takeoff of aircraft, and includes its buildings and facilities.

laska Native Regional Corporation (ANRC) [Department of Commerce-Bureau of the Census] An Alaska Native Regional Corporation (ANRC) is a corporate entity established under the Alaska Native Claims Settlement Act of 1972 to conduct both business and nonprofit affairs of Alaska Natives. Alaska is divided into 12 ANRC's that cover the entire State, except for the Annette Islands Reserve. The ANRC boundaries for the 1990 census were identified by the Bureau of Land Management. Each ANRC was designed to include Alaska Natives with a common heritage and common interests.

See also **Alaska Native Village Statistical Area (ANVSA)**.

laska Native Village Statistical Area (ANVSA) [Department of Commerce-Bureau of the Census] An Alaska Native Village Statistical Area (ANVSA) is a Census

Bureau-defined area which encompasses the settled area associated with an Alaska Native village (ANV). ANV's constitute tribes, bands, clans, groups, villages, communities, or associations in Alaska that are recognized by the Alaska Native Claims Settlement Act of 1972. ANVSA's are located within Alaska Native Regional Corporations (ANRC's) and do not cross ANRC boundaries.
ANVSA's for the 1990 census replace the ANV's from the 1980 census.
See also **Alaska Native Regional Corporation (ANRC)**.

Aleut see **race**.

all employees [Department of Labor-Bureau of Labor Statistics] All employees is a Current Employment Statistics (CES) classification used for reporting both employment, and hours and earnings data by industry and geographic area. All employees is an inclusive grouping of workers encompassing all persons who meet the program criteria of an employed person. However, in conformance with CES methodology, all employees excludes proprietors, pensioners, unpaid family workers, partners of unincorporated firms, persons on strike, and persons on unpaid leave. CES employment, hours and earnings data is also reported for constituent sub-groups of all employees, which include such classifications as production workers, construction workers, and non-supervisory workers, depending upon the subject industry. The concept of all employees is also used in the economic censuses conducted every five years by the Bureau of the Census.
See also **Current Employment Statistics (CES) program; employed persons**.

ambulatory care visit [Department of Health and Human Services-Public Health Service; Alcohol, Drug Abuse, and Mental Health Administration] An ambulatory care visit is a direct, personal visit by an ambulatory patient to a health care provider in the provider's office, a hospital outpatient department or emergency room, or a health center or clinic.

American Housing Survey (AHS) [Department of Commerce-Bureau of the Census] The American Housing Survey (AHS), formerly the Annual Housing Survey, is a Census Bureau survey designed to provide current and continuous data on selected characteristics of the nation's housing and housing-related demographic information. The survey has a core section which focuses directly on housing with periodic survey supplements on housing-related topics such as energy conservation and neighborhood quality.
There are two parts of AHS: a national sample, conducted biennially over a three month period of approximately 62,000 housing units; and a metropolitan survey covering approximately 222,000 units in 44 Metropolitan Areas (MA's) which are interviewed annually on a rotating basis over a four-year period. Data for both parts cover occupied as well as vacant housing units.

The Census Bureau conducts this survey for the Department of Housing and Urban Development, and survey results are published in a number of places, primarily in the Census Bureau's series American Housing Survey.

American Indian, Eskimo and Aleut see **race**.

American Indian reservation [Department of Commerce-Bureau of the Census] An American Indian reservation is a unit of census geography whose boundaries were identified for the 1990 census by the Bureau of Indian Affairs, Department of Interior, and State governments. An American Indian reservation is a minor civil division (MCD) in Maine and New York. There are two types of American Indian reservations, Federal and State.

An *Federal reservation* is an area with boundaries established by treaty, statute, or executive or court order. It is recognized by the Federal government as territory in which American Indian tribes have jurisdiction. Federal reservations may cross State, county, county subdivision, or place boundaries.

A *State reservation* is land held in trust by State government for the use and benefit of a given tribe. State reservations may cross county, county subdivision, or place boundaries, but not State boundaries.

See also **minor civil division (MCD); tribal designated statistical area (TDSA); tribal jurisdiction statistical area (TJSA); trust land.**

ancestry [Department of Commerce-Bureau of the Census] Ancestry is a person's self-identified origin, descent, lineage, nationality group, or country in which the person or person's parents or ancestors were born before their arrival in the United States. Questions about ancestry were asked on a sample basis as an open-ended write-in item for the 1980 Census of Population.

animal unit [Department of Agriculture-Office of Governmental and Public Affairs] An animal unit is a standard measure based on feed requirements used to combine various classes of livestock according to size, weight, age, and use.

Annual Survey of Hospitals [Department of Health and Human Services-Public Health Service; National Center for Health Statistics] The Annual Survey of Hospitals is not sponsored by any federal government agency but is conducted annually by the American Hospital Association (AHA). However, use of the survey results is widespread in federal publications, and is the main source of current, detailed information about facilities, beds, length of stay, staffing, and hospital costs for the nation. Results of the survey are published annually by the AHA in Hospital Statistics. Portions of survey results are also published annually in the Bureau of the Census' Statistical Abstract of the United States and in the National Center for Health Statistics' Health, United States.

Annual Survey of Manufactures (ASM) [Department of Commerce-Bureau of the Census]   The Annual Survey of Manufactures (ASM) presents key measures of manufacturing activity for industry groups and important industries individually. Its purpose is to provide a continuous series of basic statistics for manufactures as well as furnishing benchmarks for current business indicators and for measures of industrial production and productivity. The ASM has been conducted in each of the intercensal years since 1949 by the Bureau of the Census.

Each year, the ASM is published as a multi-volume statistical series which provides detailed data on all employees, production workers, payrolls, production worker hours, value added by manufacturing, cost of materials, value of shipments, inventories, and other key indicators of manufacturing industries. ASM data is also widely used and reprinted by the federal government, perhaps most notably in Statistical Abstract of the United States.

Currently, the ASM is made up of two components. The first is a mail survey of about 56,000 manufacturing establishments representing a total of approximately 220,000 establishments. These 220,000 establishments represent all manufacturing establishments of multi-unit companies along with all single-unit manufacturing establishments mailed schedules for the last economic census.

The non-mail survey includes all single-unit establishments that were tabulated as administrative records for the last Census of Manufactures. Although this portion contains approximately 140,000 establishments, it accounts for less than 2% of the estimated total value of manufacturing shipments. Data for this group is not sampled; instead, estimates are prepared for every establishment in the group based on selected information obtained under confidentiality constraints from the records of the Internal Revenue Service and the Social Security Administration. The corresponding estimates for the mail and non-mail surveys are combined to produce the published figures.

See also **economic census**.

Annual Survey of Occupational Injuries and Illnesses [Department of Labor-Bureau of Labor Statistics]   The Annual Survey of Occupational Injuries and Illnesses is done each year by the Bureau of Labor Statistics and is based on records kept by establishments in compliance with the Occupational Safety and Health (OSHA) Act of 1970. The survey is based on a sample of approximately 280,000 establishments in private industry and focuses on recordable occupational injuries and illnesses as defined by OSHA. The results of the survey are used to compute incidence rates and determine high risk industries. Such results are published in articles in the Monthly Labor Review and in the annual publication Occupational Injuries and Illnesses.

See also **lost workday case; occupational illness; occupational injury**.

ANRC see **Alaska Native Regional Corporation**.

nthracite [Energy Information Administration] Anthracite is a hard, black, lustrous coal containing a high percentage of fixed carbon and a low percentage of volatile matter. Anthracite is often referred to as hard coal. It includes meta-anthracite and semi-anthracite and conforms to ASTM specification D388 for anthracite.
See also **coal.**

NVSA see **Alaska Native Village Statistical Area.**

ppellate court [Department of Justice-Bureau of Justice Statistics] An appellate court is one whose primary function is to review the judgments of other courts and administrative agencies.
See also **court; intermediate appellate court.**

rea wage survey [Department of Labor-Bureau of Labor Statistics] An area wage survey is a survey which is conducted annually or biannually in a sample of metropolitan areas to provide wage data for selected office, professional, technical, maintenance, toolroom, powerplant, material movement, and custodial occupations, that are common to a wide variety of industries in the geographic areas surveyed. The occupations chosen for study are selected to provide a cross-sectional representation of the range of duties and responsibilities associated with white-collar jobs, skilled maintenance trades, and custodial and material movement jobs.
In the surveys, weekly salary data reported for individuals in white collar jobs relate to regular straight-time salaries paid for standard workweeks. Earnings information for plant workers exclude late-shift differentials and premium pay for overtime.
The industry divisions used for area wage surveys include: manufacturing; transportation, communication, and other public utilities; wholesale trade; retail trade; finance, insurance, and real estate; and selected service industries.
The area wage survey program excludes establishments employing fewer than 50 workers. For some areas, an establishment must employ a minimum of 100 workers to be included in the survey.
Survey results are published in Bureau of Labor Statistics Bulletins, reports, news releases, and in Monthly Labor Review.
See also **wages.**

rmed robbery see **personal robbery; robbery.**

rraignment [Department of Justice-Bureau of Justice Statistics] Strictly, an arraignment is the hearing before a court having jurisdiction in a criminal case in which the identity of the defendant is established, the defendant is informed of the charge(s) and of his/her rights, and the defendant is required to enter a plea. In looser, more common, constructions, arraignment is used to mean any appearance in court prior to trial in criminal proceedings.

arrest [Department of Justice-Bureau of Justice Statistics] An arrest is the taking of an adult or juvenile into physical custody by authority of law for the purpose of charging the person with a criminal offense, a delinquent act, or a status offense, terminating with the recording of a specific offense.

This **recommended** Bureau of Justice Statistics (BJS) definition differs from the legal definition of the term in many jurisdictions in that local usage does not require that the action be completed by actual specification of the offense in writing. The BJS definition of arrest also distinguishes this event from those called citations, summonses, field interrogations, or the like.

In the Uniform Crime Reports (UCR) statistics on arrests, all arrests as defined above are included, along with citations. A citation is an instance where a person is cited or summoned by police for criminal acts or is taken into custody on grounds of suspicion and no offense is recorded. However, UCR arrest totals do not include citations for minor traffic offenses, nor do they include the arrests of juveniles.

The UCR classifies arrests as to type of offense and publishes totals in a number of statistical reports, most notably the annual publication Crime in the United States.

See also **Uniform Crime Reports (UCR)**.

arson [Department of Justice-Bureau of Justice Statistics] Arson is the intentional damaging or destruction, or attempted damaging or destruction, by means of fire or explosion of the property of another without the consent of the owner, or of one's own property or that of another with the intent to defraud. Under the Uniform Crime Reports (UCR) system, only burning offenses are included.

It should be noted that arson is unique in UCR reporting. Normally when two or more offenses occur in the same criminal episode, only the most serious offense is counted. When arson is included, both offenses (arson and the most serious non-arson offense) are counted.

Arson is one of the eight Part I offenses, an index crime, and classified UCR 8.

See also **crime; index crime; Uniform Crime Reports (UCR)**.

Asian and Pacific Islanders see **race**.

ASM see **Annual Survey of Manufactures (ASM)**.

asphalt [Energy Information Administration] Asphalt is a dark brown-to-black cement-like material containing bitumens as the predominant constituents, obtained by petroleum processing. The definition includes crude asphalt as well as the following finished products: cements, fluxes, the asphalt content of emulsions exclusive of water, and petroleum distillates blended with asphalt to make cutback asphalts.

assault (simple) [Department of Justice-Bureau of Justice Statistics] Simple assault is the unlawful intentional inflicting, or attempted or threatened inflicting, of injury upon the person of another. Assault, or simple assault, differs from aggravated assault in that aggravated assault concerns serious bodily injury requiring treatment beyond simple first aid.

Historically, assault meant only the attempt or threat to inflict injury or constraint on another person. A completed act constituted the separate offense of battery, the intentional unlawful inflicting of physical violence or constraint upon the person of another. But in modern statistical usage attempted and completed acts are put together under the name assault.

In statistical reporting for the Uniform Crime Reports (UCR), assault or simple assault is classified as UCR 9, a Part II offense. In the National Crime Survey (NCS), assault is classified as a personal crime of violence.

See also **aggravated assault; National Crime Survey (NCS); personal crimes; Part I offenses; Part II offenses; Uniform Crime Reports (UCR)**.

assistance and subsidies [Department of Commerce-Bureau of the Census] Assistance and subsidies is a financial reporting category used by the Bureau of the Census for State government finances to aggregate direct cash assistance payments: to welfare recipients; for veterans' bonuses; as direct cash grants for tuition and scholarships; and as aid to non-public educational institutions.

associate degree [Department of Education-Center for Education Statistics] An associate degree is granted for the successful completion of a sub-baccalaureate program of studies, usually requiring at least two years (or equivalent) of full-time college-level study. Totals reported for associate degrees include degrees granted in cooperative and work/study programs.

attendance [Department of Education-National Center for Education Statistics] For statistical reporting purposes attendance is the presence of a student on a day when school is in session. A student may be counted present only when actually in school or present at another place at a school activity which is sponsored by the school, and personally supervised by a member or members of the school staff. Such other attendances may include authorized independent studies, work-study programs, field trips, athletic contests, music festivals, student conventions, instruction for homebound students, and similar activities when officially authorized under policies of the local school board. It does not include making up school-work at home or activities supervised or sponsored by private individuals or groups.

See also **day of attendance.**

automobile credit see **consumer installment credit.**

auxiliary unit see **establishment.**

average daily attendance (ADA) [Department of Education-Center for Education Statistics] Average daily attendance is computed by the aggregate attendance of a school during a reporting period divided by the number of days school is in session during this period. A reporting period is usually a school year. Only the days on which the pupils are under the guidance and direction of teachers are to be considered as days in session.

See also **attendance; average daily membership (ADM).**

average daily census (ADC) (hospital) 1. [Department of Health and Human Services-Public Health Service; Alcohol, Drug Abuse, and Mental Health Administration] The average daily census is a ratio which represents the average number of inpatients in a given facility per day. The ratio is computed by dividing the annual total number of inpatient days, excluding days for which patients were on overnight, weekend pass, or other short term leave, by the number of days in the year.

See also **occupancy rate (hospital).**

2. [American Hospital Association] As defined by the AHA, average daily census is the average number of inpatients, excluding newborns, receiving hospital care each day. The average daily census is computed for a given reporting period, usually a calendar year.

average daily membership (ADM) [Department of Education-Center for Education Statistics] Average daily membership is computed by the aggregate membership of a school during a reporting period divided by the number of days school is in session during this period. A reporting period is usually a school year. Only the days on which the pupils are under the guidance and direction of teachers are considered to be days in session. The average daily membership for groups of schools having varying lengths of terms is the average of the average daily memberships obtained for the individual schools.

See also **average daily attendance (ADA); membership.**

average daily patients see **average daily census (ADC) (hospital).**

average hourly earnings [Department of Labor-Bureau of Labor Statistics] Average hourly earnings is a measure of the mean hourly earnings of production or non-supervisory employees in non-agricultural establishments based on data from the Current Employment Statistics (CES) program. Average hourly earnings is computed by dividing gross payrolls by total hours in order to reflect the actual earnings of workers, including premium pay. Average hourly earnings differs from wage rates, which are the amounts stipulated for a given unit of work or time. Average hourly earnings do not represent total labor costs per hour for the employer because they exclude retroactive payments and irregular bonuses, various fringe benefits, and the employer's share of payroll taxes. Data for average hourly earnings are presented by industry and are published monthly in Employment and Earnings.

See also **average weekly earnings; average weekly hours; compensation per hour; Current Employment Statistics (CES) program; hours and earnings.**

average length of stay 1. [Department of Health and Human Services-Public Health Service; National Center for Health Statistics] In the National Health Interview Survey (NHIS), the average length of stay is the total number of patient days accumulated at the time of discharge by patients discharged during a reporting period divided by the number of patients discharged. The date of admission is counted, but not the date of discharge.

See also **National Health Interview Survey (NHIS); length of stay (hospital); length of stay (nursing home).**

2. [American Hospital Association] The average length of stay of inpatients during a given reporting period is computed by dividing the number of inpatient days by the number of admissions.

average length of term in days [Department of Education-National Center for Education Statistics] In reporting State education data, the average length of term in days is the aggregate days attendance for the State divided by the average daily attendance for the State. It is an average for the State as a whole.

average weekly earnings [Department of Labor-Bureau of Labor Statistics] Average weekly earnings is a measure of the weekly earnings of production or non-supervisory employees in non-agricultural establishments based on data from the Current Employment Statistics (CES) program. Average weekly earnings is computed by multiplying the average weekly hours by average hourly earnings. As such, it is affected not only by changes in average hourly earnings, but also by changes in the length of the work-week. The length of the work-week is affected by monthly variations in such factors as the proportion of part-time workers, stoppages for various reasons, labor turnover during the survey period, and absenteeism for which employees are not paid.

Long-time trends of average weekly earnings can be affected by structural changes in the make-up of the work force. For example, persistent long-term increases in the proportion of part-time workers in retail trade and many of the service industries have reduced average work-weeks in these industries and have affected the average weekly earnings series.

See also **average hourly earnings; average weekly hours; Current Employment Statistics (CES) program; hours and earnings.**

average weekly hours [Department of Labor-Bureau of Labor Statistics] Average weekly hours is a measure of the hours worked per week by production or non-supervisory employees in non-agricultural establishments. The measure is based on data from the Current Employment Statistics (CES) program. Average weekly hours is calculated by dividing the total hours worked by such employees by the total number of employees. Total hours worked includes overtime hours; hours paid for stand-by or reporting time; and equivalent hours for which employees received pay directly from the employer for sick leave, holidays, vacations and other leave. Data for average weekly hours are presented by industry and are published in Employment and Earnings.

See also **average weekly earnings; Current Employment Statistics (CES) program; hours and earnings.**

aviation gasoline, finished [Energy Information Administration] Finished aviation gasoline includes all grades of gasoline for use in aviation reciprocating engines, as given in ASTM specification D910. It excludes blending components that are used in blending or compounding into finished aviation gasoline.

B

achelor's degree [Department of Education-Center for Education Statistics] A bachelor's degree is granted for the successful completion of a baccalaureate program of studies, usually requiring at least four years (or equivalent) of full-time college-level study. Totals reported for bachelor's degrees include degrees granted in cooperative and work/study programs.

ail [Department of Justice-Bureau of Justice Statistics] To bail is to affect the release of an accused person from custody in return for a promise that he or she will appear at a place and time specified and submit to the jurisdiction and judgment of the court, guaranteed by a pledge to pay to the court a specified sum of money or property if the person does not appear. The preferred terminology for this sense of the term bail is, release on bail. Bail also refers to the money or property pledged to the court or actually deposited with the court to effect the release of a person from legal custody.

alance of payments [Department of Commerce-International Trade Administration] In international financial accounting, balance of payments is a complete account of the value of a nation's purchases, sales, and transfers of goods and services with other nations. All types of international transactions are included, whether they be government, business, or private in origin. Balance of trade represents only the trade portion of the balance of payments.
See also **balance of trade**.

alance of trade [Department of Commerce-International Trade Administration] The balance of trade is the import/export portion of the balance of payments. For balance of trade accounting purposes, a trade balance is a net export figure, i.e. the export value less the import value. If the net export value is positive, the balance of trade is said to be a surplus. If the net export value is negative, the balance of trade is said to be a deficit. Trade balances may be calculated not only for total trade but for subcategories and are frequently reported by regions, countries, and commodities.
See also **balance of payments**.

anker's acceptance [Board of Governors, Federal Reserve System] A banker's acceptance is a draft or bill of exchange that a bank has accepted as its own potential liability, thus pledging its credit on behalf of its customers.

arrel (petroleum) [Energy Information Administration] A barrel is a volumetric unit of measure for crude oil and petroleum products equivalent to 42 U.S. gallons.

barrels per calendar day see **operable refinery capacity.**

barrels per stream day see **operable refinery capacity.**

barrio [Department of Commerce-Bureau of the Census] A barrio is a minor civil division (MCD) in Puerto Rico.
See also **minor civil division (MCD).**

barrio-pueblo [Department of Commerce-Bureau of the Census] A barrio-pueblo is a minor civil division in Puerto Rico.
See also **minor civil division (MCD).**

base gas [Energy Information Administration] Base gas is defined as the total volume of natural gas in underground storage reservoirs that will maintain the required rate of delivery during an output cycle.

baseload [Energy Information Administration] The baseload is defined as the minimum amount of electric power delivered or required over a given period of time.

baseload capacity [Energy Information Administration] In the generation of electricity, the baseload capacity refers to the capacity of generating equipment normally operated to serve load on a round-the-clock basis.
See also **installed nameplate capacity (electric utilities).**

baseload plant [Energy Information Administration] A baseload plant is one used for the generation of electricity, usually housing high-efficiency steam-electric units, which is normally operated to take all or part of the minimum load of a system, and which consequently produces electricity at an essentially constant rate and runs continuously. These units are operated to maximize system mechanical and thermal efficiency and minimize system operating costs.

basic commodity [Department of Agriculture-Office of Governmental and Public Affairs] A basic commodity is one of six agricultural crops (corn, cotton, peanuts, rice, tobacco, and wheat) declared by federal legislation as requiring price support.

bassinets [American Hospital Association] Bassinets are a measure consisting of the total number of newborn bassinets set up and staffed for use at the end of a given reporting period. Bassinets are not included in the bed total of a hospital and do not include isolettes or neonatal intensive care units, which are included under beds.

athroom [Department of Commerce-Bureau of the Census] A bathroom is either a full bathroom or a half bathroom . A *full bathroom* is one with: a wash basin; flush toilet; either a bathtub or shower, or combination of bathtub and shower; and piped hot and cold water. A *half bathroom* is one with either a toilet, bathtub, or shower, but not all the facilities needed to be classified as a full bathroom. The Bureau of the Census collects information about bathrooms in housing units as part of various surveys concerning the characteristics of housing units. In counting a housing unit's bathrooms, the bathroom(s) must be for the exclusive use of occupants of the housing unit in order to be counted. For units with multiple bathrooms, a housing unit with one full bathroom and two half bathrooms is reported as a unit with two bathrooms. Bathrooms are a separate room in themselves, and are not counted toward the total number of rooms in a housing unit.
See also **American Housing Survey; housing unit; rooms.**

attery (crime) see **assault (simple).**

ed (hospital) 1. [Department of Health and Human Services-Public Health Service; National Center for Health Statistics] A hospital bed is any bed that is set up and staffed for use by an inpatient.
Counting beds differs slightly depending on the data collection program. In the National Master Facility Inventory (NMFI), the count is of the number of such beds at the end of the reporting period; for the American Hospital Association (AHA), it is the average number of beds during the entire period.
2. [World Health Organization] The World Health Organization (WHO) defines a hospital bed as one regularly maintained and staffed for the accommodation and full-time care of a succession of inpatients and situated in a part of the hospital where continuous medical care for inpatients is provided.
See also **hospital; occupancy rate (hospital).**

ed capacity see **institutional capacity (corrections).**

ed disability day see **disability day.**

edroom [Department of Commerce-Bureau of the Census] A bedroom is a finished room specifically designed to be used for sleeping. The Bureau of the Census collects information about the number of bedrooms in a housing unit as a part of surveys of housing units and their characteristics, most notably the decennial census, the American Housing Survey, and the Survey of Construction program. A den, a space in the attic, or a basement which could be converted into a bedroom are not counted by the Bureau as bedrooms. Those rooms used mainly for sleeping are counted as bedrooms even if they are used for other purposes. Rooms reserved for sleeping such as guest rooms, even though used infrequently, are also counted as bedrooms. Rooms which are mainly used for something else (e.g.

living rooms with sofa beds) are not counted as bedrooms. If a housing unit consists of only one room, such as a one-room efficiency apartment, it is classified by definition as having no bedroom. Bedrooms are included in the total count of rooms.
See also **American Housing Survey; rooms.**

birth rate [Department of Health and Human Services-Public Health Service; National Center for Health Statistics] The birth rate is the number of live births per unit of population. Birth rates can be reported in a number of ways, such as live births per 1,000 persons of resident population, or live births per 1,000 resident women, aged 15 to 44 years old, or for subgroups of the population as a whole (or of women), and by age, race, marital status, or geographic location.
See also **completed fertility rate; fertility rate; live birth.**

bituminous coal [Energy Information Administration] Bituminous coal is a coal that is high in carbonaceous matter having a volatility greater than anthracite and a calorific value greater than lignite. In the United States, it is often referred to as soft coal. It conforms to ASTM specification D388 for bituminous coal and is used primarily for electricity generation, coke production, and space heating.
See also **coal.**

Black (population) see **race.**

blind see **handicapped.**

block see **census block.**

block group see **census block.**

block numbering area (BNA) see **census block.**

BNA see **census block.**

Boeckh indexes [Department of Commerce-Bureau of Economic Analysis] Boeckh indexes are commonly cited construction cost indexes. E. H. Boeckh and Associates compiles monthly national cost indexes for three types of construction: residences; apartments, hotels and office buildings; and commercial and factory buildings. The original base period for these indexes is 1926-1929 = 100. These indexes are published monthly in Survey of Current Business where they have been converted to a 1982 = 100 base. Boeckh indexes are national indexes, based on averages of indexes for 20 major pricing areas. The individual indexes take into account prices for selected building materials, common and skilled labor wage rates, and sales and social security payroll taxes. They are adjusted to reflect the effect of labor shortages and labor efficiency, as determined by studies in each of the 20 pricing areas.

The selected building materials component of the index includes common brick, common lumber, portland cement, structural steel, heating and plumbing equipment, glass, hardware, and paint. Materials cost data are obtained from construction contractors and building trade associations. Weights are based on studies by the compiler of actual building costs and vary by type of structure.

See also **Engineering News-Record (ENR) indexes.**

book value [Department of Commerce-Bureau of the Census] In accounting, the book value of an asset or group of assets is the value as recorded in the business books of account. Such value may differ from the market value or even the purchase price of the asset due to depreciation. In looking at a corporation as a whole, book value is the corporation's net asset value.

borough [Department of Commerce-Bureau of the Census] A borough is a minor civil division (MCD) in New York, and an MCD equivalent in Pennsylvania. In Alaska, a borough is a county equivalent. In Connecticut and Pennsylvania, a borough is a place. In New Jersey, a borough can be either a place or an MCD equivalent.

See also **county; minor civil division (MCD); place.**

breeding unit (agriculture) [Department of Agriculture-Office of Governmental and Public Affairs] A breeding unit is a measure of a breeding herd, which includes the total number of female animals capable of giving birth in a given base period weighted by the production per head.

British Thermal Unit (Btu) [Energy Information Administration] A British Thermal Unit (Btu) is equal to the quantity of heat required to raise the temperature of 1 pound of water by one degree fahrenheit. It is a standard unit for measuring the quantity of heat energy.

brown coal see **lignite.**

Btu see **British Thermal Unit (Btu).**

budgeted capacity see **institutional capacity (corrections).**

building cost index see **Boeckh indexes; Engineering News-Record (ENR) indexes.**

burglary [Department of Justice-Bureau of Justice Statistics] By its oldest and narrowest definition, burglary is the trespassory breaking and entering of a dwelling house of another in the nighttime with the intent to commit a felony. Burglary, as defined in the Uniform Crime Reports (UCR), is broader, including the unlawful entry of any fixed structure, vehicle, or vessel used for regular residence, industry, or business, with or without force, with the intent to commit a felony or larceny. The UCR gives examples of structures, vehicles, and vessels subject to burglary, and by contrast, explicitly classifies thefts from motor vehicles, buildings open to the public, recreational vehicles, temporary structures, and coin operated devices as larceny-theft as opposed to burglary.

For statistical reporting purposes, burglary is classified as a UCR 5, a Part I offense, and a crime index offense. The UCR data reporting burglary is divided into three categories: those involving forcible entry, those constituting unlawful entry with no force used, and attempted forcible entry. Unlawful entry accompanied by the commission or attempted commission of forcible rape, robbery, or aggravated assault, or by the commission of a criminal homicide is classified as the more serious offense, in accordance with UCR convention.

See also **crime; index crime; Part I offense; Uniform Crime Reports (UCR)**.

business see **firm (business)**.

business discontinuance see **business failure**.

business failure [Department of Commerce-Bureau of Economic Analysis] A business failure is defined as a business concern that is involved in a court proceeding or a voluntary action that is likely to end in a loss to creditors. Data reported on business failures in federal publications comes from Dun & Bradstreet, Inc. All industrial and commercial enterprises which are petitioned into federal bankruptcy courts are included in these failure records. Also included are: concerns forced out of business through such actions in the State courts such as foreclosure, execution and attachment with insufficient assets to cover all claims; concerns involved in court actions such as receivership, reorganization, or arrangement; voluntary discontinuances with known losses to creditors; and voluntary compromises with creditors out of court.

The totals provided for business failures do not represent total business closings, which consist of both business failures and business discontinuances. Business discontinuances are those businesses which discontinue operations for reasons such as loss of capital, inadequate profits, ill health, or retirement, where there is no loss to creditors.

Annual and monthly failure data through June, 1975 include the 48 States and the District of Columbia; data beginning July, 1975 include Hawaii, and beginning in September, 1976, data includes Alaska.

It should be noted that failure data excludes railroad failures and failures in certain other types of businesses — banks, financial companies, holding companies, real estate and insurance brokers, amusement enterprises, shipping agents, tourist companies, transportation terminals, and some others. The reported classification of failure records by industries conforms to the Standard Industrial Classification Manual (SIC) in order to facilitate direct comparisons between failures and any other series of data based on the same official code.

Failure data is sometimes presented in the form of the *failure index*. The failure index is expressed as the annual number of failures per 10,000 listed industrial and commercial enterprises. Through 1983, the failure index was reported monthly, on an annualized basis. Since 1984, only annual data has been prepared.

business firm see **establishment; firm (business).**

business formation see **new business incorporation.**

business incorporation see **new business incorporation.**

business transfer payment [Department of Commerce-Bureau of Economic Analysis] A business transfer payment is a payment by a business to persons for which it does not perform current services. These payments include liability payments for personal injury, corporate gifts to non-profit institutions, and consumer bad debts.

Business transfer payments are an income-side component of the National Income Product Account (NIP) which, in combination with other income-side components, combine to measure the Gross National Product (GNP).

See also **Gross National Product (GNP); National Income Product Accounts (NIPA).**

butane [Energy Information Administration] Butane is a normally gaseous, paraffinic hydrocarbon extracted from natural gas or refinery gas streams. Butane includes isobutane and normal butane and is covered by ASTM specification 1835, and Natural Gas Processors Specification for commercial butane. It is used primarily for blending into motor gasoline, for residential and commercial heating, and for industrial purposes, especially the manufacture of chemicals and synthetic rubber.

butylene [Energy Information Administration] Butylene is a normally gaseous olefinic hydrocarbon recovered from refinery processes. For statistical reporting purposes, quantities are included with normal butane.

C

cancer survival rate see **relative survival rate.**

capability (electric utilities) [Energy Information Administration] The capability of an electrical generating unit, generating station, or other electrical apparatus is the maximum load that can be carried under specified conditions for a given period of time without exceeding approved limits of temperature and stress.

The *available but not needed capability* is the net capability of main generating units that are operable but not considered necessary to carry load and cannot be connected to load within 30 minutes.

The *net summer capability* is the steady hourly output which generating equipment is expected to supply to system load exclusive of auxiliary power as demonstrated by test at the time of summer peak demand.

The *running and quick start capability* is the net capability of generating units that carry load or have quick-start capability. In general, quick-start capability refers to generating units that can be available for load within 30 minutes.

See also **reserve margin (electric utilities).**

capacity factor (electric utilities) [Energy Information Administration] Capacity factor is an output measure of electric utilities. It is computed by taking the actual electricity generation during a given period and dividing it by the maximum possible generation for that same period. This fraction is then multiplied by 100 to obtain a percentage. The maximum possible generation for a month is the number of hours in the month multiplied by the net monthly maximum dependable capacity. The annual capacity factors are the computed average of the monthly values for that year. Both annual capacity factors and monthly capacity factors are reported by the Energy Information Administration.

capital consumption allowances with capital consumption adjustment [Department of Commerce-Bureau of Economic Analysis]   Capital consumption allowances with capital consumption adjustment is an income-side component of the National Income Product Account (NIP) which, in combination with other income-side components, combine to measure the Gross National Product (GNP). Capital consumption allowances with capital consumption adjustment consists of capital consumption based on the use of uniform service lives, straight-line depreciation, and replacement cost. For non-profit institutions serving individuals, it is based on the value of the current services of the fixed capital assets owned and used by these institutions; it is included in personal consumption expenditures.

Capital consumption allowances consist of depreciation charges and accidental damage to fixed capital. For non-farm business and corporate farms, depreciation is as reported on federal income tax returns. For non-corporate farms, non-profit institutions serving individuals, tax-exempt cooperatives, and owner occupied houses, depreciation is calculated by the Bureau of Economic Analysis based on their expenditures for fixed capital, uniform service lives, straight line depreciation and service costs.

The *capital consumption adjustment* for corporations is the difference between tax-return-based capital consumption allowances and capital consumption based on uniform service lives, straight-line depreciation, and replacement cost. Similar adjustments are calculated for proprietor's income, rental income of persons, and non-profit institutions serving individuals.

See also **Gross National Product (GNP); National Income Product Accounts (NIPA).**

capital expenditure see **capital outlay (government); new and used capital expenditures (manufacturing).**

capital finance accounts [Department of Commerce-Bureau of Economic Analysis] Capital finance accounts are a branch of national economic accounting that, along with input-output accounts, compliment the National Income and Product Accounts (NIPA). Capital finance accounts provide more detailed information on savings and investment than is presented in the NIPA system. Capital finance accounts present the information in the sector savings-investment accounts in such a way as to illuminate the process by which financial institutions and financial markets transform the economy's savings into investment. By presenting considerably greater detail on both the sectors and types of financial assets and liabilities than that shown in the savings-investment section of the NIPA's, these accounts show the funds available to each sector from saving and borrowing, the transfer of funds among sectors by lending and borrowing, and the use of these funds for investment.

See also **input-output accounts; Gross National Product (GNP); National Income and Product Accounts (NIPA).**

capital goods industry [Department of Commerce-Bureau of Economic Analysis] A capital goods industry is one of two types, defense capital goods industries and non-defense capital goods industries. *Non-defense capital goods industries* include those that produce the following products: non-electrical machinery (excluding machine shop and farm machinery and equipment); electrical machinery (excluding household appliances, radios, television sets and electronic components); and railroad equipment. This category also includes the non-defense production of shipbuilding, conversion, and repair; communication equipment; aircraft and aircraft parts; and ordnance. *Defense capital goods industries* include the defense production of shipbuilding, conversion, and repair; communication equipment; aircraft and aircraft parts; and ordnance.

Data for capital goods industries are reported monthly in Survey of Current Business. Defense capital goods shipments are reported in detail by the Bureau of the Census in the MA-175 report Shipments to Federal Government Agencies. See also **durable goods.**

capital outlay (government) [Department of Commerce-Bureau of the Census] Government capital outlay is direct government expenditure for contract or force account construction of buildings, roads, and other improvements, and for purchases of equipment, land, and existing structures. Also included in capital outlay are amounts for additions, replacements, and major alterations to fixed works and structures. Expenditures for repairs to such works and structures are classified as current operation expenditure, not capital outlay.
See also **direct expenditure (government).**

cargo ton-mile see **revenue ton-mile.**

carnegie unit see **credit (education).**

carryover (agriculture) [Department of Agriculture-Office of Governmental and Public Affairs] The carryover is the volume of a farm commodity not yet used at the end of a marketing year; i.e., it is the remaining stock carried over into the next year.
See also **marketing year (agriculture).**

case (crime) [Department of Justice-Bureau of Justice Statistics] At the level of police or prosecutorial investigation, a case is a set of circumstances under investigation involving one or more persons. At subsequent steps in criminal proceedings, a case is a charging document alleging the commission of one or more crimes or a single defendant charged with one or more crimes. In juvenile or correctional proceedings a case is a person who is the object of agency action.

catalyst petroleum coke [Energy Information Administration] Catalyst petroleum coke is the carbon deposited on the catalyst during many catalytic operations, such as catalytic cracking, which deactivates the catalyst. The catalyst is reactivated by burning off the catalyst petroleum coke, which is used as a fuel in the refinery process. Such carbon or coke is not recoverable in a concentrated form.
See also **catalytic cracking; petroleum coke.**

catalytic cracking [Energy Information Administration] Catalytic cracking is a refining process that consists of using a catalyst and heat to break down heavier and more complex hydrocarbon molecules into lighter and simpler molecules.

categorical assistance program [Department of Commerce-Bureau of the Census] A categorical assistance program is a specific program of State governments which includes Old Age Assistance, Aid to Families with Dependent Children (AFDC), Aid to the Blind, Aid to the Disabled, medical assistance programs, etc. The Census Bureau reports expenditures for categorical assistance programs.

categorically needy [Department of Health and Human Services-Public Health Service; Alcohol, Drug Abuse, and Mental Health Administration] The categorically needy are those persons who are aged, blind, disabled, or families and children who are otherwise eligible for Medicaid and who meet financial eligibility requirements for Aid to Families with Dependent Children (AFDC), Supplemental Security Income (SSI), or an optional state supplement program.

It is a grouping of persons made under the Medicaid program.

Catholic school [Department of Education-Center for Education Statistics] A Catholic school is a private school over which, in most cases, a parent Catholic church group exercises some control or to which it provides some sort of subsidy. Catholic schools include those affiliated with the Roman Catholic Church, including the independent Catholic schools operated by religious orders.

cause of death [Department of Health and Human Services-Public Health Service; National Center for Health Statistics] For the purpose of national mortality statistics, every death is attributed to one underlying condition, based on information reported on the death certificate and utilizing the international rules for selecting the underlying cause of death from the reported condition. That one underlying condition which is chosen is called the cause of death.

For data years 1979-1984, the International Classification of Diseases, Ninth Edition was used for coding cause of death. Earlier data used the then current edition. There are differences between editions and use of successive revisions for classification of diseases may introduce some discontinuities in cause of death statistics over time.

See also **death rate; infant mortality.**

CBD see **central business district (CBD).**

CCD see **census county division (CCD).**

CD see **certificate of deposit (CD).**

CD see **Congressional district (CD).**

CDC see **Centers for Disease Control.**

CDP see **census designated place (CDP)**.

census [Department of Commerce-Bureau of the Census] A census is a survey in which information is collected from every unit (e.g., person, company, institution) in a survey universe. It is a 100% percent sample.
See also **economic census; survey**.

census area [Department of Commerce-Bureau of the Census] A census area is a county equivalent in Alaska.
See also **county**.

census block [Department of Commerce-Bureau of the Census] A census block is the smallest unit in the geographical hierarchy used by the Bureau of the Census. Census blocks are normally a rectangular piece of land bounded by four streets and contain, on the average, about 70 people. However, a block may also be irregular in shape, or be bounded by railroad tracks, streams, or other features. Although blocks are usually compact units, in some suburban and rural areas blocks may encompass quite a large area, depending on the intersection of roads, rivers, and other physical features.

Tabulation blocks, used in census data products, are in most cases the same as *collection blocks*, used in the census enumeration. In some cases, collection blocks have been split into two or more parts required for data tabulations. For example, when a city limit runs through data collection block 101, the data for the portion inside the city is tabulated in tabulation block 101A and the portion outside in tabulation block 101B. Tabulation blocks do not cross the boundaries of counties, county subdivisions, places, census tracts, or block numbering areas (BNA's).

For the 1980 Census, data was tabulated by block for urbanized areas and in incorporated places with 10,000 or more inhabitants outside urbanized areas and in other areas which contracted with the Census Bureau for the preparation of block statistics. The 1990 census is the first for which the entire United States and its possessions are block-numbered.

A *geographic block group* (BG) is a combination of census blocks that is a sub-division of a census tract or BNA. Geographic BG's never cross census tract or BNA boundaries but may cross the boundaries of county subdivisions, places, American Indian and Alaska Native areas, urbanized areas, voting districts, and congressional districts. BG's generally contain between 250 and 550 housing units.

In the data tabulations, a geographic BG may be split into *tabulation BG's* to present data for every unique combination of county subdivision, place, voting district, etc. BG's are used in tabulating decennial census data nationwide in the 1990 census, in all block-numbered areas in the 1980 census, and in Tape Address Register (TAR) areas in the 1970 census. For purposes of data presentation, BG's are a substitute for the enumeration districts used for reporting data in many parts of the United States for the 1970 and 1980 censuses, and in all areas for pre-1970 censuses.

A *block numbering area* (BNA) is an area defined for the purpose of grouping and numbering blocks in block-numbered areas where census tracts have not been defined non-metropolitan counties. BNA's do not cross county boundaries, although they may be split by the boundaries of places, MCD's and CCD's. State agencies and the Census Bureau delineated BNA's for the 1990 census, using guidelines similar to those for the delineation of census tracts.

See also **census county division (CCD); census designated place (CDP); census enumeration district; census geography; census tract; incorporated place; Metropolitan statistical area (MSA); minor civil division (MCD); urbanized area; water area.**

census county division (CCD) [Department of Commerce-Bureau of the Census] A census county division (CCD) is a statistical subdivision of a county, roughly comparable to a minor civil division (MCD). For the 1990 census, CCD's are defined in 21 States (20 for the 1980 census) where MCD's are not legally defined, are not well known, or have frequent boundary changes and hence are not suitable for census purposes. CCD's are established cooperatively by the Bureau and both State and local governments. They are generally defined by boundary features that seldom change and can be easily located, such as roads, rivers, and powerlines.

See also **census geography; census subarea; minor civil division (MCD).**

census designated place (CDP) [Department of Commerce-Bureau of the Census] A census designated place (CDP) is a densely settled population center without legally defined corporate limits or corporate powers or functions. Each CDP has a definite residential nucleus with a dense city-type street pattern and ideally should have an overall population density of at least 1,000 persons per square mile. In addition, a CDP is a community that can be identified by a place name. Boundaries of CDP's are drawn by the Census Bureau in cooperation with State and local agencies to include, insofar as possible, all closely settled areas. However, since CDP boundaries may change with changes in the settlement pattern, a CDP with the same name as in previous censuses does not necessarily have the same boundaries.

The population-specific criteria necessary for an unincorporated area to qualify as a CDP have changed from the 1980 to the 1990 census. For more detailed information, see 1980 Census of Population and Housing: Users Guide (PHC80-R1-A) and Summary Population and Housing Characteristics, CPH1.

See also **census geography; minor civil division (MCD); place.**

census enumeration district [Department of Commerce-Bureau of the Census] A census enumeration district (ED) is an area used in the 1980 Census for data collection activities and as a tabulation area where census blocks are not defined. ED's vary widely in population size, but average about 600 persons. ED's do not cross the boundaries of legal or statistical areas such as census tracts, minor civil divisions (MCD's), census county divisions (CCD's), places, counties, congressional districts and States. About 1,000 jurisdictions in 47 States participated in a program for local definition of ED's. In areas without census blocks, ED's are the smallest unit of census geography for which statistics are prepared.

In the 1990 census, enumeration districts were replaced by tabulation block groups.

See also **census block; census county division (CCD); census geography.**

census geography [Department of Commerce-Bureau of the Census] As there is a diverse and widespread demand for information that the Bureau of the Census collects, two principal methods of geographically subdividing the nation have evolved in an effort to provide sub-national data to different data user groups. These two methods together may be referred to as census geography. One method divides the nation into political/governmental areas, which is of interest to those seeking information about political units, such as States, counties, and cities. The other divides the nation into statistical and administrative areas, which enable the Bureau to provide data along other than strict political lines. By using both of these methods of geographical organization which overlap in some ways, the Bureau is better able to satisfy differing demands from data users for sub-national information. Although each method is not fully distinct, it is best to view them on their own.

In political/governmental subdivision, the primary division of the nation is into States and the District of Columbia, and State equivalents such as Puerto Rico, Guam, Virgin Islands, American Samoa, and the Trust Territories of the Pacific Islands. States are further subdivided by congressional districts, counties and county equivalents, incorporated places, American Indian Reservations/Alaska Native Villages, and election precincts. Counties are divided into minor civil divisions (MCD's).

In statistical/administrative subdivision, the nation is divided into four regions: the Northeast, Midwest, South, and West. These regions are further subdivided into nine divisions. The divisions contain non-metropolitan areas and metropolitan areas of various levels which can cross state lines. Under statistical/administrative subdivision methodology counties may contain urban and rural areas and census designated places (CDP's). In some states, counties are subdivided into census county divisions, (CCD's).

It is within the framework of metropolitan and non-metropolitan areas that small statistical areas such as blocks, block groups, and census tracts are defined. In metropolitan areas, census blocks make up a block group, which, in combination with other block groups, make up a census tract. All central cities of metropolitan areas are composed of census tracts. Central cities contain central business districts (CBD's), and metropolitan areas contain major retail centers (MRC's) which are used in the economic censuses.

In non-metropolitan counties block groups make a up a block numbering area (BNA). In smaller places, census block groups may make up minor civil divisions (MCD's) which are part of a non-metropolitan county.

Complete definitions of specific terms of census geography are found in this dictionary under individual entries for each term. Readers should also be aware that although the above outline of census geography is accurate for the 1990 census, terminology and aggregation have changed somewhat from the 1980 and previous censuses.

As an aid to understanding these concepts, there are five basic principles which should be considered in using geographically presented census data. First, as a general rule, the larger the geographic area, the greater detail that is available. Second, for most areas, more data has been collected and is available in machine readable format than appears in printed publications. Third, the smaller the geographic area, the more likely the data will be suppressed to prevent disclosure of information about identifiable respondents. Fourth, sample data for geographic areas containing relatively few respondents are more subject to certain kinds of statistical error than are similar areas containing a larger number of respondents. Fifth, boundaries do change from survey to survey, census to census, and this may affect historical comparisons.

census subarea [Department of Commerce-Bureau of the Census] A census subarea is a statistical subdivision of a census area such as a borough in Alaska. Census subareas, first identified in 1980, replaced the various types of subdivisions used in the 1970 census.

See also **census geography; census county division (CCD); minor civil division (MCD)**.

census subdistrict [Department of Commerce-Bureau of the Census] A census subdistrict is a minor civil division (MCD) equivalent in the Virgin Islands of the United States.

See also **minor civil division (MCD)**.

census tract [Department of Commerce-Bureau of the Census] A census tract is a small, relatively permanent statistical subdivision of a county. Counties in metropolitan areas (MA's) are divided into census tracts. In addition, over 3,000 tracts have been established in 221 counties outside MA's. Six states (California, Connecticut, Delaware, Hawaii, New Jersey, and Rhode Island) and the District of Columbia have been fully tracted. Census tracts usually have between 2,500 and 8,000 persons and, when first delineated, are designed to be homogeneous with respect to population characteristics, economic status, and living conditions.

Census tracts do not cross county boundaries. Census tract boundaries are delineated with the intention of being maintained over a long time so that statistical comparisons can be made from census to census. When necessary, a tract is subdivided into two or more constituent tracts, thus reaggregation can maintain compatibility while allowing for growth.

See also **census block; census geography; Metropolitan Statistical Area (MSA).**

central administrative office see **establishment.**

central business district (CBD) [Department of Commerce-Bureau of the Census] A central business district (CBD) was a unit of census geography used prior to the 1987 economic census. In 1987, the CBD concept was eliminated.

CBD's are areas within cities that have high traffic flow, high land valuation and characterized by a high concentration of retail businesses, service businesses, offices, theatres, and hotels. A CBD follows census tract boundaries so it consists of one or more whole census tracts.

CBD's are identified only in central cities of metropolitan areas (MA's) and other cities of 50,000 or more, and are designated by local Census Statistical Area Committees in consultation with the Census Bureau. However, some eligible cities have chosen not to participate in the CBD delineation program, hence not every city has a CBD.

For the 1982 economic censuses there were 456 CBD's. Retail trade data is frequently reported for a CBD.

See also **census geography; census tract; central city; Metropolitan Statistical Area (MSA).**

central city [Department of Commerce-Bureau of the Census] In each MSA and CMSA, the largest place and, in some cases, additional places ar designated as central cities. A few PMSA's do not have central cities. The largest central city and, in some cases, up to two additional central cities are included in the title of the MA; there also are central cities that are not included in an MA title. An MA central city does not include any part of that city that extends outside the MA boundary.

See also **census geography; Consolidated Metropolitan Statistical Area (CMSA); extended city; Metropolitan Area (MA); Metropolitan Statistical Area (MSA); Primary Metropolitan Statistical Area (PMSA); urbanized area.**

certificate of deposit (CD) [Federal Reserve Bank of New York] A certificate of deposit (CD) is a time deposit at a bank, which cannot be withdrawn without penalty before a specified maturity date not less than 14 days from initial purchase

and is evidenced by a negotiable or non-negotiable instrument. CD's make up one portion of the larger federal reserve reporting category, time deposits.
See also **time deposit**.

certificate of high school equivalency [Department of Education-National Center for Education Statistics] A certificate of high school equivalency is a formal document issued by a State department of education or other authorized agency certifying that an individual has met the state requirements for high school graduation by attaining satisfactory scores on the Tests of General Education Development (GED) or another State-specified examination. Certificates of high school equivalency are official documents that frequently are accepted by employers, post-secondary educational institutions, and others in the same manner as high school diplomas.

certified route air carrier see **air carrier**.

CES see **Current Employment Statistics (CES) program**.

CEX see **Consumer Expenditure Survey (CEX)**.

charge (crime) [Department of Justice-Bureau of Justice Statistics] In criminal justice usage, a charge is an allegation that a specified person(s) has committed a specific offense, recorded in a functional document such as a record of arrest, a complaint, information or indictment, or a judgment of conviction.

charges (government) see **current charges (government)**.

child see **householder**.

CHINS see **PINS/CHINS/JINS/MINS**.

chronic condition see **condition (health)**.

c.i.f. valuation [Department of Commerce-International Trade Administration] The c.i.f. (cost, insurance, and freight) value represents the value of imports at the first port of entry in the United States. It is based on the purchase price to which is added all freight, insurance, and other charges except U.S. import duties incurred in bringing the merchandise from the country of export and placing it alongside the carrier at the first U.S. port of entry. The c.i.f. valuation is one of the three methods of import valuation used by the International Trade Administration.
See also **customs valuation; f.a.s. valuation; imports**.

city [Department of Commerce-Bureau of the Census] A city is a minor civil division (MCD) equivalent in 20 States. In all States, a city can be a place.
　　See also **minor civil division (MCD); place.**

city (independent) [Department of Commerce-Bureau of the Census] An independent city is a county equivalent or a minor civil division (MCD) equivalent in Maryland, Missouri, Nevada, and Virginia.
　　See also **county; minor civil division (MCD).**

ciudad see **minor civil division (MCD).**

civilian labor force [Department of Labor-Bureau of Labor Statistics] The civilian labor force is comprised of all persons who are not members of the armed forces age 16 years old and over who are either employed or unemployed.
　　See also **employed person; employment; labor force; unemployed persons; unemployment.**

civilian non-institutional population see **population.**

civilian physicians see **physician.**

civilian population see **population.**

class [Department of Education-National Center for Education Statistics] A class is defined as a group of students assigned to one or more teachers or other staff members for a given period of time for instruction or other activity in a situation where the teacher(s) and the students are in the presence of each other.

class A electric utility see **electric utility.**

class B electric utility see **electric utility.**

class of worker [Department of Commerce-Bureau of the Census] For the decennial censuses and in some supplements to the Current Population Survey (CPS), the Bureau of the Census asks survey respondents about their work status, and classifies workers according to the type of ownership of the employing organization. This type of classification of employees is known as class of worker. There are four classes of worker:
　　Private wage and salary workers are those who are employees of a private company, business, or individual who work for wages, salary, commission, tips, or payment in kind. Work for wages or salary from settlement houses, churches, and other non-profit organizations is included as are those self employed persons whose business is incorporated.

Government workers are those who work for any governmental unit regardless of the activity of the particular agency or level of government. For example, employees of public schools, government owned bus lines, and government-owned electric power utilities are all government workers. Government workers also include paid elected officials. Those on active duty in the armed forces are not included since class of worker data is collected for the civilian labor force only.

Self employed workers are those who work for profit or fees in their own unincorporated business, profession, or trade, including those who operate a farm. Persons whose own business is incorporated are counted as employees of their own corporation and are included in private wage and salary workers.

Unpaid family workers are those who work without pay on a farm or a business operated by a person to whom they are related by blood or marriage. These are usually the children or spouse of a business owner or farm operator. Unpaid family workers must have worked at least 15 hours per week during the reference week to be counted as unpaid family workers; persons working less than that amount of time are not considered to be at work.

The determination of class of worker is independent of occupation and industry classifications. However, class of worker does refer to the same job for which data about occupation and industry are collected.

See also **employed persons; labor force.**

class period [Department of Education-National Center for Education Statistics] The class period is that portion of the daily session set aside for instruction in classes, when most classes meet for a single such unit of time.

class size [Department of Education-Center for Education Statistics] Class size is defined as the membership of a class at a given date.

classroom [Department of Education-National Center for Education Statistics] A classroom is a space designed or adapted for regularly scheduled group instruction. This includes regular classrooms and special use classrooms such as laboratories and shops, but excludes such rooms as auditoriums, lunch rooms, libraries, and gymnasiums.

classroom teacher [Department of Education-Center for Education Statistics] A classroom teacher is a staff member assigned the professional activities of instructing pupils in self-contained classes or courses, or in classroom situations.

clearance (crime) [Department of Justice-Bureau of Justice Statistics] In Uniform Crime Reports (UCR) terminology, a clearance occurs when a known occurrence of a Part I offense is followed by an arrest or other decision which indicates a solved crime at the police level of reporting. In UCR vocabulary, a known offense is cleared when one of either two things occurs: (1) *clearance by arrest,* where a known offense is solved by the arrest and charging of at least one person, the summoning, citing or notifying of at least one person, or the citing of a juvenile to appear before juvenile authorities in connection with the offense; or (2) *clearances by exceptional means,* where police know the identity and location of a suspect and have information to support arrest, charging and prosecution, but are prevented from taking action by circumstances outside police control. Such circumstances may include that the subject is dead, already in custody in the same or other jurisdiction, or the victim of the offense has refused cooperation in the prosecution. For data reporting purposes, the UCR counts both types of clearances as offenses cleared by arrest.

A UCR clearance does not necessarily indicate the closing of a case from the law enforcement operations standpoint. Although a clearance under either method may be reported for UCR purposes, an active investigation may still continue. Conversely, the closing of a police case may or may not indicate a clearance.

See also **arrest; clearance rate (crime); Part I offense; Uniform Crime Reports (UCR).**

clearance by arrest see **clearance (crime).**

clearance by exceptional means see **clearance (crime).**

clearance rate (crime) [Department of Justice-Bureau of Justice Statistics] In Uniform Crime Reports (UCR) publications, the clearance rate is the number of offenses cleared divided by the number of offenses known to police. The clearance rate is expressed as a percent. The national UCR program annually publishes tabulations of clearances and clearance rates for all Part I offenses.

See also **clearance (crime); Part I offenses; Uniform Crime Reports (UCR).**

CLF see **civilian labor force.**

closing costs [Department of Commerce-Bureau of the Census] As measured by the Bureau of the Census for the American Housing Survey, closing costs are the total estimated costs customarily chargeable to the buyer for items which are incident to the transaction of purchasing a housing unit. These costs include the initial service charge for the mortgage, cost of title search, charges for the preparation of the deed and mortgage documents, mortgage tax, recording fees, and similar items. For houses sold with FHA-insured mortgages, closing costs include an examination or application fee. Items not included in closing costs are: deposits for unaccrued taxes, insurance premiums, and similar items that are treated as prepayable expenses.

CMHC see **federally funded community mental health center (CMHC).**

CMSA see **Consolidated Metropolitan Statistical Area (CMSA).**

coal [Energy Information Administration] As used by the Energy Information Administration, coal includes all ranks of coal conforming to ASTM specification D388.
    See also **anthracite; bituminous coal; lignite; sub-bituminous coal.**

coal coke [Energy Information Administration] Coal coke is the strong, porous residue consisting of carbon and mineral ash that is formed when the volatile constituents of bituminous coal are driven off by heat in the absence of or in limited supply of air. Coal coke is used primarily in blast furnaces for smelting ores, especially iron ore.
    See also **bituminous coal.**

college [Department of Education-Center for Education Statistics] A college is defined as a post-secondary school which offers general or liberal arts education, usually leading to an associate, bachelor's, master's, doctor's, or first professional degree. Junior colleges and community colleges are included

colony [Department of Commerce-Bureau of the Census] A colony is an American Indian reservation.
    See also **American Indian reservation.**

combined elementary and secondary school [Department of Education-Center for Education Statistics] A combined elementary and secondary school is one which encompasses instruction at both the elementary and secondary levels. Examples of combined elementary and secondary schools would be those with grade spans 1 through 12, or 5 through 12. Any such school is considered to be a combined school.

combined school see **combined elementary and secondary school.**

commercial operator (aviation) see **air carrier; aircraft operator.**

commercial paper [Federal Reserve Bank of New York] Commercial paper is the general term for unsecured, short term, negotiable, promissory notes issued by businesses and financial institutions and sold to investors, usually other companies. Typically commercial paper has an initial maturity of 270 days or less.

commercial sector see **end-use sector.**

commitment (crime) [Department of Justice-Bureau of Justice Statistics] Commitment refers to the action of a judicial officer ordering that a person subject to judicial proceedings be placed in a particular kind of confinement or residential facility, for a specific reason authorized by law. Commitment is also the result of the action, the admission to the facility.

See also **correctional facility (adult); residential facility.**

community [Department of Commerce-Bureau of the Census] A community is an American Indian reservation.

See also **American Indian reservation.**

community hospital see **hospital.**

community/junior college [Department of Education-National Center for Education Statistics] A community/junior college is an institution of higher education which usually offers the first two years of college instruction and career education, grants an associate degree, and does not grant a bachelor's degree. It is either a separately organized institution or part of a public school system or system of junior colleges. Community/junior college offerings include transfer, occupational, and general studies programs at the post-secondary instructional level and may also include adult/continuing education programs.

See also **associate degree; bachelor's degree.**

commuter air carrier see **air carrier.**

company see **firm (business).**

compensation [Department of Labor-Bureau of Labor Statistics] Compensation is defined as the total of wages and benefits paid to an employee by an employer.

See also **compensation per hour.**

compensation of employees [Department of Commerce-Bureau of Economic Analysis] Compensation of employees is a measure of the income accruing to employees as remuneration for their work. It is the sum of wages and salaries and supplements to wages and salaries. Compensation of employees is an income-side component of the National Income Product Account (NIP) which, in combination with other income-side components, combine to measure the Gross National Product (GNP).

See also **Gross National Product (GNP); National Income Product Accounts (NIPA); wages and salaries.**

compensation per hour [Department of Labor-Bureau of Labor Statistics] Compensation per hour is a measure which includes wages and salaries of employees plus employers' contributions for social insurance and private benefit plans. The data on compensation per hour published by the Bureau also includes an estimate of wages, salaries, and supplementary payments for the self-employed.

Real compensation per hour is compensation per hour adjusted to eliminate the effect of the change in the Consumer Price Index for urban consumers (CPI-U).

See also **average hourly earnings; Consumer Price Index (CPI)**.

complementary imports (agriculture) [Department of Agriculture-Office of Governmental and Public Affairs] Complementary imports are agricultural import items not produced in the United States in appreciable commercial volume, such as bananas, coffee, cocoa, tea, and spices.

completed fertility rate [Department of Health and Human Services-Public Health Service; National Center for Health Statistics] The completed fertility rate is the sum of the central birth rates over all ages (14-49 years) of childbearing for a given birth cohort.

See also **birth rate; fertility rate**.

composite indexes [Department of Commerce-Bureau of Economic Analysis] The composite indexes, short for the composite indexes of leading, coincident, and lagging cyclical indicators, are summary measures designed to signal changes in the direction of aggregate economic activity. Each index measures the average behavior of a group of economic time series that show similar timing at business cycle turns but represent widely different activities or sectors of the economy. The components of the index are selected with the help of a formal, detailed scoring system that places particular emphasis on cyclical timing. To ensure broad economic coverage with a minimum of duplication, care is taken to include in each composite index the highest scoring indicators from as many economic process groups as have the requisite timing pattern. Because the combination of prompt availability and reasonable accuracy is an especially important requirement of composite indexes, only monthly series that are available with short lag times and are not subject to large revisions are considered when selecting components of the three major composites.

The *composite index of leading indicators* is made up of 11 series which tend to lead at business cycle turns. They are: Series 1–Average weekly hours of production or non-supervisory workers; Series 5–Average weekly initial claims for unemployment insurance and State programs; Series 8–Manufactures' new orders in 1982 dollars, consumer goods and materials industries; Series 19–Index of stock prices, 500 common stocks; Series 20–Contract and orders for plant and equipment in 1982 dollars; Series 29–Index of new private housing units authorized by local building permits; Series 32–Vendor performance, companies receiving slower deliveries; Series 36–Change in manufacturing and trade inventories on hand and on order in 1982 dollars; Series 99–Change in sensitive materials prices; Series 106—Money Supply M2 in 1982 dollars; and Series 111—Change in business and consumer credit outstanding.

The *composite index of roughly coincident indicators* is made up of four series which tend to coincide with business cycle turns. They are: Series 41—Employees on nonagricultural payrolls; Series 47—Employee hours in nonagricultural establishments; Series 51—Personal income less transfer payments in 1982 dollars; and Series 57—Manufacturing and trade sales in 1982 dollars.

The *composite index of lagging indicators* is made up of six series which tend to lag at business cycle turns. They are: Series 62—Index of labor cost per unit of output, manufacturing; Series 77—Ratio, manufacturing and trade inventories to sales in 1982 dollars; Series 91—Average duration of unemployment in weeks; Series 95—Ratio, consumer installment credit outstanding to personal income; Series 101—Commercial and industrial loans outstanding in 1982 dollars; and Series 109—Average prime rate charged by banks.

The composite indexes are made available in press release form and are published monthly in Business Conditions Digest.

See also **cyclical indicator; diffusion index/rate of change.**

comunidad [Department of Commerce-Bureau of the Census] A comunidad is a census designated place (CDP) in Puerto Rico.

See also **census designated place (CDP).**

condensate see **lease condensate; plant condensate.**

condition (health) [Department of Health and Human Services-Public Health Service; National Center for Health Statistics] A health condition is a departure from a state of physical or mental well-being. Conditions, except for impairments, are coded by the National Center for Health Statistics according to International Classification of Diseases, Ninth Edition, Clinical Modification (ICD-9-CM). Based on duration, there are two categories of conditions: acute and chronic.

In the National Health Interview Survey (NHIS), an acute condition is one that has lasted less than three months and has involved either a physician visit, medical attention, or restricted activity. A chronic condition is any condition lasting three months or more, or is one classified as chronic regardless of the time of onset.

The National Nursing Home Survey (NNHS) uses a specific list of conditions classified as chronic, disregarding time of onset.

See also **disability; disability day; limitation of activity; National Health Interview Survey (NHIS); National Nursing Home Survey (NNHS).**

condominium [Department of Commerce-Bureau of the Census] A condominium describes a type of ownership of an apartment in a building or a house in a development where common areas are shared. In a condominium the owner has a deed to the individual unit and also holds a common or joint ownership in all common areas such as grounds, lobbies, and elevators.

See also **cooperative (housing); housing unit.**

onfidence game [Department of Justice-Bureau of Justice Statistics] A confidence game is the popular name for false representation to obtain money or any other thing of value where deception is accomplished through the trust placed by the victim in the character of the offender. This type of offence is included in the Uniform Crime Reports (UCR) under category 11, fraud. A confidence game is different from a swindle in that a confidence game requires trust in a person as opposed to belief in the validity of some statement or object.

See also **swindle; Uniform Crime Reports (UCR).**

onfidence interval [Department of Commerce-Bureau of the Census] The confidence interval is a range of values around an estimate having a known probability of including the value estimated and is calculated to account for the impact of sampling variability. Given a particular sampling scheme, if all possible samples were selected, then a particular estimate (E) will differ from the average estimate over all possible estimates by no more than the standard error (s.e.) of the estimate about 67% of the time. Thus a 67% confidence interval is defined as the range from E minus 1 s.e. to E plus 1 s.e. An interval from E minus 2 s.e. to E plus 2 s.e. constitutes a 95% confidence interval. If the standard error of an estimate of 2,000 were 200, then a 95% confidence interval would be from 1,600 to 2,400, and the data user could be 95% confident that the interval included the value being estimated.

onfidentiality [Department of Commerce-Bureau of the Census] The Bureau of the Census is bound by Title 13 of the U.S. Code to keep responses to its census and survey questions confidential. This confidentiality includes not only refraining from disclosing the identity of both its individual and business respondents, but also extends to refraining from publishing data which allows inference of characteristics of particular persons, housing units, establishments, etc. As a result, much small geographic area data is suppressed. The Bureau notes such suppression in its publications, frequently with the use of the symbol, D.

onfinement facility [Department of Justice-Bureau of Justice Statistics] A confinement facility is one in which all or a large majority of the prisoners are not free to depart at any time, including jails, pre-arraignment lockups, and prisons.

See also **correctional facility (adult); jail; pre-arraignment lockup; prison.**

ongressional district (CD) [Department of Commerce-Bureau of the Census] A Congressional district (CD) is one of 435 areas from which persons are elected to the U.S. House of Representatives. After each decennial census, congressional seats are apportioned and each State is responsible for establishing CD's for the purpose of electing representatives. Each CD is to be as equal in population to all other CD's in the State as practicable, based on the decennial census counts.

conservation tillage [Department of Agriculture-Office of Governmental and Public Affairs] Conservation tillage is any of several farming methods that provide for seed germination, plant growth, and weed control yet maintain effective ground cover throughout the year and disturb the soil as little as possible. The aim of conservation tillage is to reduce soil loss and energy use while maintaining crop yields and quality.

consolidated city [Department of Commerce-Bureau of the Census] A consolidated city is the primary incorporated place in a consolidated government where the county or minor civil division (MCD) performs few or no governmental functions and has few or no elected officials. The consolidated city functions as a separate government even though it is included in the consolidated government.

See also **census geography; consolidated government; incorporated place; minor civil division (MCD); semi-independent municipalities.**

consolidated government [Department of Commerce-Bureau of the Census] A consolidated government is a unit of local government for which the functions of an incorporated place and its county or minor civil division (MCD) have merged.

See also **census geography; consolidated city; incorporated place; minor civil division (MCD); semi-independent municipalities.**

Consolidated Metropolitan Statistical Area (CMSA) [Department of Commerce-Bureau of the Census] A Consolidated Metropolitan Statistical Area (CMSA) is a unit of census geography introduced in June, 1984, which, in combination with Metropolitan Area (MA), and Primary Metropolitan Statistical Area (PMSA), replaces the Standard Metropolitan Statistical Area (SMSA) and related concepts. CMSA's are designated in accordance with criteria established by the federal Office of Management and Budget (OMB). In general, CMSA's are MA's with a population of one million or more and which have component PMSA's.

See also **census geography; Metropolitan Area (MA); Primary Metropolitan Statistical Area (PMSA).**

consolidated statement (banking) [Federal Reserve Bank of New York] In a consolidated statement, transactions between a bank and its domestic subsidiaries and between the bank's head office and its domestic branches are eliminated. Transactions between domestic and foreign offices and foreign subsidiaries of the bank, or between domestic offices and Edge Act or Agreement subsidiaries of the bank are included on a net basis.

See also **agreement corporation; Edge Act corporation.**

onstruction see **new construction.**

onstruction cost index see **Boeckh indexes; (F.W.) Dodge Construction Costs; <u>Engineering News-Record</u> (ENR) indexes.**

onstruction wages see **<u>Engineering News-Record</u> (ENR) indexes.**

onstruction worker [Department of Labor-Bureau of Labor Statistics] In the Current Employment Statistics (CES) program, construction workers are a sub-group of all employees. They are employed persons up through the level of working supervisors who are engaged directly on the construction project at jobs ordinarily performed by members of the construction trades, either at the site or in shops or yards. Excluded from this category are executive and managerial personnel, professional and technical employees, and workers in routine office jobs. The Bureau of Labor Statistics publishes hours and earnings information for workers in this category.

See also **all employees; Current Employment Statistics (CES) program; employed person.**

Consumer Expenditure Survey (CEX) [Department of Labor-Bureau of Labor Statistics] The Consumer Expenditure Survey (CEX) is an ongoing survey of consumer expenditures conducted by the Bureau of the Census for the Bureau of Labor Statistics. The primary emphasis of the CEX is on collecting data relating to consumer unit expenditures for goods and services used in day-to-day living. The CEX also collects information on the amount and sources of consumer unit income, changes in savings and debts, and major demographic and economic characteristics of consumer unit members. The CEX is based on the civilian non-institutional population as well as that portion of the institutional population living in the following group quarters: boarding houses; housing facilities for students and workers; staff units in hospitals and homes for the aged, infirm, or needy; permanent living quarters in hotels, motels, and mobile home parks. Thus the CEX is not strictly speaking a household survey.

The CEX consists of two separate components: a quarterly interview panel survey in which each consumer unit in the sample is interviewed every three months over a twelve month period; and a diary or record keeping survey completed by the sample consumer units for two consecutive one-week periods with the sample spread over a twelve month period. Each component has its own questionnaire and independent sample.

The interview survey collects detailed data on an estimated 60-70% of total consumer unit expenditures. Global estimates, expense patterns for a three month period, are obtained for food and other selected items. These global estimates account for an additional 20-25% of total expenditures. For the interview survey as a whole, 20% of the sample is dropped and a new group added each quarter to improve efficiency in capturing changes in expenditure patterns.

In the diary survey, respondents are requested to report all expenditures made during their two-week participation in the survey. The diary sample is a new sample each year.

The samples for the CEX are national probability samples of consumer units designed to be representative of the urban US civilian noninstitutional population. The CEX, which collects data on expenditures, should not be confused with the Consumer Price Index, which measures the average change in prices of consumer goods and services.

See also **consumer unit, household, population.**

consumer installment credit [Board of Governors, Federal Reserve System] There are four major types of consumer installment credit: *Revolving credit* includes credit arising from purchases on credit card plans of retail stores and banks, cash advances and check credit plans of banks, and some overdraft credit arrangements. *Automobile credit* represents credit extended for the purchase of new or used passenger automobiles whether or not the credit is specifically secured by the automobile purchased. *Mobile home credit* covers credit extended for the purchase of mobile homes A final category called *other* includes personal cash loans, sales finance contracts for non-automotive goods, and home improvement loans, both FHA-insured and non-insured, made to finance the maintenance and improvement of dwelling units.

Consumer installment credit is considered a key economic indicator and is reported on by the Board of Governors of the Federal Reserve System. The Board compiles and then publishes data on consumer installment credit in its release G.19 "Consumer Installment Credit" and the Federal Reserve Bulletin. This data also appears in Survey of Current Business and Economic Indicators, along with other federal publications.

The series "Consumer Installment Credit" covers most short and intermediate term credit extended to individuals through regular business channels. This credit is usually used to finance the purchase of consumer goods and services, or to refinance debts originally incurred for such purposes, and is scheduled to be repaid (or with option of repayment) in two or more installments. Debts secured by real estate, including first liens, junior liens, and home equity loans, are excluded. Credit extended to government agencies and non-profit charitable organizations, as well as credit extended to businesses or individuals exclusively for business purposes is also excluded.

The amount of outstanding credit represents the sum of balances in the installment receivable accounts of financial institutions and retail outlets at the end of each month. Current monthly estimates are brought forward for the latest benchmark data that becomes available and classification is made on the basis of the holder. Thus installment paper sold by retail outlets is included in the figures for bank and finance companies that purchased the paper.

In addition to the amount of credit outstanding, the federal reserve also reports a net change, which measures the change during the month in the amount of consumer installment credit outstanding. The net change is defined as the amount of consumer credit extended less the amount liquidated during the month, including repayments, charge-offs, and other credits.

Consumer Price Index (CPI) [Department of Labor-Bureau of Labor Statistics] The Consumer Price Index (CPI) is a measure of the average change in prices over time of a fixed market basket of goods and services. Calculated by the Bureau of Labor Statistics, the CPI is published for two population groups: the CPI-U for urban consumers, and the CPI-W for urban wage and clerical workers. The CPI is based on prices of food, clothing, shelter and fuels, transportation fares, charges for doctors' and dentists' services, drugs, and other goods and services that people buy for day-to-day living. Prices are collected in 85 urban areas across the country from about 4,000 food stores, 24,000 rental units, and 28,000 establishments.

CPI data are issued initially in a news release about three weeks following the reference month. CPI Detailed Report is a monthly publication available approximately three weeks after the initial release which reports the CPI in detail.

The CPI, which measures the change in prices of consumer oriented goods and services, should not be confused with the Consumer Expenditure Survey (CEX), which measures the amount of money expended by representative consumers on consumer items during a given survey period.

consumer unit [Department of Labor-Bureau of Labor Statistics] A consumer unit is an entity used as the basis of the Consumer Expenditure Survey (CEX). A consumer unit comprises either: a) all the members of a particular household who are related by blood, marriage, adoption, or other legal arrangements; b) a person living alone or sharing a household with others, or living as a roomer in a private home or lodging house, or in permanent living quarters in a hotel or motel, but who is financially independent; or c) two or more persons living together who pool their income to make joint expenditure decisions. A consumer unit may or may not be a household.

See also **Consumer Expenditure Survey (CEX); household.**

contract rent see **rent.**

contractor-built house [Department of Commerce-Bureau of the Census] A contractor-built house is a house built for owner occupancy on the owner's land with construction taking place under the supervision of a single general contractor. Contractor-built houses differ from owner built houses.

See also **American Housing Survey (AHS); owner-built house.**

cooperative (housing) [Department of Commerce-Bureau of the Census] A cooperative is a building that is owned by shareholders and is organized as a corporation. Ownership of shares in the corporation entitles each shareholder to perpetual use of one or more units in the building until the owner sells the share(s).

See also **condominium; housing unit.**

corn-hog ratio [Department of Agriculture-Office of Governmental and Public Affairs] The corn-hog ratio is the number of bushels of corn that are equal in value to 100 pounds of live hogs; that is, the price of hogs per hundredweight divided by the price of corn per bushel. The corn-hog ratio may be calculated in terms of U.S. average prices received by farmers, prices received by farmers in a given area, or on the basis of central market prices rather than farm prices.

corporate profits with inventory valuation and capital consumption adjustments [Department of Commerce-Bureau of Economic Analysis] The income which comprises corporate profits is that which arises from current production. With several exceptions, this income is measured as receipts less deductions as defined in federal tax law. Among these exceptions are: receipts exclude capital gains and dividends received; deductions exclude depletion and capital losses; inventory withdrawals are valued at current replacement cost; and depreciation is on a consistent accounting basis and valued at current replacement cost. Because national income is defined as the income of U.S. residents, its profit components include income earned abroad by U.S. corporations and excludes income earned in the U.S. by foreigners.

The *inventory valuation adjustment* is the difference between the cost of inventory withdrawals as valued in determining profits before tax and the cost of withdrawals valued at the current replacement cost.

The *capital consumption adjustment* is the difference between tax-return-based capital consumption allowances and capital consumption based on uniform service lives, straight-line depreciation, and replacement cost.

Corporate profits with inventory valuation and capital consumption adjustments are an income-side component of the National Income Product Account (NIP) which, in combination with other income-side components, combine to measure the Gross National Product (GNP). They are profits of organizations treated as corporations in the National Income and Product Accounts (NIPA's); i.e., all entities required to file federal corporate tax returns including mutual financial institutions and cooperatives subject to federal income tax, private non-insured pension funds, non-profit organizations that primarily serve business, federal reserve banks, and federally sponsored credit agencies.

See also **Gross National Product (GNP); National Income Product Accounts (NIPA).**

correctional facility (adult) [Department of Justice-Bureau of Justice Statistics] An adult correctional facility is a building, part of a building, set of buildings, or area enclosing a set of buildings or structures operated by a government agency for the physical custody, or custody and treatment, of sentenced persons or persons subject to criminal proceedings. Correctional facilities include correctional institutions, jails, prisons, residential facilities, lockups and all other government facilities in which alleged or adjudicated adult offenders are confined or reside.

See also **confinement facility; jail; juvenile facility (corrections); prison; residential facility.**

correctional facility (juvenile) see **juvenile facility (corrections).**

cost of materials (manufacturing) [Department of Commerce-Bureau of the Census] In manufacturing establishments, the cost of materials is the direct charge or actual charges paid or payable for items consumed or put into production during the year, including freight charges and other direct charges incurred by the establishment in acquiring these materials. For Census Bureau reporting, manufacturers include the cost of materials or fuel consumed regardless of whether these items were purchased by the individual establishment from other companies, transferred to it from other establishments of the same company, or withdrawn from inventory during the year. In reports where an industry total is given for cost of materials, separate figures were obtained for: a) the total delivered cost of all raw materials, semifinished goods, parts, components, containers, scrap, and supplies put into production or used as operating supplies or for repair and maintenance during the year; b) the amount paid for electricity purchased; c) the amount paid for all fuels consumed for heat, power, or the generation of electricity; d) the cost of work done by others on parts furnished by manufacturing establishments; and, e) the cost of products bought and resold in the same condition. The total excludes the cost of services used such as advertising, insurance, telephone, etc., and research, developmental and consulting services of other establishments. It also excludes overhead costs such as depreciation charges, rent, interest, royalties, etc. Materials, machinery, and equipment used on plant expansion or capitalized repairs which are chargeable to fixed assets accounts are also excluded.

cost per student [Department of Education-National Center for Education Statistics] Cost per student is an expenditure measure of an educational institution or authority. It is calculated by current expenditures for a given period of time and/or for given programs divided by an appropriate student unit of measure such as average daily attendance (ADA) or students in average daily membership (ADM).

See also **average daily attendance (ADA); average daily membership (ADM)**.

counselor [Department of Education-National Center for Education Statistics] A counselor is a staff member performing assigned professional services having the purpose of assisting pupils in making plans and choices in relation to education, vocation, or personal development.

counterfeiting [Department of Justice-Bureau of Justice Statistics] Counterfeiting is the manufacture or attempted manufacture of a copy or imitation of a negotiable instrument with value set by law or convention, or the possession of such a copy without authorization, with the intent to defraud by claiming the genuineness of the copy. Counterfeiting is classified with forgery under the Uniform Crime Reports (UCR) as UCR 10. In many statutes, counterfeiting is included within the definition of forgery. Where a distinction is made, it rests on the fact that a counterfeiting presupposes the prior existence of an officially issued item of value which provides a model for the perpetrator. Examples include currency, coins, postage stamps, ration coupons, food stamps, bearer bonds, etc. This kind of model is absent in a forgery.

See also **forgery; fraud; Uniform Crime Reports (UCR)**.

county [Department of Commerce-Bureau of the Census] A county is a basic political unit of census geography. Counties and their equivalents in the United States represent the primary political and administrative divisions of States. Counties are called parishes in Louisiana. In Alaska, the boroughs and census areas are treated as county equivalents for census purposes. The five boroughs of New York City are also counties. Several cities are independent of any county organization and, because they constitute primary divisions with their states, are accorded the same treatment as counties in economic census' tabulations. The District of Columbia is considered a county equivalent.

See also **census geography**.

county group [Department of Commerce-Bureau of the Census] A county group is an area with a population of 100,000 or more, generally a group of contiguous counties, and identified on one of the 1980 Census public-use microdata samples. The term county group is applied loosely, since some of the areas included are single counties, single cities, groups of places, or groups of towns and townships in New England and a few other States, all of which meet the 100,000 minimum population criterion.

course [Department of Education-National Center for Education Statistics] A course is an organization of subject matter and related learning experiences provided for the instruction of students on a regular or systematic basis, usually for a predetermined period of time such as a semester, a regular school term, or a two week workshop. Credit toward graduation or completion of a program of studies generally is given students for the successful completion of a course.

court [Department of Justice-Bureau of Justice Statistics] A court is an agency or unit of the judicial branch of government, authorized or established by statute or constitution, and consisting of one or more judicial officers, which has the authority to decide upon cases, controversies in law, and disputed matters of fact brought before it. There are two basic types of courts: those having original jurisdiction to make decisions regarding matters of fact and law; and those having appellate jurisdiction to review issues of law in connection with decisions made in specific cases previously adjudicated by other courts and decisions made by administrative agencies. However, individual courts are frequently authorized to exercise both original and appellate jurisdiction, depending upon the subject matter of individual cases. For statistical purposes these courts are classified according to their primary function as trial courts if they primarily hear cases from the beginning, and as appellate courts if they primarily perform appellate reviews of court or administrative agency decisions.

In most States there are two levels of trial court: those with limited (special) jurisdiction; and those with general jurisdiction. In about half of the States there are two levels of appellate court: intermediate appellate courts; and courts of last resort. Whether a given court deals with criminal cases only depends upon the structure of the court system of a given State; however, most courts handle both civil and criminal matters.

See also **appellate court; court of general jurisdiction; court of last resort; court of limited (special) jurisdiction; intermediate appellate court; trial court.**

court of general jurisdiction [Department of Justice-Bureau of Justice Statistics] A court of general jurisdiction is a trial court having original jurisdiction over all subject matter not specifically assigned to a court of limited (special) jurisdiction. Courts of general trial jurisdiction frequently are also given jurisdiction over certain kinds of appeal matters. These courts are usually called superior courts, district courts, or circuit courts.

See also **court; court of limited (special) jurisdiction.**

court of last resort [Department of Justice-Bureau of Justice Statistics] A court of last resort is an appellate court having final jurisdiction over appeals within a given State.

See also **court.**

court of limited (special) jurisdiction [Department of Justice-Bureau of Justice Statistics] A court of limited (special) jurisdiction is a trial court having original jurisdiction over only that subject matter specifically assigned to it by law. Limited jurisdiction courts also go by such names as municipal court, justice court, magistrate court, family court, probate court, and traffic court.

See also **court**.

court probation [Department of Justice-Bureau of Justice Statistics] Court probation is a criminal court requirement that a defendant or offender fulfill specified conditions of behavior in lieu of a sentence to confinement but without assignment to a probation agency's supervisory caseload. Court probation is sometimes referred to as unsupervised probation, summary probation, or informal probation.

coverage error see **non-sampling error**.

CPI see **Consumer Price Index (CPI)**.

CPI-U see **Consumer Price Index (CPI)**.

CPI-W see **Consumer Price Index (CPI)**.

CPS see **Current Population Survey (CPS)**.

credit (education) [Department of Education-Center for Education Statistics] A credit is defined as the unit of value awarded for the successful completion of certain courses, and is intended to indicate the quantity of course instruction in relation to the total requirements for a diploma, certificate, or degree. Credits are frequently expressed in terms such as carnegie units, semester credit hours, and quarter credit hours.

credit union [Federal Reserve Bank of New York] A credit union is a cooperative thrift and loan association composed of persons who generally are employees of the same company, are members of the same union or other organization, or have some other common tie. Members purchase ownership shares similar to savings accounts and are permitted to borrow from the association. A credit union share draft may be negotiable or non-negotiable and is functionally equivalent to an interest bearing checking account.

crime [Department of Justice-Bureau of Justice Statistics] A crime is an act committed or omitted in violation of a law forbidding or commanding it for which the possible penalties for an adult upon conviction include incarceration, for which a corporation can be penalized by fine or forfeit, or for which a juvenile can be adjudged delinquent or transferred to criminal court for prosecution. The term crime excludes certain infractions, violations, and petty offenses for which imprisonment is not a possible penalty such as traffic offenses. In most jurisdictions, felonies and misdemeanors are the two major classes of crimes.

There are two major programs which measure crime in the United States. The Uniform Crime Reports (UCR) is based on crimes known to police. Every month, most police agencies report on crime to the FBI, which administers the UCR. For statistical reporting purposes the UCR classifies crime into two groupings: Part I offenses, which include eight serious crimes, and Part II offenses which include 18 less serious crimes. The terms crime and criminal offense are used interchangeably for this program.

The second major program is the National Crime Survey (NCS) which is based on a household survey and is administered by the Bureau of Justice Statistics. Crime is broadly divided into two categories, household crime and personal crime, and data on the occurrence of these crimes are based on interviews. The definitions of specific NCS crimes vary from UCR terminology, and the overall results of the survey differ from those obtained by the FBI. The central concepts involved in the NCS are those of criminal incidents and victimization.

See also **crime index; criminal incident; felony; household crimes; misdemeanor; National Crime Survey (NCS); offenses known to police; Part I offenses; Part II offenses; personal crimes; Uniform Crime Reports (UCR); victimization.**

crime index [Department of Justice-Bureau of Justice Statistics] In Uniform Crime Reports (UCR) terminology, the crime index is a set of numbers indicating the volume, fluctuation, and distribution of crimes reported to local law enforcement agencies. The crime index is made up of eight index, or serious, crimes which are all of the eight Part I offenses except UCR 1b, negligent manslaughter. The crime index is reported for the United States as a whole and for geographic subdivisions, based on reports of UCR index crimes. In the national UCR publication Crime in the United States, index crime data are presented in the form of numbers, rates, or percentage changes in relation to areas, population, and periods of time. Crime rates are presented for index crimes as a whole, and the two component groups of index crimes, violent crimes and property crimes.

See also **crime; index crime; Part I offense; property crime; Uniform Crime Reports (UCR); violent crime.**

crime rate [Department of Justice-Bureau of Justice Statistics] The crime rate is the number of crimes known to police divided by a unit of population. The Uniform Crime Reports (UCR) computes crime rates for all UCR crime index crimes for the nation, all 50 States, and selected subdivisions of states and publishes them annually in Crime in the United States.

See also **crime; crime index; index crime; Uniform Crime Reports (UCR).**

crimes against property see **property crime.**

crimes known to police see **offenses known to police.**

crimes of violence see **violent crime.**

criminal homicide [Department of Justice-Bureau of Justice Statistics] Criminal homicide is defined as the causing of the death of another person without legal justification or excuse. Criminal homicide includes both murder and non-negligent manslaughter, Uniform Crime Reports (UCR) category 1a, as well as negligent manslaughter, UCR category 1b. In UCR statistics, 1a and 1b together constitute the Part I offense, criminal homicide, but only 1a is a crime index offense.

See also **crime; index crime; murder and non-negligent manslaughter; negligent manslaughter; Part I offenses; Uniform Crime Reports (UCR).**

criminal incident [Department of Justice-Bureau of Justice Statistics] A criminal incident is a term used in the National Crime Survey (NCS) encompassing a criminal event which involves one or more victims and one or more offenders. In NCS terminology, a critical distinction is made between a criminal incident and a victimization. Only one criminal incident is recorded for any continuous sequence of criminal behavior, even though it may contain acts which constitute two or more NCS offenses, or involve two or more distinct victims. One victimization is recorded for each distinct person or household harmed as a result of a given criminal incident. The NCS represents a different methodological approach for measuring crime than the Uniform Crime Reports (UCR).

See also **National Crime Survey (NCS); Uniform Crime Reports (UCR); victimization.**

criminal mischief [Department of Justice-Bureau of Justice Statistics] Criminal mischief is defined as intentionally destroying or damaging, or attempting to destroy or damage, the property of another without his consent, usually by a means other than burning. Sometimes known as malicious mischief, criminal mischief is classified by the Uniform Crime Reports (UCR) as vandalism (UCR 14).

See also **Uniform Crime Reports (UCR).**

criminal offense see **crime.**

cross-compliance (agriculture) [Department of Agriculture-Office of Governmental and Public Affairs] Cross-compliance is a government farm program term which means that if a farmer wishes to participate in a program for one crop by meeting the qualifications for production adjustment payments and loans for that crop, the farmer must also meet the program provisions for other major program crops which the farmer grows.

Crude Materials Index see **stage of processing (SOP).**

crude oil [Energy Information Administration] Crude oil is a mixture of hydrocarbons that existed in liquid phase in underground reservoirs and remains liquid at atmospheric pressure after passing through surface separating facilities. For statistical reporting purposes, crude oil includes lease condensate and liquid hydrocarbons produced from tar sands, gilsonite, and oil shale. Drip gases are also included, but topped crude oil and other unfinished oils are excluded. Liquids produced at natural gas processing plants and mixed with crude oil are excluded where they are identifiable.

See also **crude oil wellhead price; heavy oil; proved reserves, crude oil.**

crude oil wellhead price [Energy Information Administration] Crude oil wellhead price is the average price at which all domestic crude oil is purchased. Prior to February 1976, the domestic crude oil wellhead price represented an estimate of average prices posted; after February 1976, the wellhead price represents an average of first sale prices.

current charges (government) [Department of Commerce-Bureau of the Census] Current charges are amounts received by a government from the public for performance of specific services benefiting the person charged, as well as from the sales of commodities and services. Current charges includes fees, assessments, and other reimbursements for current services, rents and sales derived from commodities or services furnished incident to the performance of particular functions, gross income of commercial activities, etc. Current charges excludes intergovernmental revenue, interdepartmental charges and transfers, and receipts from liquor store sales. Current charges are distinguished from license taxes, which relate to privileges granted by government or regulatory measures for the protection of the public.

See also **intergovernmental revenue.**

Current Employment Statistics (CES) program [Department of Labor-Bureau of Labor Statistics] The Current Employment Statistics (CES) program is an integrated Federal-State program administered by the Bureau of Labor Statistics which gathers data on employment, hours, and earnings of employees in nonagricultural establishments, including government. The CES presents the data gathered by: industry and on a national, state, and area basis. The CES is based on payroll reports from over 290,000 establishments which report voluntarily to the Bureau of Labor Statistics on a monthly basis. On the national level, over 3,500 separately published series are produced each month, detailing employment, hours and earnings by industry. For industry detail, the information collected is used to prepare estimates at the four-digit Standard Industrial Classification (SIC) code level for manufacturing industries and at the three-digit SIC level for most non-manufacturing industries. In addition to the monthly data, additional information is published in the June issue of <u>Employment and Earnings</u> for a number of industries which do not meet established publications standards.

It is important to note that although both provide data on employment, there are significant differences between the CES and the Current Population Survey (CPS). These differences arise from the fact that the former is based on a payroll survey of establishments, while the latter is based on a survey of households. As a result of this fundamental distinction, data from the surveys are not comparable. The Bureau sees the differing roles of both surveys as complimentary, providing an important focus in each of their respective areas.

See also **Current Population Survey (CPS); Standard Industrial Classification (SIC) program.**

current expenditures (elementary/secondary) [Department of Education-Center for Education Statistics] Current expenditures are those expenditures for operating local public schools excluding capital outlay and interest on school debt. Current expenditures include such items as salaries for school personnel, fixed charges, student transportation, school books and materials, and energy costs.

current-fund expenditures (higher education) [Department of Education-Center for Education Statistics] Current-fund expenditures in higher education represent money spent to meet current operating costs including salaries, wages, utilities, student services, public services, research libraries, scholarships and fellowships, auxiliary enterprises, hospitals, and independent operations. They exclude loans, capital expenditures, and investments.

See also **expenditures (education).**

current-fund revenues (higher education) [Department of Education-Center for Education Statistics] Current-fund revenues in higher education are monies received during the current fiscal year from revenue which can be used to pay obligations currently due, along with surpluses reappropriated for the current fiscal year.

See also **expenditures (education).**

Current Population Survey (CPS) [Department of Commerce-Bureau of the Census] The Current Population Survey (CPS) is the oldest and largest Bureau of the Census survey. It is a household survey conducted monthly from a probability sample of approximately 60,000 occupied households and provides a wealth of statistical information about persons 16 years of age and over. The primary focus of the CPS is to collect data about the labor force. Statistics coming from the

CPS include data on employment and unemployment; personal characteristic of workers such as age, sex, race, marital and family status; hours of work; occupational data; and some information concerning those outside the labor force such as disabled persons and students. In addition, the CPS regularly provides a large amount of detail on the economic and social characteristics of the population as it is frequently used for a program of special inquiries to obtain detailed information from particular segments or for particular characteristics of the population. In many cases these inquiries are repeated annually in the same month for some topics. These annual topics include the earnings and total incomes of individuals and families, the immunization of children, fertility, alimony and child support, employee benefits, immigration, school enrollment, and voting and registration. As a result, CPS data is probably the most far-reaching and important intercensal information collected.

The time period covered by each monthly survey is a calendar week, and since July, 1955, the Sunday through Saturday calendar week is that week which contains the 12th day of the month.

Each month during the calendar week containing the 19th day of the month, interviewers contact some responsible person in each of the sample households in the CPS. Of the occupied housing units available for enumeration, about 4-5% are not interviewed in a given month because the residents are not found at home after repeated calls, are temporarily absent, refuse to cooperate, or are unavailable for other reasons.

At the time of the first enumeration of a household, the interviewer visits the household and prepares a roster of the household members including their personal characteristics such as date of birth, sex, race, ethnic origin, marital status, educational attainment, and veteran status; and their relationship to the person maintaining the household. This roster is updated at each subsequent interview. Personal visits are required in the first, second and fifth month that a household is in the sample. In other months, the interview may be conducted by telephone. Approximately two thirds of the households in any given month are interviewed by telephone.

The processing of collected data follows a rigorous methodology and estimating methods include a non-interview adjustment, staged ratio estimates and a final composite estimate. CPS data is used not only by the Department of Labor but by a wide variety of government agencies, along with researchers in business and academia.

customs valuation [Department of Commerce-International Trade Administration] Customs valuation is one of the three methods of valuing imports. The Customs value represents the value of imports appraised by the U.S. Customs Service and is primarily used for the collection of import duties. Methodologically, customs and f.a.s. valuation data are similar since both represent a value in the foreign country and both exclude all charges incurred in bringing the merchandise to the

United States. Customs valuation replaced f.a.s. valuation for the International Trade Administration beginning with the compilation of January, 1982, data.
See also **c.i.f. valuation; f.a.s. valuation; imports**.

cyclical indicator [Department of Commerce-Bureau of Economic Analysis] A cyclical indicator is one of the measures of specific areas of the economy which have been singled out and categorized as leaders, coinciders, or laggers based on their general conformity to cyclical movements in aggregate economic activity. Cyclical indicators are classified by the Bureau of Economic Analysis (BEA) by both economic process and their average timing at business cycle peaks, business cycle troughs, and at peaks and troughs combined. Although the approximately 150 indicators which the BEA watches have been selected primarily on the basis of their cyclical behavior, they have also proven useful in forecasting, measuring, and interpreting short term fluctuations in aggregate economic activity.

Of these 150 indicators, about three quarters are individual cyclical indicators; the remaining quarter are related analytic measures: composite indexes, diffusion indexes, and rates of change). At present, there are 112 individual time series classified by economic process and grouped into seven areas: employment and unemployment; production and income; consumption, trade, orders, and delivery; fixed capital investment; inventories and inventory investment; prices, costs, and profits; money and credit. These include the 21 indicators used in the construction of the composite indexes. Each of the 112 series are charted, and peaks and troughs are indicated. These charts are published monthly in <u>Business Conditions Digest</u>.
See also **composite indexes; diffusion index/rate of change**.

D

dangerous weapon see **deadly weapon.**

day (hospital) [Department of Health and Human Services-Public Health Service; National Center for Health Statistics] According to the American Hospital Association (AHA) and the National Master Facility Inventory (NMFI), days or inpatient days are the number of adult and pediatric days of care rendered during a reporting period. Days of care for newborns are excluded.

In the National Health Interview Survey (NHIS), hospital days during the year refer to the total number of hospital days occurring in the 12 month period prior to the interview week. A hospital day is a night spent in the hospital for persons admitted as inpatients to a hospital.

In the National Hospital Discharge Survey (NHDS), days of care refer to the total number of patient days accumulated by patients at the time of discharge from non-federal short stay hospitals during a reporting period. All days from and including the date of admission but not including the date of discharge are counted.

See also **hospital; inpatient days (hospital); National Health Interview Survey (NHIS); National Hospital Discharge Survey (NHDS); National Master Facility Inventory (NMFI).**

day in session (education) [Department of Education-National Center for Education Statistics] A day in session is a day on which school is open and the students are under the guidance and direction of teachers. On some days the school plant may be closed and the student body as a whole engaged in school activities outside the school plant under the guidance and direction of teachers. Such days are also considered as days in session. Days on which the teaching facility is closed for such reasons as holidays, teachers' institutes, and inclement weather are not considered as days in session.

day of absence [Department of Education-National Center for Education Statistics] A day of absence is a school day during which a student is in membership but not in attendance.

See also **attendance; membership.**

day of attendance [Department of Education-National Center for Education Statistics] A day of attendance is a school day during which a student is present for the entire school session and is under the guidance and direction of teachers. For statistical reporting purposes, when a student is present for only part of a session, his attendance is counted according to the nearest half day of attendance. If overcrowded conditions make it necessary for a school to hold two separate sessions per day, a student attendance for all of either session is considered as having completed a full day of attendance. An excused absence during examination periods or because of sickness or for any other reason is not counted as a day of attendance. Attendance at a State-approved half day session for kindergarten or prekindergarten also is considered as a full day of attendance; for example if one group of 100 pupils attends a prekindergarten in the morning and a different group of 100 pupils attends in the afternoon, the aggregate attendance for the day is 200. However, when computing ratios for various purposes, persons attending curtailed sessions are counted as if they were in attendance for a portion of the session. For example, for purposes of obtaining statistical comparability only, student-staff ratios involving kindergarten and pre-kindergarten students attending a half day session are computed as though these students were in attendance for half days.

day of membership [Department of Education-National Center for Education Statistics] For a given pupil, a day of membership includes all days that school is in session, from the date the pupil presents him/herself at school and is placed on the current roll, until that student withdraws from membership in the class or school.
   see also **membership**.

day school [Department of Education-National Center for Education Statistics] A day school is a school attended by students during a part of the day, as distinguished from a residential school where students are boarded and lodged as well as taught.

days of care see **day (hospital)**.

deadly weapon [Department of Justice-Bureau of Justice Statistics] A deadly weapon is an instrument designed to inflict serious bodily injury or death or capable of being used for such a purpose. A statutory distinction is sometimes made between a deadly weapon which is specifically designed to cause serious injury or death, and a dangerous weapon which is one capable under certain circumstances of causing serious injury or death.
   See also **aggravated assault**.

deaf see **handicapped**.

deaf-blind see **handicapped**.

death see **cause of death; infant mortality**.

death rate [Department of Health and Human Services-Public Health Service; National Center for Health Statistics] The death rate is the number of deaths per unit of population, usually per 1,000 persons. Most death rates in the United

States are the result of dividing the number of deaths in a population in a given period by the resident population at the middle of that period. Death rates may be restricted to deaths in specific age, race, sex, or geographic groups, or they may be related to the entire population. Death rates are frequently age adjusted.

See also **age adjustment; fetal death rate; late fetal death rate; live birth; neonatal mortality rate; perinatal mortality rate; perinatal mortality ratio; postneonatal mortality rate.**

debt (government) [Department of Commerce-Bureau of the Census] State and sub-state government debt includes all short-term credit obligations of the government and its agencies and all long-term credit obligations, whether backed by the government's full faith and credit or non-guaranteed. Debt also includes judgments, mortgages, revenue bonds, general obligation bonds, notes, and interest bearing warrants. Debt excludes non-interest-bearing short-term obligations, interfund obligations other than formal debt instruments of the government held by its funds as investments, amounts owed in a trust or agency capacity, advances and contingent loans from other governments, and rights of individuals to benefit from government social insurance funds. The reporting of debt by government is usually divided into the categories of long-term and short-term debt.

Long term debts are debts payable more than one year after the date of issue. The amount reported as the long-term debt issued is the par value of long-term debt obligations incurred during the fiscal period concerned including funding and refunding obligations. Debt obligations authorized but not actually incurred during the fiscal period are not included.

Long-term debt offsets are cash and investment assets of sinking funds and other reserve funds, however designated, which are specifically held for redemption of long-term debt. Such offsets include bond reserve funds, deposits with fiscal agents for the redemption of uncancelled debt, balances in refunding bond accounts held pending completion of refunding transactions, and any credit paper or other assets of credit funds which are pledged to the ultimate redemption of debt incurred to finance loan activities of such funds. Assets held for debt redemption are included up to the amount of the specific debt for which they were accumulated. Any excess of assets over the amount of such debt and any separately recorded amounts held for future interest payments are excluded.

The *long-term debt retired* is the par value of long-term debt obligations liquidated by repayment or exchange, including debt retired by refunding obligations. The amount reported as the *long-term debt redeemed* is the par value of long term debt retired during the fiscal year other than amounts retired as a result of refunding operations. This includes amounts redeemed from current revenues of fund balances and from assets accumulated for debt redemption.

Short-term debts are interest bearing debts payable within one year from date of issue. Short-term debt includes bond anticipation notes, bank loans, tax anticipation notes, and warrants. Amounts reported for short-term debts include obligations having no fixed maturity date if they are payable from a tax levied for collection in the year of their issuance.

See also **full faith and credit; general obligation debt; refunding (government finance).**

defense capital goods industry see **capital goods industry.**

deficiency payment (agriculture) [Department of Commerce-Bureau of the Census] A deficiency payment is paid to a farmer by the federal government when farm prices are below the target price. Deficiency payments are computed by subtracting from the target price the higher of: a) the loan rate; or b) the national average market price of a commodity during the first five months of the marketing year. Generally the federal government pays this difference to a farmer who qualifies by meeting all farm program conditions for that portion of the farmer's production specified in the farm program.

See also **target price (agriculture).**

delinquency [Department of Justice-Bureau of Justice Statistics] In the broadest usage, delinquency is juvenile actions or conduct in violation of criminal law, juvenile status offenses, and other juvenile behavior. Common usage frequently includes not only criminal offenses, but also status offenses, violations of accepted conventions of behavior, or tendencies to engage in such conduct. In an effort to order the concept of delinquency, the Bureau of Justice Statistics has recommended the following four terms: A *delinquent act* is an act committed by a juvenile for which an adult could be prosecuted in a criminal court, but for which a juvenile can be adjudicated in a juvenile court or prosecuted in a court having criminal jurisdiction if the juvenile court transfers jurisdiction. Generally, a delinquent act is a felony or misdemeanor level offense in States employing these terms. A *delinquent* is a juvenile who has been adjudged by a judicial officer of a juvenile court to have committed a delinquent act. A *status offense* is an act or conduct which is declared by statute to be an offense when committed or engaged in by a juvenile and which can only be adjudicated in a juvenile court. Typical status offenses are violation of curfew, running away from home, truancy, possession of an alcoholic beverage, incorrigibility, having delinquent tendencies, and being in need of supervision. Status offense ordinarily refers to juvenile conduct, but the term also refers to adults who were charged with the status of being vagrant or an addict. A *status offender* is a juvenile who has been adjudged by a judicial officer of a juvenile court to have committed a status offense.

See also **juvenile; PINS/CHINS/JINS/MINS.**

delinquent see **delinquency.**

delinquent act see **delinquency.**

demand (electric utilities) [Energy Information Administration] In the generation of electricity, demand is the rate at which electric energy is delivered to or by a system, part of a system, or piece of equipment, at a given instant, or averaged over any designated period of time.

demographic data [Department of Commerce-Bureau of the Census] Demographic data are statistics related to the size, density, distribution, social structure, and related characteristics of human populations. As used by the Census Bureau, the term often refers to socioeconomic data obtained from censuses and surveys of persons, households, and housing units; as distinguished from economic data which are collected from business establishments and organizations.
See also **census; economic census; survey.**

density (population) see **population density.**

dental visit [Department of Health and Human Services-Public Health Service; National Center for Health Statistics] The National Health Interview Survey (NHIS) counts visits to a dentist's office for treatment or advice, including services by a technician or hygienist acting under the supervision of a dentist, as dental visits. Dental services provided to hospital inpatients are not included.
See also **National Health Interview Survey (NHIS).**

depository institution [Federal Reserve Bank of New York] Depository institution is a term which includes commercial banks, savings banks, savings and loan associations, credit unions, foreign bank branches and agencies in the United States, Edge Act corporations, and agreement corporations.
See also **agreement corporation; Edge Act corporation.**

depreciable assets [Department of Commerce-Bureau of the Census] Depreciable assets are capital assets, items of property whose value can be depreciated over time for accounting and tax purposes. In the economic censuses, the definition of fixed depreciable assets is consistent with the definition of capital expenditures. For example, expenditures include actual capital outlays during the year, rather than the value of equipment put in place and buildings completed during the year. Accordingly, the value of assets at the end of the year includes the value of construction in progress. Respondents to the economic census were asked to make sure that assets at the beginning of the year, plus new and used capital expenditures, less retirements, equalled assets at the end of the year.
See also **new and used capital expenditures (manufacturing); retirements (capital assets).**

depreciation charges [Department of Commerce-Bureau of the Census] In the economic censuses, depreciation charges include all depreciation and amortization charged during the year against assets. Depreciation charged against fixed assets acquired since the beginning of the year and against assets sold or retired during the year are components of this category. Depreciation charges do not include accumulated depreciation.

See also **retirements (capital assets)**.

design capacity see **institutional capacity (corrections)**.

detention [Department of Justice-Bureau of Justice Statistics] Detention is the legally authorized confinement of a person subject to criminal or juvenile court proceedings until the point of commitment to a correctional facility or until release.

Dictionary of Occupational Titles (DOT) [Department of Labor-U.S. Employment Service] The Dictionary of Occupational Titles (DOT), first published in 1939, provides a comprehensive system of defining and classifying jobs. In order to look at the millions of jobs in the U.S. economy in an organized way, DOT groups jobs into occupations based on their similarities and defines the structure and content of all listed occupations. Occupational definitions are the result of comprehensive studies of how similar jobs are performed in establishments all over the nation and are composites of data collected from diverse sources. The term occupation as used in DOT refers to this collective description of a number of individual jobs performed, with minor variations, in many establishments.

There are six parts to an occupational definition: the occupational code number; the occupational title; the industry designation; alternative titles, if any; the body of the definition; and undefined related titles, if any. DOT classifications are used in private industry as well as a variety of government data programs, perhaps most notable in the Occupational Employment Statistics survey, OES.

DOT differs from the Standard Occupational Classification (SOC) system which results from an interagency effort to promote compatibility in occupational classification. Although they are separate systems, there is a significant degree of compatibility between DOT and SOC.

See also **Occupational Employment Statistics (OES) survey; Standard Occupational Classification (SOC) system**.

diesel fuel see **distillate fuel oil**.

diffusion index/rate of change [Department of Commerce-Bureau of Economic Analysis] Many of the Bureau of Economic Analysis' economic time series, measures in specific areas of the economy which are tracked over time, are aggregates consisting of numerous components. A diffusion index summarizes how the individual components of an aggregate move over a given time span. It indicates the percentage of components that are rising, with half of the unchanged components considered as rising. Because diffusion indexes computed over short time spans are highly erratic, they are computed from the changes over the relatively longer time periods of six or nine months or three or four quarters, in addition to one month or one quarter periods. Longer spans help to highlight the trends underlying the short term fluctuations.

Although movements in diffusion indexes and in rates of change for the same aggregates are generally positively correlated, these two measures present information about two related but distinct aspects of economic change. Diffusion indexes measure the prevailing direction or scope of change, while rates of change measure the degree as well as the overall direction. Thus diffusion indexes (which measure only direction) indicate how widespread a direction of movement is among the components, while rates of change measure the magnitude and direction of change in the aggregate series.

It should be noted that cyclical changes in diffusion indexes tend to lead those of the corresponding aggregates. Diffusion indexes are published in Business Conditions Digest (BCD) for the component series included in each of the major composite indexes and for the components of some other series, such as industrial production, stock prices, and expenditures for plant and equipment.

Rates of change are also shown in BCD for a number of economic time series, including the major composite indexes and other important indicators of economic activity. Rates of change are shown for one and three or six month time spans, or for one and four quarter time spans. As is the case for diffusion indexes, cyclical movements in the rates of change tend to lead those of corresponding indexes or aggregates, and thus, they tend to lead at business cycle turns as well.

See also **composite indexes; cyclical indicators.**

DIME [Department of Commerce-Bureau of the Census] DIME (dual independent map encoding) is a technique used to edit geographic base files for completeness. Sometimes the term DIME file is used synonymously with geographic base file (GBF).

See also **GBF/DIME file.**

direct expenditure (government) [Department of Commerce-Bureau of the Census] Government direct expenditures are payments to employees, suppliers, contractors, beneficiaries, and other final recipients of government payments. Direct expenditures are all expenditures other than intergovernmental expenditures.

See also **expenditure (government); general expenditure (government); intergovernmental expenditure.**

disability [Department of Health and Human Services-Public Health Service; National Center for Health Statistics] A disability is any temporary or long term reduction of a person's activity as a result of an acute or chronic condition. A disability is often measured in terms of the number of days that a person's activity has been reduced. The 1980 Census collected data on persons with a work disability and those with a public transportation disability.

See also **condition (health); disability day; public transportation disability; work disability.**

disability day [Department of Health and Human Services-Public Health Service; National Center for Health Statistics] For the National Health Interview Survey (NHIS), a disability day is a day on which a person's usual activity is reduced because of illness or injury. There are four types of disability days on which the NHIS reports. They are:

A *restricted-activity day* is a day on which a person cuts down on his or her usual activities because of illness or injury.

A *bed-disability day* is a day on which a person stays in bed more than half of the daylight hours or normal waking hours because of a specific illness or injury. All hospital days are bed-disability days.

A *work-loss day* is a day on which a person did not work at his or her job or business for at least half of his or her normal workday because of a specific illness or injury. Work loss days are determined only for employed persons

A *school-loss day* is a day on which a child did not attend school for at least half of his or her normal schoolday because of a specific illness or injury. School-loss days are determined only for children 6 to 16 years of age.

These four types of disability days are not mutually exclusive; thus, a bed-disability day may also be a work-loss day, etc.

See also **disability; National Health Interview Survey (NHIS).**

discharge (hospital) [Department of Health and Human Services-Public Health Service; National Center for Health Statistics] In the National Health Interview Survey (NHIS), a hospital discharge is the completion of any continuous period of stay of one night or more in a hospital as an inpatient, excepting the period of stay of a well newborn infant.

In the National Hospital Discharge Survey (NHDS), the American Hospital Association (AHA), and the National Master Facility Inventory (NMFI), a discharge is the formal release of an inpatient by a hospital, i.e. the termination of a period of hospitalization, including stays of 0 nights, by death or by disposition to a place of residence, nursing home, or another hospital. Newborn infants are excluded.

See also **discharges (hospital-mental health).**

discharges (hospital-mental health) [Department of Health and Human Services-Public Health Service; Alcohol, Drug Abuse, and Mental Health Administration] For persons hospitalized for mental disorders, discharges represent the number of persons released or discharged from inpatient care, including transfers to non-inpatient components and non-psychiatric wards of non-federal general hospitals.

Discharges exclude deaths. For survey reporting purposes, if one person is discharged more than once during a year, each discharge is counted separately.
See also **discharge (hospital)**.

discontinuer see **dropout**.

discount house [Federal Reserve Bank of New York] A discount house is an organization which purchases and discounts trade and banker's acceptances, bills of exchange, and various forms of commercial paper.
See also **banker's acceptance; commercial paper**.

discount rate [Federal Reserve Bank of New York] The discount rate is the interest rate the Federal Reserve Bank charges on advances. It is payable when the advance is repaid. The discount rate is expressed in annual terms and interest charges are computed on the basis of the number of days funds are actually advanced. Thus charges on a one day advance would be 1/365 of the discount rate. The discount rate is fixed by directors of each Federal Reserve Bank every 14 days, subject to the review of Board of Governors of the Federal Reserve System.

disease see **notifiable disease; cause of death; prevalence (health)**.

disposable income see **disposable personal income**.

disposable personal income [Department of Commerce-Bureau of Economic Analysis] Disposable personal income represents a portion of personal income available to persons for spending and saving. It is equal to personal income less personal tax and non-tax payments. Personal tax and non-tax payments are tax payments net of refunds excluding contributions for social insurance that are not chargeable to business expenses, and certain personal payments to general government that are treated like taxes. Personal taxes include income taxes, estate and gift taxes, personal property taxes, and motor vehicle licenses. Non-tax payments include passport fees, fines and penalties, donations, tuition and fees paid to schools and hospitals mainly operated by the government.
See also **income; income after taxes; income before taxes; money income; personal income**.

distillate fuel oil [Energy Information Administration] Distillate fuel oil is one of several light fuel oils distilled in the refining process. Included are products known as No. 1, No. 2, and No. 4 fuel oils; and No. 1, No. 2, and No. 4 diesel fuels; that conform to either ASTM specification D396 or D975. These products are used primarily for space heating, as on and off highway diesel engine fuel including railroad engine fuel and fuel for agricultural machinery and for electric power generation.

district [Department of Commerce-Bureau of the Census] A district is a minor civil division in Pennsylvania, Virginia, and West Virginia.
See also **minor civil division (MCD)**.

division [Department of Commerce-Bureau of the Census] A division is a principal statistical unit of census geography. The nation is divided into four regions: the Northeast, Midwest or North Central, South, and West. These regions are further subdivided into nine divisions: *New England Division* (Maine, New Hampshire, Vermont, Massachusetts, Rhode Island, Connecticut) and the *Mid Atlantic Division* (New York, New Jersey, Pennsylvania) are in the Northeast. The *East North Central Division* (Ohio, Indiana, Illinois, Michigan, Wisconsin) and *West North Central Division* (Minnesota, Iowa, Missouri, North Dakota, South Dakota, Nebraska, Kansas) are in the Midwest. The *South Atlantic Division* (Delaware, Maryland, District of Columbia, Virginia, West Virginia, North Carolina, South Carolina, Georgia, Florida), *East South Central Division* (Kentucky Tennessee, Alabama, Mississippi), and *West South Central Division* (Arkansas, Louisiana, Oklahoma, Texas) are in the South. The *Mountain Division* (Montana, Idaho, Wyoming, Colorado, New Mexico, Arizona, Utah, Nevada) and *Pacific Division* (Washington, Oregon, California, Alaska, Hawaii) are in the West.
See also **census geography; region**.

divorce see **marital status**.

doctor's degree [Department of Education-Center for Education Statistics] A doctor's degree is an earned degree carrying the title of doctor, such as Ph.D. (Doctor of Philosophy), Ed.D. (Doctor of Education), or D.B.A. (Doctor of Business Administration). First professional degrees such as M.D. (Medical Doctor), D.D.S. (Doctor of Dental Surgery), and J.D. (Juris Doctor) are not included as doctor's degrees.

(F.W.) Dodge Construction Contracts [Department of Commerce-Bureau of Economic Analysis] Each month, Survey of Current Business publishes data concerning the total value of construction in the 50 States and the District of Columbia, based on material from Dodge Reports, a publication of McGraw-Hill. This series is called Dodge Construction Contracts. The valuation figures provided represent actual construction costs. Construction costs are all costs of construction, exclusive of land, architectural fees and, in the case of manufactured buildings, the cost of the equipment that is not an integral part of the structure. The monthly indexes of total value of construction are based on seasonally adjusted data. The annual indexes are separately based and are not averages of monthly figures. Annual totals are also widely republished by the federal government, most notably in Statistical Abstract of the United States.

domestic services [Department of Labor-Bureau of Labor Statistics] Domestic services is a type of expenditure detailed in the Consumer Expenditure Survey (CEX). It includes consumer unit expenditures for babysitters, day care tuition, care of invalids, and domestic and other duties.

See also **Consumer Expenditure Survey (CEX); consumer unit.**

DOT see **Dictionary of Occupation Titles (DOT).**

double sessions (education) [Department of Education-National Center for Education Statistics] A double session is a school day consisting of separate sessions for two groups of pupils in the same instructional space. For example a double session may include one room used by one fourth grade class in the morning and by another fourth grade class in the afternoon; or one school building used by high school juniors and seniors during a morning session and by freshmen and sophomores during an afternoon session.

dropout [Department of Education-National Center for Education Statistics] A dropout is a student who leaves school for any reason except death before graduation or completion of a program of studies without transferring to another school. The term dropout is used most often to designate an elementary or secondary school student who has been in membership during the regular school term and who withdraws from membership before graduating from secondary school or before completing an equivalent program of studies. Such an individual is considered a dropout whether the dropping out occurs before or after the pupil has passed the compulsory school attendance age, and, where applicable, whether or not the pupil has completed a minimum required amount of schoolwork. The term dropout is used synonymously with the term discontinuer.

See also **elementary school; membership; secondary school.**

dry natural gas see **natural gas.**

DSM-III [Department of Health and Human Services-Public Health Service; Alcohol, Drug Abuse, and Mental Health Administration] DSM-III (Diagnostic and Statistical Manual of Mental Disorders, 3rd edition) is a volume prepared by the American Psychiatric Association which defines and groups mental disorders and is used for statistical classification purposes in mental health studies.

See also **mental disorder.**

durable goods 1. [Department of Commerce-Bureau of the Census] Durable goods are manufactured products with an expected lifetime of more than three years.

See also **non-durable goods.**

2. [Department of Commerce-Bureau of Economic Analysis] Durable goods are those produced by the following industries: stone, clay and glass products;

69

primary metals; fabricated metal products; machinery; transportation; and instruments and related products.

See also **household durable goods; non-durable goods.**

duration of unemployment [Department of Labor-Bureau of Labor Statistics] Duration of unemployment represents the length of time, through the current survey week, during which persons classified as unemployed have been continuously looking for work. Thus duration of unemployment is a measure of an in-progress spell of joblessness. For persons on layoff, duration of unemployment represents the number of full weeks since the termination of their most recent employment.

A period of two weeks or more during which a person was employed or ceased looking for work is considered to break the continuity of the present period of seeking work.

Two useful measures of duration of unemployment are the mean and the median. Mean duration is the arithmetic average computed from single weeks of unemployment. Median duration is the midpoint of a distribution of weeks of unemployment.

Data on duration of unemployment comes from the Current Population Survey (CPS).

See also **Current Population Survey (CPS); labor force; unemployment.**

E

earner [Department of Labor-Bureau of Labor Statistics] In the Consumer Expenditure Survey (CEX), an earner is a member of a consumer unit, 14 years old or over, who reported having worked at least one week during the 12 months prior to the interview date. The concept of earner as used in the CEX is distinct from the concept of an employed person or a member of the civilian labor force.

See also **Consumer Expenditure Survey (CEX).**

earnings [Department of Commerce-Bureau of the Census] Earnings is defined as an income aggregation representing the sum of wage and salary income, and self employment income. Earnings are those sources of income most appropriately interrelated with labor force characteristics, such as hours and weeks worked, or occupation.

See also **income.**

ECI see **Employment Cost Index.**

economic census [Department of Commerce-Bureau of the Census] The economic censuses provide basic business data on establishments, employment, payroll, sales, receipts, value of shipments, operating and capital expenditures assets and inventories. Results of each economic census are published separately, and in summary form they appear in Statistical Abstract of the United States.

The Bureau of the Census conducts economic censuses every five years in years ending in 2 or 7. The economic censuses cover seven sectors: retail trade, wholesale trade, service industries, construction industries, manufactures, mineral industries, and transportation; along with an economic census of Puerto Rico and outlying areas under U.S. sovereignty or jurisdiction. As part of the economic census programs, there are also surveys of minority-owned businesses and women-owned businesses. The Enterprise Statistics Program is also part of the economic censuses.

While economic censuses are intended to provide fairly complete enumerations, there is a need for intercensal data as well. To meet this need the Bureau has a number of programs which provide current statistics, the results of which are published in Current Business Reports, the Annual Survey of Manufactures, Current Industrial Reports, and their Quarterly Financial Report. County Business Patterns is another source of annual business and economic statistics, but it is based largely on administrative records. A key difference between the censuses and the surveys that update them is that the censuses present a relatively complete, detailed picture of the economic sectors they cover, from the national to the local level, while the surveys generally have less geographic, industry, and related detail.

economic maximum yield (agriculture) [Department of Agriculture-Office of Governmental and Public Affairs] The economic maximum yield is the most that can be produced by full and efficient application of technology known by all farmers. The concept assumes no limitation on management, materials, equipment, capital, and experience.

economic times series [Department of Labor-Bureau of the Census] The term time series refers to information collected or recorded at intervals through time (weekly, monthly, annually, etc.). An economic time series collects or records economic information over a period of time. Examples of economic time series are: monthly reports of employment in the United States, annual data on retail sales for the State of New York, and monthly steel production. An economic time series may be made up of simple counts such as unemployment, dollar values such as income, or other types of data. They may also present information in the form of an index such as the Consumer Price Index. Economic time series are usually shown in tabular form or in charts and graphs.

ED see **census enumeration district.**

Edge Act corporation [Federal Reserve Bank of New York] An Edge Act corporation is a State chartered U.S. corporation which engages in international banking and finance and does not accept domestic deposits. In practice, Edge Act corporations are usually majority owned by a U.S. banking organization.
    See also **agreement corporation.**

educational attainment [Department of Education-Center for Education Statistics] Educational attainment is the highest grade of regular school attended and completed.

efficiency (housing) [Department of Commerce-Bureau of the Census] An efficiency is a one room apartment or studio apartment which has no room specifically designated for sleeping.
    See also **bedroom; room.**

election precinct see **precinct (election).**

electric utility [Energy Information Administration] An electric utility is a corporation, person, agency, authority, or other entity that owns or operates facilities for the generation, transmission, distribution, or sale of electricity, primarily for use by the public.
    Class A electric utilities are those having annual electric operating revenues of $2.5 million or more. Class B electric utilities are those having annual electric operating revenues of more than $1.0 million, but less than $2.5 million.

lectricity exchange see **net interstate sales of electricity.**

lectricity generation [Energy Information Administration] There are two frequently used measures of electricity generation, gross electricity generation and net electricity generation.

Gross electricity generation is the total amount of electrical energy produced by a generating station or stations, measured at the generator terminal.

Net electricity generation is a measure which is equal to gross electricity generation less electricity consumed at the generating plant for station use. Electricity required for pumping at pumped-storage plants is regarded as plant use and is deducted from gross generation. Net electricity generation is the main measure of electricity generation used in the United States.

lectricity sales [Energy Information Administration] As a measure, electricity sales is comprised of the gross electricity output measured at the generator terminals, minus power plant use and transmission and distribution losses. Included in sales to each end-use sector are the following: commercial sales of electricity include sales to businesses that generally require less than 1,000 kilowatts of service; industrial sales of electricity include sales to businesses that generally require more than 1,000 kilowatts of service; residential sales of electricity are sales to residences for household purposes; other sales of electricity include sales to government, railways, street lighting authorities, and sales not elsewhere included.

See also **end-use sector; net interstate sales of electricity.**

lementary school [Department of Education-Center for Education Statistics] An elementary school is any school classified as elementary by State and local practice and composed of any span of grades not above grade 8. A preschool or kindergarten is included under this heading only if it is an integral part of an elementary school or a regularly established school system.

limination (utilities) [Energy Information Administration] In accounting by utilities, consolidated company accounts do not include intersegment revenues and expenditures. Elimination is a procedure performed by the Energy Information Administration in reporting accounting data which eliminates revenue and expenditures resulting from transactions between segments.

mbezzlement [Department of Justice-Bureau of Justice Statistics] Embezzlement is the misappropriation, misapplication, or illegal disposal of legally entrusted property by the person(s) to whom it was entrusted, with intent to defraud the legal owner or intended beneficiary. Embezzlement is classified in the Uniform Crime Reports (UCR) as UCR 12.

See also **Uniform Crime Reports (UCR).**

employed persons 1. [Department of Labor-Bureau of Labor Statistics] Data published by the Bureau of Labor Statistics concerning employed persons comes from two main sources, the Current Employment Statistics (CES) program, a payroll survey of establishments, and the Current Population Survey (CPS), a monthly survey of households. Each survey uses a different concept of employed person for its count, hence two separate definitions of employment are required.

1a. In CES data, employed persons are those persons who worked during, or received pay for, any part of the pay period which includes the 12th day of the month. Exceptions include: national figures for federal government establishments represent the number of civilian persons who occupied positions on the last day of the calendar month, and intermittent workers are counted if they performed any service during the month. Workers on an establishment payroll who are on paid sick leave where pay is received directly from the employer, on paid holiday, or paid vacation, or who worked only part of the specified pay period, are counted as employed. Temporary employees are also included.

Persons on the payroll of more than one establishment during the pay period are counted in each establishment which reports them, whether the duplication is due to turnover or dual jobholding.

Persons are considered employed if they receive pay for any part of the specified pay period, but are not considered employed if they receive no pay at all for the pay period. Since proprietors, the self employed, and unpaid family workers do not have the status of paid employees, they are not included. Domestic workers in households are also excluded from the data for non-agricultural establishments.

CES gathers data for hours and earnings for all employed persons as well as three sub-categories of all employees, depending on the industry.

1b. For CPS data, employed persons comprise all those who, during the survey week, did any work at all as paid employees, or in their own business profession, or on their own farm, or worked 15 hours or more as unpaid workers in a family-operated enterprise. It also includes those who did not work but had jobs or businesses from which they were temporarily absent due to illness, bad weather, vacation, labor-management dispute, or various personal reasons - whether or not they were paid by their employers for the time off and whether or not they were seeking other jobs. Members of the armed forces stationed in the United States are also included in total employment. Also included in CPS total employment are employed citizens of foreign countries temporarily in the United States, who are not living on the premises of an embassy.

Excluded from employed persons are those persons whose only activity consisted of work around their own home such as housework, painting, or repairing, or volunteer work for religious, charitable and similar organizations. Also excluded are those who are temporarily absent from a job due to layoff, and those who were waiting to begin a new job within 30 days.

In the CPS, each person is counted only once. Those who held more than one job are counted in the job at which they worked the greatest number of hours during the survey week. Thus the CPS universe is larger than the CES universe, and excludes potential duplication.

See also **class of worker; Current Employment Statistics (CES); Current Population Survey (CPS); employment; hours of work; labor force; population; unemployment.**

2. [Department of Commerce-Bureau of the Census] The CPS is done monthly by the Bureau and is the main source of employment data. However, the Census began a new, ongoing survey program in 1983, the Survey of Income and Program Participation (SIPP), which is also a household survey that collects data on employment and unemployment. There is one significant difference in employment and unemployment definitions between CPS and SIPP. For CPS, those who are temporarily absent from a job due to layoff, and those who were waiting to begin a new job within 30 days are considered unemployed. Under SIPP methodology, such persons are considered to be employed.

See also **class of worker; Survey of Income and Program Participation (SIPP).**

mployment [Department of Labor-Bureau of Labor Statistics] Employment is the total number of employed persons. Data published by the Bureau of Labor Statistics concerning employment comes from two main sources, the Current Employment Statistics (CES) program, a payroll survey of establishments and the Current Population Survey (CPS), a monthly survey of households. Each survey uses a different concept of employed person for its count, along with different collection and estimating techniques hence two separate definitions of employment are required.

1. In the CES, employment represents the total number of employed persons working full or part-time in non-agricultural establishments during a specific payroll period.

2. For the CPS, employment is the total number of all employed persons, including members of the armed forces stationed in the United States, during a survey week. CPS employment numbers include agricultural workers and armed services personnel as well as proprietors, self employed persons, domestic workers employed in households, and some family workers, thus they encompass a larger universe than CES data. There are other significant differences between the two surveys as well.

See also **employed persons; class of worker; Current Employment Statistics (CES) program; Current Population Survey (CPS); hours of work; labor force; unemployment.**

mployment and Wages program see **ES-202 program.**

employment benchmark [Department of Labor-Bureau of Labor Statistics] An employment benchmark is a reasonably complete count of employment used to adjust estimates derived from a sample. Adjustment is usually done annually. For the Current Employment Statistics (CES) program, the basic source of benchmark data is data collected from employers by State employment security agencies as a byproduct of the unemployment insurance system. About 98% of all employees on non-agricultural payrolls are covered by the unemployment insurance system.

See also **Current Employment Statistics (CES); employed persons; employment.**

Employment Cost Index (ECI) [Department of Labor-Bureau of Labor Statistics] The Employment Cost Index (ECI) is a measure of the rate of change in employee compensation. Employee compensation includes wages, salaries, and employers' cost for employee benefits. The ECI is more comprehensive than simple wage measures in that it includes costs incurred by employers for employee benefits in addition to wages and salaries. Also, it covers all establishments and occupations in both the private non-farm and public sectors. It excludes the self employed, owner-managers, private household workers, federal government workers, and unpaid family workers.

The ECI measures the change in the cost of employing by using a fixed set of labor inputs, so it is not affected over time by changes in the composition of the labor force. Data is based on a sample of more than 3,000 private industry establishments and 700 establishments in state and local government, and a sample of jobs within those establishments. The survey is timely in that statistics are published quarterly in news releases approximately one month after their reference date. The ECI is also published in Current Wage Developments and Monthly Labor Review.

As the measure of change in the price of labor, the ECI enables users to compare rates of change in detailed occupational, industrial, geographic, union coverage, and ownership submeasures.

See also **compensation.**

employment status see **labor force.**

end-use consumption see **end-use energy consumption.**

end-use energy consumption [Energy Information Administration] End-use energy consumption is a measure which represents total energy consumption less losses incurred in the generation, transmission, and distribution of electricity, and less power plant use and unaccounted-for system energy losses. As end-use energy consumption is typically reported by consuming sector, it is also equal to the sum of fossil fuel consumption in the residential, commercial, industrial, and transportation end-use sectors, plus electric utility sales to these sectors and generation of hydroelectric power by non-electric utilities.

See also **end-use sector.**

nd-use sector [Energy Information Administration] In general, end-use sector reporting presents energy consumption based on the kind of activity in which the ultimate end-user of that energy is engaged. Among the ways energy and fuel consumption is reported by the Energy Information Administration, consumption by end-use sector is the most common.

There are four end-use sectors: The *residential sector* represents consumption by private households for space heating, water heating, air conditioning, lighting, refrigeration, cooking and other household uses. The *commercial sector* represents consumption by non-manufacturing establishments including hotels, motels, restaurants, wholesale businesses, retail stores, laundries, service businesses, hospitals, educational institutions, and federal, State, and local governments. The *industrial sector* includes establishments primarily engaged in the processing of unfinished materials into another form of product, including mining, manufacturing, and petroleum refining establishments. The *transportation sector* represents sales of fuels for use in public and private vehicles that move people and commodities, including fuel for automobiles, trucks, buses, motorcycles, railroads and railways, aircraft, ships and barges, and natural gas pipelines.

Sometimes data is provided for a fifth sector, the *electric utility sector,* which is used to report sales of fuels like coal, petroleum, and natural gas to publicly and privately owned establishments that generate electricity primarily for use by the public.

See also **electricity sales; natural gas.**

ndowment [Department of Education-Center for Education Statistics] An endowment is a trust fund set aside to provide a perpetual source of revenue from the proceeds of the endowment investments. Endowment funds are often created by donations from benefactors of an institution who may designate the use of the endowment revenue. Normally institutions or their representatives manage the investments, but they are not permitted to spend the endowment fund itself, only the proceeds from the investments.

nergy weighted industrial output [Energy Information Administration] The energy weighted industrial output is a measure which represents the weighted sum of real output for all manufacturing industries, agriculture, construction, and mining to the two digit Standard Industrial Classification (SIC) code level. The weight for each industry is the ratio for between the quantity of end-use energy consumption and the value of real output.

See also **Standard Industrial Classification (SIC).**

engaged in housework see **labor force.**

Engineering News-Record (ENR) **indexes** [Department of Commerce-Bureau of Economic Analysis] Each month, Survey of Current Business re-publishes four Engineering News-Record (ENR) indexes concerned with construction: the new construction planning index, the construction cost index, the building cost index, and construction hourly wage rates.

New construction planning index: The new construction planning index covers new construction plans for public and private construction projects excluding one and two family homes in the continental United States and Alaska which are valued at $750,000 or more which have entered the planning stages. The data comes from the Dodge Major Projects Database and is issued monthly and annually.

Construction cost index and *building cost index:* Each of the cost indexes cover construction costs and each has four components, three for material items and one for labor. The three material items for both indexes are the same: a) the average mill price for structural steel shapes; b) a 20 city average of wholesale prices for portland cement; and c) a 20 city average of wholesale prices for 2" x 4" S4S pine and fir in carload lots. The labor component of the construction cost index, which is designed to show the movement of construction costs in general, is the common labor rate, the ENR 20 city average, while the labor component of the building cost index is the ENR 20 city average for three skilled labor trades, carpenters, bricklayers, and structural iron workers. The component series are weighted by a formula according to their relative importance as determined by the compilers.

Both cost indexes measure the effects of wage-rate and material-price trends. They are not adjusted for productivity, managerial efficiency, competitive conditions, contractor overhead and profit, design changes or other less tangible cost factors.

Construction hourly wage rates: The construction hourly wage rates are presented for common and skilled labor and represent the hourly wages as of the 1st of each month. The data are compiled from monthly reports of correspondents in 20 cities. The rates shown are arithmetic averages of wages actually paid in the 20 cities and cover take home pay plus fringe benefits, including welfare fund, pension fund, etc. The data reflect retroactive wage increases. The skilled labor rates are averages from three principal trades: bricklayers, carpenters, and structural ironworkers. The common labor rates are averages for building and heavy construction workers.

See also **Boeckh indexes; (F.W.) Dodge Construction Costs.**

enrollment [Department of Education-Center for Education Statistics] Enrollment is defined as the total number of students registered in a given school unit at a given time, usually in the fall of a year.

See also **full time enrollment (higher education); part-time enrollment (higher education); post-baccalaureate enrollment.**

enterprise see **firm (business).**

enumeration district see **census enumeration district.**

ES-202 program [Department of Labor-Bureau of Labor Statistics] The ES-202 program is a cooperative endeavor of the Bureau of Labor Statistics (BLS) and the employment security agencies of the 50 States, the District of Columbia, Puerto Rico, and the Virgin Islands. Using quarterly reports representing approximately 5.5 million reporting units submitted by the agencies, BLS summarizes employment and wage data for workers covered by State unemployment insurance laws, and for civilian workers covered by the program of Unemployment Compensation for Federal Employees (UCFE).

The ES-202 program is a comprehensive and accurate source of employment and wage data, by industry at the national, State, and county levels. It is so extensive as to provide a virtual census of non-agricultural employees and their wages. In addition, about 40% of all workers in agriculture are covered. Data from the program is presented primarily in <u>Employment and Wages</u>, an annual BLS publication.

Eskimo see **race.**

establishment [Executive Office of the President-Office of Management and Budget; Statistical Policy Division] An establishment is an economic unit, generally at a single physical location where business is conducted or where services or industrial operations are performed. Examples of establishments include a factory, mill, store, hotel, movie theatre, mine, farm, ranch, bank, railroad depot, airline terminal, sales office, warehouse, or central administrative office.

Where distinct and separate economic activities are performed at a single physical location, each activity is treated as a separate establishment, if a) no one industry description in the classification includes such combined activities; b) the employment in each economic activity is significant, and c) reports can be prepared on the number of employees, their wages and salaries, sales or receipts, and other establishment type data.

For activities such as construction, transportation, communication, electric, gas, sanitary services, and similar physically dispersed operations, establishments are represented by those relatively permanent main or branch offices, terminals, stations, etc., which are either a) directly responsible for supervising such activities, or b) the base from which personnel operate to carry out these activities. Hence, the individual sites, projects, fields, networks, lines, or systems of such dispersed activities are not ordinarily considered to be establishments.

An establishment is not necessarily identical with an enterprise or company, as an enterprise or company may consist of one or more establishments. Also, an establishment is to be distinguished from sub-units, departments, or divisions. Supplemental interpretations of the definition of an establishment are included in the industry descriptions in the Standard Industrial Classification Manual (SIC) where appropriate.

Central administrative offices and auxiliary units are recognized as special types of establishments. A *central administrative office* is an establishment primarily engaged in general administrative supervisory, accounting, purchasing, engineering and systems planning, advertising, legal, financial, or related management functions performed centrally for other establishments of the same company. Central administrative offices characteristically do not produce any products nor do they provide any services for the general public, other companies, or the government.

An *auxiliary unit* is an establishment primarily engaged in performing supporting services for other establishments of the same company, rather than for the general public or for other business firms Auxiliaries include such diverse activities as research, development and testing laboratories of manufacturing firms; central warehouses for the company's own merchandise; central garages for the company's own vehicles,; sales promotion offices and the like.

This definition of establishment and the related concepts of central administrative office and auxiliary unit are widely used by both the Department of Commerce, and the Department of Labor.

See also **enterprise, firm (business)**.

estimation error see **non-sampling error**.

ethane [Energy Information Administration] Ethane is a normally gaseous, paraffinic hydrocarbon extracted from natural gas or refinery gas streams. Ethane is used primarily as petrochemical feedstock for eventual production of chemicals and plastic materials.

ethylene [Energy Information Administration] Ethylene is a normally gaseous, olefinic hydrocarbon recovered from refinery processes. For statistical reporting purposes, quantities are included with ethane data.

See also **ethane**.

eurodollar [Federal Reserve Bank of New York] A eurodollar is a U.S. dollar held outside the United States, usually as a deposit in a commercial bank. Such deposits may be owned by either U.S. residents or non-residents. Eurodollars are used by banks, corporations, and foreign governments in international commerce.

expenditure (government) [Department of Commerce-Bureau of the Census] Government expenditure includes all amounts of money paid out by a government net of recoveries and other correcting transactions, other than those for the retirement of debt, investment in securities, extension of credit, or as agency transactions. Note that a government's expenditures includes only external transactions of the government and excludes non-cash transactions such as the provision of perquisites or other payments in kind. Aggregate expenditures for groups of governments exclude intergovernmental transactions among the governments.

See also **agency and private trust transaction; direct expenditure (government); general expenditure (government); intergovernmental expenditure.**

expenditures (education) [Department of Education-Center for Education Statistics] Expenditures in education are charges incurred which are presumed to benefit the current fiscal year. For elementary/secondary schools, these include all charges for current outlays plus capital outlays and interest on school debt. For institutions of higher education, these include current outlays plus capital outlays.

See also **current expenditures (elementary/secondary); current-fund expenditures (higher education); expenditures per pupil.**

expenditures per pupil [Department of Education-Center for Education Statistics] Expenditures per pupil are charges incurred for a particular period of time divided by a student unit of measure, such as average daily attendance (ADA) or average daily membership (ADM).

See also **average daily attendance (ADA); average daily membership (ADM); current expenditures (elementary/secondary).**

experienced worker [Department of Labor-Bureau of Labor Statistics] An experienced worker is any employed civilian labor force (CLF) member or any unemployed CLF member who has worked at any time in the past.

See also **civilian labor force; labor force.**

exports 1. [Department of Commerce-Bureau of Economic Analysis] Exports are goods and services provided by U.S. residents to foreigners. Combined with imports, they are used in computing the Gross National Product.

See also **Gross National Product (GNP); net export of goods and services.**

2. [Department of Commerce-Bureau of Economic Analysis] In foreign trade statistics, total exports reflect exports from the U.S. customs area of domestic and foreign merchandise by both the government and non-government shippers. There are six exceptions/exclusions: (1) merchandise shipped in transit through the United States from one foreign country to another; (2) goods destined for the

U.S. Armed Forces or U.S. diplomatic missions abroad for their own use; (3) bunker fuel and supplies and equipment for vessels and planes engaged in foreign trade; (4) non-monetary gold and silver in the form of ore, sweepings, scrap, base and refined bullion, etc.; (5) issued monetary coins of all component metals; and (6) items of relatively small statistical importance, such as low-value non-commercial shipments by mail, household and personal effects of travelers, and goods for the personal use of U.S. government employees abroad, etc. Included in the export figures reported in the Bureau's Foreign Trade reports are Department of Defense Military Assistance Program Grants-Aid shipments and economic assistance shipments under the Foreign Assistance Act. The data also reflect shipments of agricultural commodities under the Agricultural Trade Development and Assistance Act of 1954.

The value reported in export statistics is defined as the value at the U.S. port of export based on the selling price (or cost if not sold), including inland freight, insurance, and other charges to the U.S. port of export. The value, as defined, is equivalent to an f.a.s. valuation, excluding the cost of loading the goods aboard the exporting carrier and transportation or other costs beyond the port of export.

See also **f.a.s. valuation.**

extended city [Department of Commerce-Bureau of the Census] An extended city is an incorporated place located in an urbanized area, of which one or more portions are classified as rural. To be treated as an extended city, a city must contain one or more areas that are each at least five square miles in extent and have a population density of less than 100 persons per square mile. Together, such areas must constitute at least 25% of the land area of the legal city or include at least 25 square miles. For the 1990 census, this classification has also been applied to certain places outside urbanized areas. Only the urban part is considered to be the central city of an urbanized area.

See also **central city; incorporated place; Metropolitan Area (MA); urban/rural area.**

extortion [Department of Justice-Bureau of Justice Statistics] Extortion is defined as unlawfully obtaining or attempting to obtain something of value from another by compelling the other person to deliver it by threat of eventual physical injury or other harm to that person or his/her property, or a third person. Extortion differs from robbery in that in robbery there is an immediate confrontation between offender and victim, and the threatened injury is physical and imminent. Extortion is usually categorized as a type of theft offense.

See also **larceny-theft; robbery.**

extraction loss [Energy Information Administration] Extraction loss is the reduction in volume of natural gas due to the removal of natural gas constituents, such as ethane, propane, and butane, at natural gas processing plants.

F

failure index see **business failure.**

family [Department of Commerce-Bureau of the Census] A family is defined as a type of household in which two or more persons including the householder live together who are related by birth, marriage, or adoption. All such related persons in one housing unit are considered as members of one family. This includes related sub-families. However, non-family members who are not related to the householder, including non-related sub families such as a roomer or boarder and his or her spouse, are not counted as family members but as unrelated individuals living in a family household.

The measure, *persons per family,* excludes such unrelated individuals living in family households; however, such persons are included in the measure, persons per household.

A person maintaining a household alone, or two or more unrelated persons maintaining a household are regarded as a household, but not a family. Thus some households do not contain families. Additionally, for Census Bureau purposes, a housing unit can contain only one household, and a household may contain only one family.

See also **family type; household; householder; sub-family; unrelated individual.**

family farm [Department of Agriculture-Office of Governmental and Public Affairs] A family farm is one where the operator and the operator's family make most of the day-to-day management decisions, supply the equity capital, and supply a significant part of the labor needs.

See also **farm; farm operator.**

family income see **income.**

family type [Department of Commerce-Bureau of the Census] Families are classified by type according to the sex of the householder and the presence of a spouse and children. The three main types of family households are: *married couple families,* in which a husband and wife live together; *male householder, no wife present,* in which a male householder lives together with other members of his family but without a wife; and *female householder, no husband present,* in which a female householder lives together with other members of her family but without a husband.

See also **family; household; householder; sub-family.**

farm [Department of Commerce-Bureau of the Census] As defined by the Bureau of the Census and adopted by the Department of Agriculture, a farm is any place from which $1,000 or more of agricultural products were sold, or would have been sold during a given year. Control of the farm may be exercised through ownership or management, or through a lease, rental or cropping arrangement. In the case of landowners who have one or more tenants or renters, the land operated by each is counted as a separate farm. This definition has been in effect since 1974.

farm income [Department of Commerce-Bureau of the Census] Farm income is reported on both a gross and net basis. Gross farm income comprises cash receipts from farm marketings of crops and livestock, federal government payments made directly to farmers for farm-related activities, rental value of farm homes, value of farm products consumed in farm homes, and other farm-related income such as machine hire and custom work.

Net farm income is gross farm income less production expenses. Net farm income is measured in two ways: net farm income before inventory adjustment which does not include the changes in value of inventory such as crops and livestock, at the end of the year; and net farm income after inventory adjustment.

See also **farm; farm marketings.**

farm marketings [Department of Commerce-Bureau of the Census] Farm marketings are an aggregate representing the total value of agricultural products sold by farmers. Marketings are computed by multiplying the amount of farm product marketed by the price received per unit of production at the local market.

farm operator [Department of Agriculture-Office of Governmental and Public Affairs] A farm operator is a person who operates a farm by either doing or supervising the work and by making day-to-day operating decisions.

See also **farm.**

farm prices see **index of prices received by farmers**

farmland [Department of Commerce-Bureau of the Census] Farmland is all land under the control of a farm operator, including land not actually under cultivation or not used for pasture or grazing. Rent free land is included as part of a farm only if the operator has sole use of it. Farmland includes grazing lands controlled by grazing associations leased on a per acre basis. Land used for pasture or grazing on a per head basis that is neither owned nor leased by the farm operator is not included.

See also **farm operator.**

f.a.s. valuation [Department of Commerce-International Trade Administration] The f.a.s. (free alongside ship) import valuation method was used from 1974 to 1981 and represented the transaction value of imports at the foreign port of export. It was based on the purchase price and generally included all charges incurred in

placing the merchandise alongside the carrier at the foreign port of export. U.S. import duties, freight, insurance, and other charges incurred in bringing the merchandise to the United States were excluded. f.a.s. data were replaced with Customs valuation data beginning in 1982.
See also **c.i.f. valuation; customs valuation; imports.**

Federal-Aid Highway Construction Composite Index [Department of Commerce-Bureau of Economic Analysis] The Federal-Aid Highway Construction Composite index is a price index with 1967 = 100 which measures price changes for fixed amounts of items represented. It is a composite derived from actual contract prices for specified amounts of the following items: common excavation; surfacing including portland cement concrete pavement and bituminous concrete pavement; and structures including reinforcing steel, structural steel, and structural concrete. The index is published monthly in Survey of Current Business.
See also **federal-aid highway system.**

federal-aid highway system [Department of Transportation-Federal Highway Administration] The federal-aid highway system is a classification system of highways promulgated by the Department of Transportation for use in the distribution of federal aid. Federal law provides that federal funds be matched in varying proportions with State funds for the planning, engineering, right of way acquisition, and construction of highways. Effective July 1, 1976 a new federal-aid highway system was adopted, classifying highways into three systems.

The *federal-aid primary system* is comprised of a network of main roads important to interstate, statewide, and regional travel. The primary system consists of main rural roads and their extensions into or through urban areas. The National System of Interstate and Defense Highways, commonly called interstate highways, are part of the federal-aid primary system.

The *federal-aid secondary system* consists of rural roads of a more local nature, such as those which connect county seats and the larger population centers not served by the primary system.

The *federal-aid urban system* is located in urban places with 5,000 or more persons and consists of major urban roads and streets except those on the primary system.

The Federal Highway Administration also classifies highways in functional systems. Although the two systems are interrelated, with the exception of classification of interstate highways, the two systems do not correspond with each other.
See also **functional systems (highways).**

federal funds (banking) [Federal Reserve Bank of New York] Federal funds are funds that are available to a bank immediately without clearing. Federal Reserve regulations require banks to keep some such funds with the regional Federal Reserve bank as a reserve requirement. As the reserve requirements of an individual bank change frequently, federal funds are often bought and sold by banks to meet their needs for immediately available funds. The rate of interest charged by a lending bank is called the federal funds rate, which is almost always somewhat lower than the Federal Reserve discount rate. Although federal funds transactions take place at a Federal Reserve bank, the Federal Reserve System plays no part in the transaction other than to make the necessary transfers as directed by member banks.

See also **reserve requirement**.

federal hospital see **hospital**.

Federal Information Processing Standards (FIPS) code [Department of Commerce-Bureau of the Census] Federal Information Processing Standards (FIPS) code is an identification code assigned for a variety of geographic entities, including American Indian and Alaska Native areas, congressional districts, counties, county subdivisions, Metropolitan Areas, places, and States. The objective of the FIPS codes is to improve the use of data resources of the Federal government and avoid unnecessary duplication and incompatibilities in the collection, processing, and dissemination of data.

See also **United States Postal Service (USPS) code**.

federal marketing orders and agreements (agriculture) [Department of Agriculture-Office of Governmental and Public Affairs] Federal marketing orders and agreements are a means to permit agricultural producers collectively to influence the supply, demand, and/or price for a particular crop or commodity in order to improve the orderly marketing of that crop or commodity. They are authorized by, and based on, enabling legislation. Once approved by a required number of producers of the regulated commodity (usually two-thirds), the marketing order is binding on all handlers of the commodity in the area of regulation.

A federal marketing agreement may contain more diversified provisions, but it is enforceable with respect to those producers or handlers who voluntarily enter into the agreement with the Secretary of Agriculture.

federal physician see **physician**.

federally funded community mental health center (CMHC) [Department of Health and Human Services-Public Health Service; Alcohol, Drug Abuse, and Mental Health Administration] A federally funded community mental health center (CMHC) is a legal entity through which comprehensive mental health services are provided to a specific geographic area. This mental health delivery system may be implemented by a single organization or by a group of affiliated organizations that make available at least the following essential mental health services: inpatient, partial, outpatient, and emergency care, consultation, and education. Further, one

of the component organizations of a CMHC must be the recipient of federal funds under P.L. 88-164 (construction) and/or P.L. 89-105 (staffing) as amended. This definition is applicable to survey data obtained prior to 1981.
See also **mental health organization.**

feed grain [Department of Agriculture-Office of Governmental and Public Affairs] Feed grain is any of several grains that are used for livestock or poultry feed.

felony [Department of Justice-Bureau of Justice Statistics] A felony is a criminal offense punishable by death or by incarceration in a prison facility. In most jurisdictions, felonies are one of two major classes of crimes, the other being misdemeanors. The distinctive feature of the felony class is that although the upper limit of potential penalties depends upon the particular crime and ranges from as little as two years of confinement to death or life imprisonment, the lower limit for the entire class is relatively unvarying, usually one year.
See also **misdemeanor; prison.**

fertility rate [Department of Commerce-Bureau of the Census] The fertility rate is the number of births in a given population divided by the number of women of childbearing age in that population. Fertility rates in the United States are most frequently reported for women aged 18 to 44 years old and are collected as part of the Current Population Survey (CPS). In addition to national presentations, data is collected and prepared for subgroups of all women by age, race, region of residence, labor force status, and the like.

CPS fertility rates are based on women who have had a birth within the past year, and not on the actual number of births themselves. This may in effect understate fertility in that multiple births and women who have had more than one birth within the year are counted only once. CPS data excludes women who had a birth during the year but did not survive until the survey date, and women who were not part of the CPS survey universe.
See also **birth rate; completed fertility rate; Current Population Survey (CPS).**

fetal death rate [Department of Health and Human Services-Public Health Service; National Center for Health Statistics] The fetal death rate is the number of fetal deaths with stated or presumed gestation of 20 weeks or more per 1,000 live births plus fetal deaths.
See also **infant mortality; late fetal death rate; live birth; neonatal mortality rate; perinatal mortality rate; perinatal mortality ratio; postneonatal mortality rate.**

financing (housing) [Department of Commerce-Bureau of the Census] The type of financing of housing units is reported by the Bureau of the Census in the American Housing Survey (AHS) and other surveys. The type of financing reported such as Veteran's Administration (VA), Federal Housing Administration (FHA), or conventional loans, is the type of financing at the time the original sales agreement was signed or deposit accepted. This methodology is different from both the VA and FHA, which usually report financing data at the time of closing. As changes do occur between signing and settlement, it is possible that discrepancies may be found in comparing Census Bureau data with that of other agencies.

fines and forfeits [Department of Commerce-Bureau of the Census] Fines and forfeits is a category of government revenue consisting of moneys received from penalties imposed for violations of law and forfeits on amounts on deposit as performance guarantees. The category fines and forfeits does not include penalties on delinquent taxes.

See also **revenue (government)**.

finished goods see **stage of processing (SOP)**.

Finished Goods Price Index see **stage of processing (SOP)**.

FIPS see **Federal Information Processing Standards (FIPS) code**.

firm (business) [Department of Commerce-Bureau of the Census] In business enterprise, a firm is a legal entity engaged in economic activity which, for a given survey period, filed an IRS form 1040, Schedule C; 1065; 1120; or 1120S. A firm may operate one or more place of business or have no fixed business location. Although the term firm is often used interchangeably with company, business, and enterprise, it does differ from an establishment, which is a single physical location at which business is conducted.

See also **establishment**.

first listed diagnosis [Department of Health and Human Services-Public Health Service; National Center for Health Statistics] In the National Hospital Discharge Survey (NHDS), the first listed diagnosis is the diagnosis listed first on the face sheet of the medical record.

See also **National Hospital Discharge Survey (NHDS)**.

first professional degree [Department of Education-Center for Education Statistics] A first professional degree is one that signifies both completion of the academic requirements for beginning practice in a given profession and a level of skill beyond that normally required for a bachelor's degree. This degree is usually based on a program requiring at least two academic years of work to complete, including both prior required college work and the professional program itself. By Center for Education Statistics definition, first professional degrees are awarded in the fields of dentistry (D.D.S. or D.M.D.), medicine (M.D.), optometry (O.D.), osteopathic medicine (D.O.), pharmacy (D.Phar.), podiatric medicine (D.P.M.), veterinary medicine (D.V.M.), chiropractic (D.C. or D.C.M.), law (J.D.), and theological professions (M.Div. of M.H.L.).

first professional enrollment [Department of Education-Center for Education Statistics] First professional enrollment is the number of students enrolled in a professional school or program which requires at least two years of academic college work for entrance and a total of at least six years for a degree. By Center for Education Statistics definition, first professional enrollment includes only students in ten specific programs.

See also **first professional degree; graduate enrollment; post-baccalaureate enrollment.**

fiscal year [Department of Commerce-Bureau of the Census] A fiscal year is the 12 month period at the end of which the government, corporation, or other reporting entity determines its financial condition and the result of its operations and closes its books.

floor area [Department of Commerce-Bureau of the Census] For the American Housing Survey (AHS), the Bureau of the Census defines floor area as all completed finished floor space, including space in basements and attics with finished walls, floors, and ceilings.

The measurement is based on exterior dimensions. Measurements are taken to the outside of exterior walls for detached houses. Half stories are measured to the outside of enclosing partitions. Row houses are measured from the center line of party walls to the outside surface of exterior walls. In certain cases when interior dimensions are provided to the Bureau, the figure is converted by multiplying by 1.08; when the square footage provided is of uncertain methodology, the standard conversion factor is 1.04.

food at home [Department of Labor-Bureau of Labor Statistics] Food at home is an expenditure detailed in the Consumer Expenditure Survey (CEX). It refers to the total cost of food spent at grocery stores or other food stores during the interview period for consumption at home. It is calculated by multiplying the number of visits to a grocery or other food store by the average amount spent per visit. As such, food at home includes non-food items.

food away from home [Department of Labor-Bureau of Labor Statistics] Food away from home is an expenditure detailed in the Consumer Expenditure Survey (CEX). It includes all meals at restaurants and carryouts; meals (breakfast or lunch) at school; board; meals as pay; special catered affairs such as weddings, bar-mitzvahs, and confirmations; and meals away from home on trips.

food grain [Department of Agriculture-Office of Governmental and Public Affairs] Food grain is cereal seeds most commonly used for human food, chiefly wheat and rice.

forcible rape [Department of Justice-Bureau of Justice Statistics] Forcible rape is sexual intercourse or attempted sexual intercourse with a female against her will, by force or threat of force. Forcible rape is classified by the Uniform Crime Reports (UCR) as UCR 2.

For the National Crime Survey (NCS) forcible rape is called rape and is defined, counted, and classified differently. Rape is carnal knowledge through the use of force or threat of force, including attempts. Statutory rape without force is excluded; however, both heterosexual and homosexual rapes are included. For the NCS, rape is classified as a personal crime of violence.

See also **crime; index crime; National Crime Survey (NCS); Part I offense; personal crimes; rape; Uniform Crime Reports (UCR)**.

forgery [Department of Justice-Bureau of Justice Statistics] Forgery is the creation or alteration of a written or printed document which if validly executed would constitute a record of a legally binding transaction, with the intent to defraud by affirming it to be the act of an unknowing second person. Forgery is also the creation of an art object with intent to misrepresent the creator. In most statutes, counterfeiting is included within the definition of forgery. Where a distinction is made, it rests on the fact that forged materials are of relevance to the legal affairs of specific persons while counterfeited materials, most typically money, have intrinsic value set by social convention or governmental authority.

Forgery is classified with counterfeiting under the Uniform Crime Reports (UCR) as UCR 10. In UCR terminology, forgery is somewhat broader in that it includes offenses for making, manufacturing, altering, possessing, selling, or distributing or attempting to make, manufacture, alter, sell, distribute or receive "anything false in the semblance of that which is true."

See also **counterfeiting; fraud; Uniform Crime Reports (UCR)**.

former smoker [Department of Health and Human Services-Public Health Service; National Center for Health Statistics] A former smoker is any person who has smoked at least 100 cigarettes during his or her entire life but who reports smoking no cigarettes at the present time.

forward contracting [Department of Agriculture-Office of Governmental and Public Affairs] Forward contracting is a method of selling crops before harvest by which the buyer agrees to pay a specified price to the grower for all or a portion of the grower's crops.

fraud [Department of Justice-Bureau of Justice Statistics] In Uniform Crime Reports (UCR) terminology fraud is the conversion or obtaining of money or other thing of value by false pretenses, except forgery, counterfeiting, and embezzlement. Fraud is classified as UCR 11.

See also **counterfeiting; embezzlement; forgery; Uniform Crime Reports (UCR).**

freestanding psychiatric outpatient clinic [Department of Health and Human Services-Public Health Service; Alcohol, Drug Abuse, and Mental Health Administration] A freestanding psychiatric outpatient clinic is an administratively distinct organization that is not part of another organization (e.g. a hospital) and whose primary purpose is to provide <u>only</u> ambulatory mental health services on either a regular or emergency basis. The medical responsibility for all patients/clients and direction of the mental health program is generally assumed by a psychiatrist. This definition is applicable to survey data obtained prior to 1981.

See also **mental health organization.**

freestanding psychiatric partial care organization [Department of Health and Human Services-Public Health Service; Alcohol, Drug Abuse, and Mental Health Administration] A freestanding psychiatric partial care organization is an administratively distinct organization that is not part of another psychiatric organization. It comprises programs for non-residential patients who generally require more time (three or more hours) than that provided through an outpatient visit, but who require less than 24 hours in the organization. This definition is applicable to survey data obtained prior to 1981.

See also **mental health organization.**

FTE see **full time equivalent.**

full faith and credit [Department of Commerce-Bureau of the Census] Full faith and credit is a type of pledge made by a government in regard to issuance of long term debt. In full faith and credit debt the government pledges its credit unconditionally, implying the power of taxation. Full faith and credit debt includes debt payable initially from specific taxes on non-tax sources, but represents a liability payable from any other available resource if the specifically pledged sources are insufficient.

Full faith and credit debit differs from non-guaranteed debt, which is long term debt payable solely from specifically pledged sources or from specific non-property taxes. Non-guaranteed debt includes only debt that does not constitute an obligation against any other resource of the government if the pledged sources are insufficient.

See also **general obligation debt; long-term debt.**

full-time employee (health) [Department of Health and Human Services-Public Health Service; National Center for Health Statistics] For the American Hospital Association (AHA) and the National Master Facility Inventory (NMFI) full-time employees are those who work 35 hours a week or more.

See also **full-time equivalent employees (health); National Master Facility Inventory (NMFI)**.

full-time enrollment (higher education) [Department of Education-Center for Education Statistics] In higher education, full-time enrollment is the number of students enrolled in higher education courses with total credit load equal to at least 75% of the normal full-time course load.

full-time equivalent (mental health) [Department of Health and Human Services-Public Health Service; Alcohol, Drug Abuse, and Mental Health Administration] Full-time equivalent is the total hours worked by all full-time employees, part-time employees, and trainees in each staff discipline of a mental health organization in one week, divided by 40. Full-time equivalent indicates the number of person weeks.

See also **full-time staff (mental health)**.

full-time equivalent employees (health) [Department of Health and Human Services-Public Health Service; National Center for Health Statistics] The American Hospital Association (AHA) and the National Master Facility Inventory (NMFI) use an estimate of full-time equivalent employees that counts two part-time employees as one full-time employee.

The National Nursing Home Survey (NNHS) uses an estimate of full-time employees that counts 35 hours of part-time employee work per week as the equivalent of one full-time employee.

See also **full time employee (health); National Master Facility Inventory (NMFI); National Nursing Home Survey (NNHS)**.

full-time equivalent (FTE) enrollment (higher education) [Department of Education-Center for Education Statistics] For institutions of higher education, full-time equivalent (FTE) enrollment is enrollment of full-time students, plus the full-time equivalent of part-time students as reported by institutions. In the absence of an equivalent reported by an institution, the full time equivalent enrollment is estimated by adding one third of the part-time enrollment to full-time enrollment.

See also **full time enrollment (higher education)**.

full-time staff (mental health) [Department of Health and Human Services-Public Health Service; Alcohol, Drug Abuse, and Mental Health Administration] Full-

time staff is persons (excluding trainees) employed 35 hours or more per week in a particular setting.
See also **full-time equivalents (mental health)**.

full-time worker see **hours of work; labor force**.

functional illiterate [Department of Education-National Center for Education Statistics] A functional illiterate is an adult who is unable to read, write, and compute sufficiently well to meet the requirements of adult life. For purposes of many adult/continuing education programs, this is includes adults who have not gone beyond the eighth grade or who cannot read, write, and compute at or above the eighth grade level of performance.

functional systems (highways) [Department of Transportation-Federal Highway Administration] Functional systems for classifying highways have become the primary mileage categorization scheme used in the United States. The functional classification categories in current use result in the assignment of streets and highways into groups according to the character of service they are intended to provide. Functional classification defines the role that a particular road or street plays in serving the flow of trips through a highway network.

There are two functional systems, rural and urban. *Rural highways* are made up of four categories: principal arterial including interstate and other principal arterial highways shown independently; minor arterial; collector including major and minor collectors shown separately; and local.

Urban highways are also made up of four categories: principal arterial including interstate, other freeways and expressways, and other principal arterial highways - each shown independently; minor arterial; collector; and local.

In addition, the Federal Highway Administration uses a separate classification system, the federal-aid highway system, for the distribution of federal aid. Although the two systems are interrelated, with the exception of classification of interstate highways, the two systems do not correspond with each other.
See also **federal-aid highway system**.

fund (government finance) [Department of Commerce-Bureau of the Census] A fund is an accounting device established to control receipt and disbursement of income from sources set aside to support specific activities or attain certain objectives. In the accounts of individual States, each fund is treated as a distinct fiscal entity; however, in most Census Bureau reports, transactions of funds are consolidated.

funding (government finance) [Department of Commerce-Bureau of the Census] In government finance, funding refers to the issuance of bonds or other long term debt in exchange for, or to provide funds to retire, outstanding short term debt.

futures contract [Department of Agriculture-Office of Governmental and Public Affairs] A futures contract is an agreement between two people, one who sells and agrees to deliver, and one who buys and agrees to receive a certain kind, quality, and quantity of product to be delivered during a specified delivery month at a specified price.

FY see **fiscal year.**

G

gas see **natural gas.**

GBF/DIME file [Department of Commerce-Bureau of the Census] GBF/DIME is an acronym (geographic base file/dual independent map encoding) for a geographic reference file that can be used to assign geographic codes to census or other records with addresses. Such files are computerized representations of much of the geographic information within the built-up portion of an area. The basic unit of analysis is the street segment with block by block address ranges, census geographic codes, and x-y coordinate values for intersections.

general aviation [Department of Transportation-Federal Aviation Administration] General aviation is that portion of civil aviation which encompasses all facets of civil aviation except that of air carriers.
See also **air carrier.**

general expenditure (government) [Department of Commerce-Bureau of the Census] Government general expenditures include all government expenditures other than those specifically classified as Liquor Store Expenditure, Insurance Trust Expenditure, or Utility Expenditure.
See also **direct expenditure (government); expenditure (government).**

general hospital see **hospital.**

general hospital with separate psychiatric service(s) [Department of Health and Human Services-Public Health Service; Alcohol, Drug Abuse, and Mental Health Administration] A general hospital with separate psychiatric service(s) is a licensed non-federal general hospital or VA medical center that knowingly and routinely admits patients to either a separate psychiatric inpatient or outpatient setting for the express purpose of diagnosing and treating psychiatric illness.
See also **hospital; mental health organization; separate psychiatric inpatient setting, separate psychiatric outpatient setting.**

general imports see **imports.**

general obligation debt [Department of Commerce-Bureau of the Census] General obligation debt is a type of long term debt in which the issuer has pledged its full faith and credit. It includes debt payable in the first instance from particular earmarked taxes such as motor fuels or property taxes.
See also **debt (government); full faith and credit.**

general revenue (government)   [Department of Commerce-Bureau of the Census] General revenues consist of all government revenues except Liquor Store Revenue, Insurance Trust Revenue, and Utility Revenue. The basis of the distinction which excludes these three revenue sources is not the fund or administrative unit receiving particular amounts, but rather the nature of the revenue sources concerned; i.e., in Liquor Store Revenue, Insurance Trust Revenue, and Utility Revenue the government is selling a service or product.
See also **revenue (government)**.

general revenue sharing   [Department of Commerce-Bureau of the Census] General revenue sharing is funds distributed to states by the federal government under the State and Local Fiscal Assistance Act of 1972.

general sales or gross receipts taxes   see **sales and gross receipts taxes**.

geography   see **census geography**.

gestation   [Department of Health and Human Services-Public Health Service; National Center for Health Statistics] For both the National Vital Statistics System and the Centers for Disease Control's (CDC's) abortion surveillance, the period of gestation begins with the first day of the last normal menstrual period and ends with the day of birth.
See also **abortion**.

gigawatt (GW)   [Energy Information Administration] A gigawatt is equal to one billion watts.
See also **watt (W)**.

gigawatthour (GWh)   [Energy Information Administration] A gigawatthour is equal to one billion watthours.
See also **watthour (Wh)**.

GNP   see **Gross National Product (GNP)**.

gore   [Department of Commerce-Bureau of the Census] A gore is a minor civil division (MCD) in Maine and Vermont.
See also **minor civil division (MCD)**.

government appropriation   [Department of Education-Center for Education Statistics] Government appropriation is an amount other than a grant or contract received from or made available to an institution through an act of a legislative body.
See also **government grant or contract**.

government grant or contract [Department of Education-Center for Education Statistics] A government grant or contract consists of revenues from a government agency for a specific research project or other program.
See also **government appropriation.**

government purchases of goods and services [Department of Commerce-Bureau of Economic Analysis] Government purchases of goods and services include compensation of government employees and purchases from business and from foreigners. Transfer payments, interest paid by government, and subsidies are excluded. Gross investment by government enterprises is included, but their current outlays are not. Net purchases of used goods are included, and sales and purchases of land and financial assets are excluded. Government purchases of goods and services are a product-side component of the National Income Product Account (NIP) which, in combination with other product-side components, combine to measure the Gross National Product (GNP).
See also **Gross National Product (GNP); National Income Product Accounts (NIPA).**

government worker see **class of worker.**

graduate [Department of Education-Center for Education Statistics] A graduate is an individual who has received formal recognition for the successful completion of a prescribed program of studies.

graduate enrollment [Department of Education-Center for Education Statistics] Graduate enrollment is defined as the number of students who hold the bachelor's or first professional degree, or the equivalent, and who are working towards a master's or doctor's degree. First professional students are counted separately. Graduate enrollment data measure those students who are registered at a particular time during the fall of the year. At some institutions, graduate enrollment also includes students who are in post-baccalaureate classes but not in degree programs. In specific publications of the Center for Education Statistics, graduate enrollment includes all students in regular graduate programs and all students in post-baccalaureate classes but not in degree programs.
See also **first professional enrollment; post-baccalaureate enrollment.**

grant [Department of Commerce-Bureau of the Census] A grant is a minor civil division (MCD) in New Hampshire and Vermont.
See also **minor civil division (MCD).**

gross farm income see **farm income.**

Gross National Product (GNP) [Department of Commerce-Bureau of Economic Analysis] The Gross National Product (GNP) is a measure of the nation's output in terms of goods and services. It is the most widely used measure of the nation's production. GNP is primarily used to track the cyclical ups and downs of the economy and to monitor economic growth. In conjunction with measures of labor and capital input, it provides indicators of the nation's productivity.

The usefulness of the GNP stems in part from its being the keystone of a set of measures that show the output of the economy—its size, its composition, and its use and the economic process or mechanism by which output is produced and distributed. These measures are in a set of accounts, the National Income and Product Accounts (NIPA's) that show production, distribution, consumption, and savings. The first of the NIPA's, the national income and product account (NIP), shows GNP measured two ways. The first way is as charges against the GNP. These are the *income side components,* consisting of the sum of: compensation of employees; proprietors' income with inventory valuation and capital consumption adjustments; rental income of persons with capital consumption adjustment; corporate profits with inventory valuation and capital consumption adjustments; net interest; business transfer payments; indirect business tax and non-tax liability less subsidies less current surplus of government enterprises; and capital consumption allowances with capital consumption adjustment. The second way NIP shows GNP measured is as the measure of goods and services sold to final users. These are the *product-side components,* which are the sum of personal consumption expenditures; gross private domestic investment; net export of goods and services; and government purchases of goods and services.

The National Income and Product Account (NIP) shows GNP both ways and is a summary of the other four NIPA's. Together they represent activity in the four sectors of the nation's economy: business, household, government, and foreign.

See also **business transfer payment; capital consumption allowances with capital consumption adjustment; compensation of employees; corporate profits with inventory valuation and capital consumption adjustments; government purchases of goods and services; gross private domestic investment; implicit price deflator; indirect business tax and non-tax liability; National Income and Product Accounts (NIPA); net export of goods and services; net interest; personal consumption expenditures; proprietor's income with inventory valuation and capital consumption adjustments; rental income of persons with capital consumption adjustment.**

gross private domestic investment [Department of Commerce-Bureau of Economic Analysis] Gross private domestic investment includes fixed capital goods (structures and equipment) purchased by private business and non-profit institutions and the value of the change in the physical volume of inventories held by private business. The former includes private purchases of new residential structures purchased for tenant or owner occupancy. Net purchases of used goods are also included. Gross private domestic investment is a product-side component of the National Income Product Account (NIP) which, in combination with other product-side components, combine to measure the Gross National Product (GNP).

See also **Gross National Product (GNP); National Income Product Accounts (NIPA)**.

gross rent see **rent.**

group quarters [Department of Commerce-Bureau of the Census] Group quarters are a type of living quarters other than housing units. In general, group quarters are living arrangements for institutional inmates or for other groups containing nine or more persons who are not related to the person in charge of the quarters.

Group quarters are divided into two sub-categories, *other group quarters or non-institutional group quarters* and *institutions.* Institutions include: schools, hospitals, and wards for the physically or mentally handicapped; hospitals or wards for mental or chronic diseases; nursing, convalescent, and rest homes; hospitals and wards for drug/alcohol abuse; juvenile institutions; detention centers and correctional institutions. Other or noninstitutional group quarters include non-institutional, non-household living arrangements such as rooming and boarding houses, communes, convents, monasteries, and homes or halfway houses for drug/alcohol abuse. The following are considered noninstitutional group quarters regardless of the number of people sharing the unit: military barracks, college dormitories, sorority and fraternity houses, staff members quarters in institutions, missions, Salvation Army shelters, homes for unmarried mothers, farm and non-farm workers dormitories, and emergency shelter for homeless persons.

Note that some group quarters that were considered institutions in the 1980 census were re-categorized as noninstitutional group quarters for the 1990 census.

See also **housing unit; living quarters.**

guaranteed price level see **target price (agriculture).**

GW see **gigawatt (GW).**

GWh see **gigawatthour (GWh).**

H

halfway house (corrections) see **juvenile facility.**

halfway house (mental health) [Department of Health and Human Services-Public Health Service; Alcohol, Drug Abuse, and Mental Health Administration] A halfway house is an organization that prepares a previously hospitalized patient for return to home and community environment by providing transitional living quarters and assistance in the activities of daily living.
See also **mental health organization.**

handbook method [Department of Labor-Bureau of Labor Statistics] The handbook method is a series of computational steps designed to produce comparable estimates of total employment and unemployment in each of the States. The handbook method is based on a 1950 publication of the Department of Labor's Bureau of Employment Security, Techniques for Estimating Unemployment, and has been updated and adjusted to incorporate methods from the Current Population Survey (CPS).
See also **Current Population Survey (CPS).**

handicapped [Department of Education-Center for Education Statistics] Handicapped is defined as those children evaluated as having any of the following impairments, who because of these impairments need special education and related services. These definitions apply specifically to data from the US Office of Special Education and Rehabilitative Services.
A *deaf* student has a hearing impairment which is so severe that the student is impaired on processing linguistic information through hearing with or without amplification and which adversely affects educational performance.
A *deaf-blind* student has concomitant hearing and visual impairments which cause such severe communication and other developmental and educational problems that the student cannot be accommodated in special education programs solely for deaf or blind students.
A *hard of hearing* student has a hearing impairment, whether permanent or fluctuating, which adversely affects the student's educational performance but which is not included under the definition of deaf.
A *mentally retarded* student has significantly subaverage general intellectual functioning, existing concurrently with defects in adaptive behavior and manifested during the developmental period, which adversely affect the child's educational performance.
A *multi-handicapped* student has concomitant impairments such as mentally retarded-blind, mentally retarded-orthopedically impaired, etc., the combination of which causes such severe educational problems that the student cannot be ac-

commodated in special education programs solely for one of the impairments. This term does not include deaf-blind students but does include those students who are severely or profoundly mentally retarded.

An *orthopedically impaired* student has a severe orthopedic impairment which adversely affects a student's education performance. The term includes impairment resulting from congenital anomaly, disease, or other causes.

An *other health impaired* student has limited strength, vitality, or alertness due to chronic or acute health problems such as a heart condition, tuberculosis, rheumatic fever, nephritis, asthma, sickle cell anemia, hemophilia, epilepsy, lead poisoning, leukemia, or diabetes, which adversely affects the student's educational performance.

A *seriously emotionally disturbed* student exhibits one or more of the following characteristics over a long period of time, to a marked degree, and adversely affecting educational performance: an inability to learn which cannot be explained by intellectual, sensory, or health factors; an inability to build and maintain satisfactory interpersonal relationships with peers and teachers; inappropriate types of behavior or feelings under normal circumstances; a general pervasive mood of unhappiness or depression; or a tendency to develop physical symptoms or fears associated with personal or school problems. This term does not include children who are socially maladjusted unless they also display one or more of the listed characteristics.

A *specific learning disabled* student has a disorder in one or more of the basic psychological processes involved in understanding or in using spoken or written language which may manifest itself in an imperfect ability to listen, think, speak, read, write, spell, or do mathematical calculations. The term includes such conditions as perceptual handicaps, brain injury, minimal brain dysfunction, dyslexia, and developmental aphasia. The term does not include children who have learning problems which are primarily the result of visual, hearing, or environmental, cultural, or economic disadvantage.

A *speech impaired* student has a communication disorder, such as stuttering, impaired articulation, language impairment, or voice impairment, which adversely affects the student's educational performance.

A *visually handicapped* student has a visual impairment which, even with correction, adversely affects the student's educational performance. The term includes partially seeing and blind children.

See also **special education**.

hard coal see **anthracite**.

hard of hearing see **handicapped**.

harvested acres [Department of Agriculture-Office of Governmental and Public Affairs] The number of acres actually harvested for a particular crop are referred to as harvested acres. The number of harvested acres are usually somewhat smaller at the national level than the number of planted acres due to abandonment brought on by weather damage, other disasters, or market prices too low to cover harvesting costs.

health limitation of activity see **limitation of activity.**

health maintenance organization (HMO) [Department of Health and Human Services-Public Health Service; National Center for Health Statistics] A health maintenance organization (HMO) is a prepaid health plan delivering comprehensive care to members through designated providers, having a fixed monthly payment for health care services, and requiring members to be in the plan for a specified period of time (usually one year). HMO's are distinguished by the relationship of the providers to the plan.

There are two HMO model types. The group type is an HMO that delivers health services through a physician group controlled by the HMO, or an HMO that contracts with one or more independent group practices to provide health services. The Individual Practice Association (IPA) type is an HMO that contracts directly with physicians in independent practice, and/or contracts with one or more associations of physicians in independent practice, and/or contracts with one or more multispecialty group practices but is predominantly organized around solo-single specialty practices.

heavy oil [Energy Information Administration] Heavy oil includes No. 4, No. 5, and No. 6 fuel oils, crude oil, and topped crude oil used as fuel at electric utility plants for the generation of electricity. The term is applied only to fuel consumed by the electric utility sector.

See also **crude oil; end-use sector.**

help wanted-advertising index [Department of Commerce-Bureau of Economic Analysis] The help-wanted advertising index is an index of help-wanted advertising volume in the classified sections of leading newspapers. Currently there are 51 newspapers on which the index is based, one in each of 51 cities, representing 51 labor market areas, (LMA's), covering over 50% of the total non-agricultural employment. 1967 = 100 in this index.

The index is adjusted to account for the number of Sundays in a month and by a weighting formula for cities used when producing regional aggregates. The data is also seasonally adjusted.

The index concerns only ads published in the classified sections of newspapers, and excludes ads placed in the financial, sports, and other sections. Also, it is based on the number of ads, not the number of jobs advertised.

The index is produced by the Conference Board, Inc., and is republished in a number of federal publications including Survey of Current Business. See also **labor market area (LMA)**.

high school [Department of Education-Center for Education Statistics] A high school is a secondary school offering the final years of high school work necessary for graduation. A high school usually includes grades 10, 11, 12 in a 6-3-3 plan or grades 9, 10, 11, and 12 in a 6-2-4 plan.
See also **secondary school**.

high school diploma [Department of Education-National Center for Education Statistics] A high school diploma is a formal document certifying the successful completion of a prescribed secondary school program of studies. In some states or communities, high school diplomas are differentiated by type such as an academic diploma, a general diploma, or a vocational diploma.
See also **secondary school**.

high school equivalence diploma see **certificate of high school equivalency**.

higher education [Department of Education-Center for Education Statistics] Higher Education is defined as study beyond secondary school at an institution that offers programs terminating in an associate, baccalaureate, or higher degree.

higher education institutions [Department of Education-Center for Education Statistics] The Center for Education Statistics classifies an institution of higher education into one of seven categories.

A *comprehensive institution* is characterized by diverse post-baccalaureate programs including first-professional programs but is not engaged in significant doctoral-level education.

A *doctoral-granting institution* is characterized by a significant level and breadth of activity in commitment to doctoral-level education as measured by the number of doctorate recipients and the diversity in the doctoral-level program offerings.

A *general baccalaureate institution* is characterized by primary emphasis on general undergraduate baccalaureate-level education. It is not significantly engaged in post-baccalaureate education.

A *new institution* is a new addition to the Higher Education General Information Survey universe, though not necessarily newly organized. When degrees and award dates become available, a new institution will be reclassified into one of the six other categories.

A *non-degree-granting institution* offers undergraduate or graduate study but does not confer degrees or awards. In many of the Center's publications, this type of institution is classified under specialized.

A *specialized institution* is a baccalaureate or post-baccalaureate institution emphasizing one area of study plus closely related specialties, such as business or engineering. The programmatic emphasis is measured by the percentage of degrees granted in the program area.

A *two year institution* confers at least 75% of its degrees and awards for work below the bachelor's level.

These seven groups replace the two traditional classifications which are still found in some publications. Four-year institutions were defined as those institutions legally authorized to offer and offering at least a four year program of college level studies wholly or principally creditable toward a baccalaureate degree. In some published statistics a further division is made. A university is a post-secondary institution which typically comprises one or more graduate professional schools. Other four year institutions include the remainder of the non-university four year institutions. Two-year institutions were defined as those institutions legally authorized to offer and offering at least a two-year program of college-level studies which terminates in an associate degree or is principally creditable toward a baccalaureate degree.

See also **associate degree; bachelor's degree; doctor's degree; first professional degree; master's degree.**

highway see **federal-aid highway system; functional systems (highways).**

hispanic origin [Department of Commerce-Bureau of the Census] The Bureau of the Census in many of its censuses and surveys asks persons if they are of hispanic origin. Classification as being a person of hispanic origin is based on responses of the respondents.

The Bureau has established four main subcategories of hispanic origin: Mexican, Puerto Rican, Cuban, and other hispanic. It is important to recognize that hispanic origin is not a racial classification, even though data for persons of hispanic origin is reported in close proximity to data on race. Persons may be of any race and be of hispanic origin. Hispanic origin is often used interchangeably with hispanic, and Spanish origin.

See also **race.**

home ownership see **tenure (housing).**

homicide see **criminal homicide.**

hospital [Department of Health and Human Services-Public Health Service; National Center for Health Statistics] According to the American Hospital Association (AHA) and the National Master Facility Inventory (NMFI), a hospital is an institution licensed as a hospital whose primary function is to provide diagnostic and therapeutic patient services for medical conditions. Hospitals must have at least six beds, an organized physician staff, and continuous nursing services under the supervision of registered nurses.

AHA data on hospitals differs slightly from those of the NMFI, because data from the NMFI reflect osteopathic hospitals as well as hospitals not registered with the AHA. Non-AHA hospitals comprise 5-10% of all hospitals in the country.

Although not widely used for reporting data about hospitals in the United States, the World Health Organization (WHO) standards consider an entity a hospital if it is permanently staffed by at least one physician, can offer inpatient accommodation, and can provide medical and nursing care.

Hospitals may be classified by type of service and ownership.

A *general hospital* provides both diagnostic and treatment services for patients with a variety of medical conditions, both surgical and non-surgical. Excluded are hospitals, usually in rural areas, that provide a more limited range of care. According to WHO these hospitals provide medical and nursing care for more than one category of medical discipline, e.g., general medicine, specialized medicine, general surgery, specialized surgery, and obstetrics.

A *psychiatric hospital* is one whose major type of service is psychiatric care.

A *specialty hospital*, such as psychiatric, tuberculosis, chronic disease, rehabilitation, maternity, and alcoholic and narcotic, provides a particular type of service to its patients.

A *non-federal government hospital* is operated by State or local governments.

A *voluntary nonprofit hospital* is operated by a church or other nonprofit organization.

A *proprietary hospital* is operated for profit by individuals, partnerships, or corporations.

Hospitals are also classified according to length of stay. The definition of short stay and long stay vary between the different data-gathering organizations. A short stay hospital in the National Hospital Discharge Survey (NHDS) is one in which the average length of stay is less than 30 days. The AHA and NMFI define short term hospitals as hospitals in which more than half the patients are admitted to units with an average length of stay of less than 30 days, and long term hospitals as ones in which more than half the patients are admitted to units with an average length of stay of 30 days or more. The NHIS defines a short stay hospital as any hospital or hospital department in which the type of service provided is general; maternity; eye, ear, nose, and throat; children's; or osteopathic. Long-term hospitals are those in which the average length of stay is 30 days or more.

A *community hospital* is any non-federal short stay hospital classified by the AHA according to one of the following services: general medical and surgical; obstetrics and gynecology; eye, ear, nose, and throat; rehabilitation; orthopedic; other specialty; children's general; children's eye, ear, nose and throat; children's rehabilitation; children's orthopedic; and children's other specialty.

A *noncommunity hospital* is a federal hospital, long term hospital, hospital unit of an institution, psychiatric hospital, a hospital for tuberculosis and other respiratory diseases, an institution for the mentally retarded, or an alcoholism and chemical-dependency hospital.

A *registered hospital* is a hospital registered with the AHA.

See also **general hospital with separate psychiatric service(s); National Master Facility Inventory (NMFI); National Hospital Discharge Survey (NHDS); psychiatric hospital.**

hospital average daily census see **average daily census (hospital).**

hospital day see **day (hospital).**

hospital physician see **physician.**

hours and earnings [Department of Labor-Bureau of Labor Statistics] Hours and earnings is a series of statistical data based on reports of gross payrolls and the corresponding paid hours. Hours and earnings data are obtained from the Current Employment Statistics (CES) program and are reported by the Bureau for all employees and relevant subgroups of all employees in The Employment Situation and Employment and Earnings.

See also **aggregate payrolls; average hourly earnings; total hours.**

hours of work [Department of Commerce-Bureau of the Census] The Current Population Survey (CPS) collects data on the hours that employed persons work. Hours of work statistics focus on the actual number of hours worked during the survey week. This focus is important in understanding the data when atypical situations arise. For example, in a survey conducted for a week containing the Columbus Day holiday persons who usually work 40 hours per week but were off on Columbus Day, would be reported as working 32 hours, even though they are paid for the holiday. Likewise, for persons working more than one job, the data refer to the number of hours worked in all jobs during the week.

For classification purposes, persons who worked 35 hours or more during a survey week are designated as *full-time;* those who worked 1-34 hours are designated as *part-time.* Part-time workers are classified by their usual status at their present job and by their reason for working part-time hours during the survey week. Persons are said to work *part-time for economic reasons* which include slack work, materials shortages, repairs to plant or equipment, start or termination of a job during the survey week, and inability to find full-time work; or *part-time for other reasons* which include labor-management disputes, bad weather, own illness, vacations, demands of home housework, school, or no desire for full-time work. Persons on full-time schedules include both those who worked full-time during the survey week as well as those who worked 1-34 hours for non-economic reasons but who usually work full-time.

See also **employed persons.**

household [Department of Commerce-Bureau of the Census] A household includes all the persons occupying a housing unit. For the Bureau of the Census, persons not living in households live in group quarters. In census terminology households, in combination with group quarters, make up the larger category, living quarters.

There are two main types of households: *family households*, which consist of two or more persons related by birth, marriage, or adoption living together; and *non-family households*, which consist of a person living alone, or two or more unrelated individuals living together.

The measure, *persons per household*, includes all persons living in the household regardless of their relationship to the householder.

See also **family; family type; group quarters; householder; housing unit; living quarters; unrelated individual.**

household burglary see **household crimes.**

household crimes [Department of Justice-Bureau of Justice Statistics] Household crimes is a term used in the National Crime Survey (NCS). The NCS defines two broad areas of crime, household crimes and personal crimes. Household crimes include: household burglary, the unlawful or forcible entry or attempted forcible entry of a residence, usually, but not necessarily, attended by theft; household larceny, the theft or attempted theft of money or property from a residence or its immediate vicinity; and motor vehicle theft, the stealing or unauthorized taking of a motor vehicle, including attempts at such acts.

There are some special aspects of NCS terminology and usage which should be noted. Thefts or attempted thefts from residences which are accompanied by un-lawful or forcible entry of the residence are classified as household burglary. Household larceny is limited to those instances where the person committing or attempting the theft had a legal right to be present in or about the residence. For the NCS, motor vehicles include automobiles, trucks, motorcycles, and any other motorized vehicles legally allowed on public roads and highways.

NCS crime data is based on a household survey and differs substantially from Uniform Crime Reports (UCR) data which is based on crimes known to police. Definitions of crimes for both programs are somewhat different as well.

See also **crime; criminal incident; National Crime Survey (NCS); personal crimes; Uniform Crime Reports (UCR); victimization.**

household durable goods [Department of Commerce-Bureau of Economic Analysis] Household durable goods are a subcategory of durable goods which includes household furniture; kitchen articles and pottery; cutlery, hand tools, and hardware; household appliances; radios and television sets; ophthalmic goods, watches, watch cases, and clocks; and miscellaneous personal goods.

See also **durable goods.**

household income see **income.**

household larceny see **household crimes.**

household type see **household.**

householder [Department of Commerce-Bureau of the Census] The householder is the person in whose name a housing unit is owned, being bought, or rented and who is listed in column 1 of the 1990 census questionnaire. All the people living in a household are defined by their relationship to the householder.

A *spouse* is a person married to and living with a householder. This category includes persons in formal marriages, as well as persons in common-law marriages.

A *child* is a son or daughter by birth, a stepchild, or adopted child of the householder, regardless of the child's age or marital status.   Sons-in-law, daughters-in-law, and foster children are excluded.

An *other relative* is any household member related to the householder by birth, marriage, or adoption, but not included in the spouse or child categories. Other relatives include grandchildren, brothers, sisters, parents, brothers-in-law, nieces, cousins, etc.

A *nonrelative* is any household member not related to the householder by marriage or birth.   Nonrelatives include roomers, boarders, foster children, roommates, and unmarried partners.

See also **household; reference person.**

housekeeping residential building [Department of Commerce-Bureau of the Census] A housekeeping residential building is a building consisting primarily of housing units.

See also **housing unit.**

housing completion [Department of Commerce-Bureau of the Census] A housing unit is considered completed when all finished flooring, or carpeting, if used in place of finished flooring, has been installed.   If the building is occupied before all construction is finished, a housing unit is classified as completed at the time of occupancy.

In privately owned buildings with two or more housing units, all the units in the building are counted as completed when 50% or more of the units are occupied or available for occupancy. Housing units started but not completed are counted as being under construction.

See also **American Housing Survey (AHS); housing start; housing unit.**

ousing costs [Department of Commerce-Bureau of the Census] The American Housing Survey (AHS) collects data on housing costs from home owners and renters. As the methodology of the AHS differs from other Census Bureau Surveys, AHS housing costs data is not directly comparable to other housing cost data, most notably data from the Consumer Expenditure Survey (CEX).

Housing costs are computed differently for owners and renters. The AHS computes monthly housing costs for owner-occupied units by adding monthly payments for mortgage loan, installment loan or contract, real estate taxes including taxes on mobile homes or trailer sites if the site is owned, property insurance, homeowners association fee, cooperative or condominium fee, mobile home park fee, land rent, utilities, fuels, and garbage and trash collection.

For renter-occupied housing units, the AHS computed housing costs by summing the contract rent, estimated average utility costs, and fuel costs. Property insurance and garbage and trash collection are included if these items are paid for by the renter. Renter housing units occupied without payment of cash rent are tabulated separately.

See also **American Housing Survey (AHS).**

ousing start [Department of Commerce-Bureau of the Census] A housing start is when construction of a new housing unit is started. This is defined for privately owned housing units as the beginning of excavation for the footing or foundation of a building and for public housing units as when the construction contract is awarded. All housing units in a multi-family building are counted as being started when excavation for the building itself is started.

Housing units started but not completed are counted as being under construction.

Counts of housing starts exclude starts for the construction of group quarters such as dormitories and rooming houses; transient accommodations such as hotels, motels, and tourist courts; and mobile homes.

Publicly owned housing are those housing units in buildings for which construction contracts were awarded by federal, State, and local governments. Units in structures built by private developers for sale upon completion to local public housing authorities under the Department of Housing and Urban Development (HUD) turnkey program are classified as privately owned.

See also **housing completion; housing unit; housekeeping residential building.**

ousing tenure see **tenure (housing).**

housing unit [Department of Commerce-Bureau of the Census] A housing unit is a type of living quarters. A housing unit may be a house, apartment, mobile home or trailer, group of rooms, or single room occupied as a separate living quarter, or, if vacant, intended for occupancy as a separate living quarter. Separate living quarters are those in which the occupants live and eat separately from any other persons in the building and which have direct access from the outside of the building or through a common hall.

Both occupied and vacant housing units are counted in many censuses and surveys. Vacant mobile homes are included in most surveys if they are intended for occupancy on the site where they stand. Vacant mobile homes on dealer's sales lots, at the factory, or in storage yards are excluded.

Most housing unit data is for year-round housing units, i.e. all occupied housing units plus vacant housing units intended for year round use. Vacant units held for seasonal use or migratory labor are customarily excluded.

See also **American Housing Survey (AHS); bathroom; bedroom; closing costs; condominium; cooperative (housing); floor area; housing completion; housing start; group quarters; occupancy status; rooms; seasonal housing unit; specified owner-occupied housing units; story (housing); tenure (housing); value (housing).**

hub see **air traffic hub.**

I

ICD see **International Classification of Diseases, Ninth Edition** (ICD).

ICD-9-CM see **International Classification of Diseases, Ninth Edition, Clinical Modification** (ICD-9-CM).

ICDA-8 see **International Classification of Diseases, Ninth Edition, Clinical Modification** (ICD-9-CM).

IFR see **instrument flight rules** (IFR).

illness see **condition (health); occupational illness.**

implicit price deflator (Gross National Product, GNP) [Department of Commerce-Bureau of Economic Analysis] The Gross National Product (GNP) implicit price deflator is a weighted average of the detailed price indexes used in the deflation of the GNP. To deflate the GNP is to express it in dollars of constant purchasing power. In each reporting period, the implicit price deflator uses as weights the composition of constant dollar output in that period. Changes in the implicit price deflator reflect both changes in the composition of output as well as changes in prices.
See also **Gross National Product (GNP).**

imports 1. [Department of Commerce-Bureau of Economic Analysis] Imports are goods and services provided by foreigners to U.S. residents. Combined with exports, they are used in computing the Gross National Product.
See also **Gross National Product (GNP); net exports of goods and services.**
2. [Department of Commerce-Bureau of Economic Analysis] In foreign trade statistics imports reflect the total government and non-government imports of merchandise into the U.S. customs area without regard to whether the importation involves a commercial transaction. The import statistics are a complete record of merchandise that physically moves into the United States from foreign countries. The following are excluded: American goods returned to the United States by the armed forces; shipments of relatively small statistical significance, such as personal and household effects, temporary imports, and low-value non-dutiable imports by mail; monetary coins of all component metals; and in-transit shipments of all types.
General imports are a combination of entries for immediate consumption and entries into bonded warehouses.
Imports for consumption are a combination of entries for immediate consumption and withdrawals from warehouses for consumption.

111

Since 1982, the value of imports is the customs import value, the price actually paid or payable for merchandise when sold for exportation to the United States, excluding U.S. import duties, freight, insurance, and other charges incurred in bringing the merchandise to the United States. In the case of transactions between related parties, the relationship between buyer and seller should not influence the customs value.

See also **c.i.f. valuation; customs valuation; f.a.s. valuation.**

imports for consumption see **imports.**

in school see **labor force.**

incidence [Department of Health and Human Services-Public Health Service; National Center for Health Statistics] Incidence is the number of cases of disease having their onset during a prescribed period of time. Incidence of disease is most often expressed as a rate. Incidence is also a measure of morbidity or other events that occur within a specified period of time.

incident see **criminal incident.**

income [Department of Commerce-Bureau of the Census] Income has different meanings depending on both the agency or department collecting income data, as well as the specific program under which the data is being collected. To really understand income data, it is essential to identify the source of data and to be aware of the specific definitions and limitations in effect for that program at the time the data was collected.

The concept of income can vary not only between federal departments but within a Department itself such as in the Department of Commerce, where there are differences between the Census Bureau and the Bureau of Economic Analysis (BEA). This can make for substantial confusion among data users because what is reported as income by, say, the Social Security Administration, is not comparable with that reported from decennial census data, and both of which are not comparable to data in the Survey of Current Business. Even if the definition is the same in two programs, there may be methodological differences in collecting the data such as whether data is drawn from household surveys or administrative records, along with differences in editing and presentation of the data. Data users trying to cross program or department lines in using income data may quickly find themselves comparing apples to oranges. Income may be reported in aggregate, median, mean, and per capita amounts. As with other definition differences, data users should be aware of the specific methodology of how these measures are computed.

Although such an extensive programmatic review is not appropriate here, some guidelines can be provided for the most frequently reported measure, personal income. Generally, *personal income* is the current income received by persons from all sources, minus their personal contributions for social insurance. For the BEA, persons include individuals, owners of unincorporated firms, non-profit institutions serving individuals, private trust funds, and private non-insured welfare funds. Personal income includes transfers from government and business, such as Social Security benefits, public assistance, etc., but excludes transfers among persons. Also included are certain non-monetary types of income, chiefly estimated net rental value to owner-occupants of their homes, the value of services furnished without payment by financial intermediaries, and food and fuel produced and consumed on farms. Personal income has two main subcategories, disposable personal income and money income.

For the decennial census of population, the Bureau of the Census has modified this concept. Non-profit institutions are not included. Also excluded is the value of in kind income, the value of specified services, the income of persons who died prior to enumeration, and certain other income. It includes employee contributions for Social insurance. Some other significant differences exist in personal income in other programs.

See also **disposable income; income after taxes; income before taxes; money income; personal income.**

Income after taxes [Department of Labor-Bureau of Labor Statistics] In the Consumer Expenditure Survey (CEX), income after taxes is income before taxes less personal taxes. Personal taxes include federal income taxes, state and local income taxes, and other taxes including personal property taxes paid, and social security taxes for the self-employed. These amounts include both taxes withheld in the survey year and additional taxes paid in the survey year to cover any underpayment or under-withholding of taxes in the year prior to the survey. As defined here, the concept of income after taxes is unique to the CEX.

See also **Consumer Expenditure Survey (CEX); income before taxes.**

Income before taxes [Department of Labor-Bureau of Labor Statistics] In the Consumer Expenditure Survey (CEX), income before taxes is the total money earnings and selected money receipts during the 12 months prior to the interview date. Income before taxes includes wages and salaries for all consumer unit members 14 years old and over; self-employment income including losses; Social Security, private and government retirement income; interest, dividends, rental income, and other property income; unemployment and workers' compensation; veterans' benefits; public assistance, supplemental security income, and food stamps; regular contributions for support including alimony and child support; other income such as money for the care of foster children; cash scholarships, fellowships, or stipends not based on working; and meals and rent as pay. As defined here, the concept of income before taxes is unique to the CEX.

See also **Consumer Expenditure Survey (CEX).**

incorporated place [Department of Commerce-Bureau of the Census] An incorporated place is best understood as a unit of census geography. It is a political unit incorporated as a city, a borough, a village, or a town, with the following exceptions. Boroughs in Alaska are treated as county equivalents. In New York, there are five boroughs and they represent minor civil divisions (MCD'S) in the five counties comprising New York City. The towns in the New England States, New York and Wisconsin are MCD's similar to the townships found in other States, and are not necessarily thickly settled centers of population such as cities, towns, villages, and boroughs in other States. Some towns in these States have powers and functions similar to incorporated places; in Michigan, New Jersey, and Pennsylvania, some townships do also. Nevertheless, such towns and townships are not classified as incorporated places.

MCD's which may be incorporated in a legal sense of the word are not classified by the Bureau as incorporated places because, without this restriction, all of the towns of the New England States, New York, and Wisconsin, and all of the townships in Michigan, New Jersey, and Pennsylvania would have to be treated as incorporated places without any consideration of the nature of population settlement.

In most States, incorporated places are subdivisions of the minor civil division (MCD) or census county division (CCD) in which they are located, such as a village located within, and legally a part of, a township. In some States, incorporated places are independent of surrounding towns or townships and therefore are treated as MCD's. In a few States, the pattern is mixed.

See also **census geography; census county division (CCD); census designated place (CDP); minor civil division (MCD); place.**

independent city see **city (independent).**

index crime [Department of Justice-Bureau of Justice Statistics] An index crime is one of the eight Part I offenses tracked by the Uniform Crime Reports (UCR) crime index, excluding part 1b., negligent manslaughter. Index crimes are divided into two categories. The *violent crimes* are murder and non-negligent manslaughter, forcible rape, robbery, and aggravated assault. The *property crimes* are burglary, larceny-theft, motor vehicle theft, and arson. Crime rates for index crimes are published annually in Crime in the United States.

See also **crime; crime index; Part I offenses; Uniform Crime Reports (UCR).**

index of crime see **crime index.**

index of coincident indicators see **composite indexes.**

index of lagging economic indicators see **composite indexes.**

index of leading economic indicators see **composite indexes.**

index of prices paid by farmers [Department of Agriculture-National Agricultural Statistics Service] The index of prices paid by farmers for commodities and services including interest, taxes, and farm wages, is made up of five major components: commodities used in farm production; commodities used in family living; interest paid per acre for loans secured by farm real estate; taxes payable per acre on farm real estate; and wages paid to hired farm labor.

The index of prices paid by farmers is a fixed weight price index computed on 1971-1973 base weight period. The index is converted to 1910-1914 = 100, and 1977 = 100 for publication in Agricultural Prices and other federal publications.

See also **index of prices received by farmers; parity index; parity price; parity ratio.**

index of prices received by farmers [Department of Agriculture-National Agricultural Statistics Service] The index of prices received by farmers is for their products sold at the point of first sale, usually a local market, or the point to which farmers deliver their products. The reported prices received by farmers are tabulated and averaged by the States, and the State estimates of average prices are weighted by marketing or production estimates to arrive at a national average.

The index of prices received by farmers has two major groups: crops, and livestock and livestock products. The index is a fixed weight aggregative index modified from the Laspeyres formula. It is computed on 1971-1973 base weight period and is converted to 1910-1914 = 100, and 1977 = 100 for publication in Agricultural Prices and other federal publications.

See also **index of prices paid by farmers; parity index; parity price; parity ratio.**

indirect business tax and non tax liability [Department of Commerce-Bureau of Economic Analysis] Indirect business tax and non tax liability, less subsidies less current surplus of government enterprise, is an income-side component of the National Income Product Account (NIP) which, in combination with other income-side components, combine to measure the Gross National Product (GNP). It includes tax liabilities that are chargeable to business expense in the calculation of profit-type incomes and certain other business liabilities to government agencies treated as taxes.

Indirect business taxes include sales, excise, and property taxes, and the windfall profits tax on crude oil production. Taxes on corporate income are excluded; these taxes cannot be calculated until profits are known and in that sense are not a business expense. Employer contributions for social insurance are excluded.

Non-tax liability includes regulatory and inspection fees, special assessments, fines and penalties, rents and royalties, and donations. Non-taxes exclude business purchases from government of goods and services that are similar to business purchases of intermediate products from other businesses. Government receipts from the sale of such products are netted against government purchases so that they do not appear in the Gross National Product (GNP).

Subsidies less current surplus of government enterprises are the money grants paid by government to business including government enterprises at another level of government less the sales receipts and subsidies received from other levels of government, less their current expenses. In the calculation of their current surplus, no deduction is made for depreciation charges and net interest paid. Subsidies and current surplus are combined because deficits incurred by government enterprises may result from selling goods to businesses at lower than market prices in lieu of giving them subsidies. For the same reason, the current surplus of government enterprises is not counted as a profit-type income or as a factor charge.

See also **Gross National Product (GNP); National Income Product Accounts (NIPA)**.

industrial price program see **Producer Price Index (PPI)**.

industrial sector see **end-use sector.**

industry classification see **Standard Industrial Classification (SIC) program.**

industry wage surveys [Department of Labor-Bureau of Labor Statistics] The industry wage surveys program is conducted by the Bureau of Labor Statistics (BLS) in selected manufacturing and non-manufacturing industries which provides wage data for selected occupations. The BLS selects occupations for wage surveys to present a range of activities performed by workers in the industry during a specified payroll month.

In selecting the primarily non-supervisory occupations, consideration is given to their prevalence in the industry, definiteness and clarity of duties, use as reference points in collective bargaining, and importance in representing the industry's wage structure. Twenty-five manufacturing and fifteen non-manufacturing industry surveys, accounting for about 22 million employees, are conducted at the three or four digit SIC (Standard Industrial Classification) level of industry detail. The majority are on a five year cycle, but a number of comparatively low-wage industries are on a three year cycle. The program covers a broad cross section of the national economy including automobile and steel manufacturing as well as banking, computer data services and hospitals. Survey results are published in BLS Bulletins, reports, news releases, and in Monthly Labor Review.

See also **Standard Industrial Classification (SIC) program; wages.**

infant mortality [Department of Health and Human Services-Public Health Service; National Center for Health Statistics] Infant mortality is the death of live-born children who have not reached their first birthday. Infant mortality is usually expressed as a rate, such as the number of infant deaths during a year per 1,000 live births reported in the year.

See also **fetal death rate; late fetal death rate; live birth; neonatal mortality rate; perinatal mortality rate; perinatal mortality ratio; postneonatal mortality rate.**

informal probation see **court probation.**

injury see **occupational injury.**

inland water see **water area.**

inmate see **prisoner.**

inpatient see **patient.**

inpatient days (hospital) [Department of Health and Human Services-Public Health Service; Alcohol, Drug Abuse, and Mental Health Administration] Inpatient days is a measure of the number of days persons were physically present for 24 hours in the inpatient service departments of a hospital during a survey period. Survey periods are usually one year. Inpatient days excludes days for which patients were on overnight or weekend passes, or other short term leave. One person physically present for 24 hours in an inpatient service department equals one inpatient day.

See also **day (hospital).**

inpatient episodes see **patient care episodes (mental health).**

input-output accounts [Department of Commerce-Bureau of Economic Analysis] Input-output (I-O) accounts are a branch of national economic accounting that complement the National Income and Product Accounts (NIPA). Information on the flows of goods and services that make up the production relationships among industries is missing from the NIPA system but is provided by I-O accounts. I-O accounting can be viewed as a deconsolidation, along detailed industry lines, of national product accounts, with a separate production account presented for each industry.

The NIPA's and I-O accounts present the Gross National Product (GNP) in terms of final product flows, or final demand in I-O terminology and in terms of charges against GNP, or value added in I-O terminology. The distinctive feature of the I-O accounts is the presentation of detailed information for each industry on the consumption of purchased materials and services that are canceled in arriving at an unduplicated measure of production for the business sector NIPA accounts.

See also **capital finance accounts; Gross National Product (GNP); National Income and Product Accounts (NIPA).**

installed nameplate capacity (electric utilities) [Energy Information Administration] Installed nameplate capacity is the full-load continuous rating of an electrical generator, prime mover, or other electrical equipment, under specified conditions as designated by the manufacturer. Installed nameplate capacity is usually indicated on a nameplate physically attached to the equipment.

institution of higher education see **higher education.**

institutional capacity (corrections) [Department of Justice-Bureau of Justice Statistics] Institutional capacity is an officially stated number of inmates which a confinement or residential facility is or was intended to house. Institutional capacity is a term of broad possible meaning. The following terms are commonly used to indicate more limited meanings.

The *design capacity* or *bed capacity* is the number of inmates a correctional facility was originally designed to house, or currently has the capacity to house as a result of later, planned modifications. It excludes extraordinary arrangements to accommodate overcrowded conditions.

The *rated capacity* is the number of inmates which a correctional facility can house without overcrowding determined by comparison with some set of explicit standards applied to groups of facilities.

The *operational capacity, staff capacity* or *budgeted capacity* is the number of inmates a correctional facility can house while in conformity with a set of standards relating to what are considered appropriate staff to inmates and staff to bed ratios. This capacity, determined by administrative decisions relating to such factors as budgetary or personnel limits, is often less than the design or rated capacity.

The *measured capacity* of a facility is the number of persons who can be housed in a facility allowing a minimum of 60 square feet of floor space per person.

See also **jail; prison.**

instructional staff [Department of Education-Center for Education Statistics] In local schools, the instructional staff includes all public elementary and secondary day school positions that involve teaching or the improvement of the teaching-learning situation. Instructional staff includes consultants or supervisors of instruction, principals, teachers, guidance personnel, librarians, psychological personnel, and other instructional staff. Excluded are administrative staff, attendance personnel, clerical personnel, and other non-instructional personnel. Instructional staff is measured in full-time equivalent positions, not the number of different individuals occupying the positions during the school year.

See also **day school; elementary school; non-supervisory instructional staff; secondary school.**

instrument flight rules (IFR) [Department of Transportation-Federal Aviation Administration] Instrument flight rules (IFR) govern the procedures for conducting instrument flight (as opposed to visual flight) of aircraft. The term is also used to describe certain aircraft operations, and types of flight plans.

See also **aircraft operation; visual flight rules (VFR).**

insurance trust expenditures see **insurance trust system.**

insurance trust revenues see **insurance trust system.**

insurance trust system [Department of Commerce-Bureau of the Census] An insurance trust system is a State administered plan for compulsory or voluntary social insurance through accumulation of assets from contributions, assessments, premiums, and similar amounts collected from employers and employees for use in making cash benefit payments to eligible persons covered by the system. Social insurance is insurance protection of persons or their survivors against economic hazards arising from retirement, disability, death, accident, illness, unemployment, and the like.

An insurance trust system as a reporting category of government financial information includes financial data for employee retirement programs, unemployment and workers' compensation programs, and similar State programs. Each such program is treated as an entity with its transactions including intragovernmental amounts. However, such intragovernmental transactions are excluded from the insurance trust components of State revenues and expenditures.

Amounts reported as insurance trust expenditures include cash payments to beneficiaries including withdrawals of retirement contributions. Insurance trust expenditures exclude the cost of administering insurance trust activities, State contributions to programs administered by the State or federal government, intergovernmental expenditures for support of locally administered employee retirement systems, and non-contributory gratuities paid to former employees.

Amounts reported as insurance trust revenues include revenues from contributions required of employers and employees, and earnings on assets. They exclude any contributions by a State to a social insurance system it administers. Note that tax proceeds, donations, and any other forms of revenue are classified as general revenue, even though such amounts may be received specifically for insurance trust purposes.

insured unemployment see **unemployment.**

interest expenditure (government) [Department of Commerce-Bureau of the Census] Interest expenditure is government expenditure for the use of borrowed money. The Bureau of the Census reports on government interest expenditures in its census and surveys of governmental finance.

intergovernmental expenditure [Department of Commerce-Bureau of the Census] Intergovernmental expenditure is that amount paid by a government to other governments as fiscal aid in the form of shared revenues and grants-in-aid, as reimbursements for performance of general government activities such as care of prisoners, contractual research, or in lieu of taxes. Intergovernmental expenditure excludes amounts paid to other governments for the purchase of commodities, property, or utility services; any tax imposed and paid as such; and employer contributions for social insurance.
    See also **expenditure (government)**.

intergovernmental revenue [Department of Commerce-Bureau of the Census] Intergovernmental revenue is that amount received by a government from other governments as fiscal aid in the form of shared revenues and grants-in-aid as reimbursement for performance of general government functions and specific services for the paying government such as care of prisoners or contractual research, or in lieu of taxes. Intergovernmental revenue excludes amounts received from other governments for the sale of property, commodities, and utility services; and employer contributions from paying governments to receiving government for retirement systems, and the like. For financial reporting purposes, all intergovernmental revenue is classified as general revenue.
    See also **revenue (government)**.

intermediate appellate court [Department of Justice-Bureau of Justice Statistics] An intermediate appellate court is a court of which the primary function is to review the judgments of trial courts and the decisions of administrative agencies and whose decisions are, in turn, usually reviewable by a higher appellate court in the same State.
    See also **appellate court; court**.

intermediate care facility see **nursing home certification**.

intermediate goods see **stage of processing (SOP)**.

Intermediate Materials Index see **stage of processing (SOP)**.

internal point [Department of Commerce-Bureau of the Census] An internal point is a set of geographic latitude and longitude coordinates that is located within a

specified geographic entity. This point represents the approximate geographic center of that entity.
See also **census geography**.

International Classification of Diseases, Ninth Edition (ICD) [Department of Health and Human Services-Public Health Service; National Center for Health Statistics] The International Classification of Diseases, Ninth Edition (ICD) is a volume which is used to classify mortality information for statistical purposes. It was published in 1977, and represents the most recent revision of a work first used in 1900. The ninth revision has been used to classify mortality information since 1979. Most of the diseases are arranged according to their principal anatomical site, with special chapters for infective and parasitic diseases; neoplasms; endocrine, metabolic and nutritional diseases; mental disease; complications of pregnancy and childbirth; certain diseases peculiar to the perinatal period and ill-defined conditions. In addition, two supplemental classifications are provided: the classification of factors influencing health status and contact with health services, and the classification of external causes of injury and poisoning.

ICD is completely compatible with the International Classification of Diseases, Ninth Edition, Clinical Modification (ICD-9-CM).

See also **International Classification of Diseases, Ninth Edition, Clinical Modification** (ICD-9-CM).

International Classification of Diseases, Ninth Edition, Clinical Modification (ICD-9-CM) [Department of Health and Human Services-Public Health Service; National Center for Health Statistics] The International Classification of Diseases, Ninth Edition, Clinical Modification (ICD-9-CM) is a volume which is used to classify morbidity information for statistical purposes. It replaces ICDA-8 (International Classification of Diseases, Ninth Revision, Adapted for Use in the United States). Most of the diseases are arranged according to their principal anatomical site, with special chapters for infective and parasitic diseases; neoplasms; endocrine, metabolic and nutritional diseases; mental disease; complications of pregnancy and childbirth; certain diseases peculiar to the perinatal period and ill-defined conditions. In addition, two supplemental classifications are provided: the classification of factors influencing health status and contact with health services, and the classification of external causes of injury and poisoning.

ICD-9-CM is completely compatible with the International Classification of Diseases, Ninth Edition (ICD).

See also **International Classification of Diseases, Ninth Edition** (ICD).

interruptible gas [Energy Information Administration] Interruptible gas is gas sold to customers with a provision that permits curtailment or cessation of service at the discretion of the distributing company under certain circumstances as specified by contract.

interstate highway see **federal-aid highway system; functional systems (highways)**.

Inventory of Long-Term Care Places see **National Master Facility Inventory (NMFI)**.

island [Department of Commerce-Bureau of the Census]   An island is a county equivalent in the Virgin Islands of the United States.
    See also **county**.

J

jail [Department of Justice-Bureau of Justice Statistics] Jail is defined as a confinement facility administered by an agency of local government, typically a law enforcement agency, which holds persons detained pending adjudication and/or persons committed after adjudication, usually those committed on sentences of one year or less. Jail is intended for adults but sometimes also contains juveniles.

In a number of jurisdictions facilities have been established that hold only arrested persons who are awaiting first appearance in court for arraignment or pretrial release consideration. These are not considered to be jails, but pre-arraignment lockups.

Jails are different from prisons, which are administered by States. However, in five States, Delaware, Connecticut, Hawaii, Rhode Island, and Vermont, all adult confinement facilities are administered at the State level.

See also **confinement facility; correctional facility (adult); pre-arraignment lockup; prison.**

jet fuel [Energy Information Administration] As a category for statistical reporting, jet fuel includes both naphtha-type and kerosene-type jet fuels meeting standards for use in jet aircraft turbine engines or meeting ASTM specification D1655. Although most jet fuel is used in aircraft, some is used for other purposes, such as fuel for turbines to produce electricity.

JINS see **PINS/CHINS/JINS/MINS.**

job leavers see **reason for unemployment.**

job losers see **reason for unemployment.**

joint area [Department of Commerce-Bureau of the Census] A joint area is an American Indian reservation equivalent.

See also **American Indian reservation.**

junior college see **community/junior college.**

junior high school [Department of Education-Center for Education Statistics] A junior high school is a separately organized and administered secondary school, intermediate between elementary and senior high schools, usually including grades 7, 8, and 9 (in a 6-3-3 plan) or grades 7 and 8 (in a 6-2-4 plan).

See also **elementary school; secondary school.**

junior-senior high school [Department of Education-National Center for Education Statistics] A junior-senior high school is a secondary school organized on a junior-senior high school basis and administered under one head as a unit. This includes secondary schools organized on a two year junior and four year senior high school plan, a three year junior and a three year senior high school plan, and any other plan based on a junior-senior organization.

juvenile [Department of Justice-Bureau of Justice Statistics] In the context of the administration of justice, a juvenile is a person subject to juvenile court proceedings because a statutorily defined event or condition caused by or affecting that person was alleged to have occurred while his or her age was below the statutorily specified age limit of original jurisdiction of a juvenile court. Court jurisdiction is determined by age at the time of the event, not at the time of judicial proceedings, and continues in juvenile offender cases until the case is terminated or the case is transferred to adult court for prosecution. The age limit defining the legal categories juvenile and adult varies among States and also varies with respect to specified crimes within States. However, the generally applicable age limit within a given state is most often the 18th birthday.
    See also **aftercare (corrections); delinquency; PINS/CHINS/JINS/MINS.**

juvenile facility (corrections) [Department of Justice-Bureau of Justice Statistics] A juvenile facility is a building, part of a building, set of buildings, or area enclosing a set of buildings or structures, which is used for the custody and/or care and treatment of juveniles who have been administratively determined to be in need of care or who have been formally alleged or adjudged to be delinquents, status offenders or dependents. Juvenile facilities may be operated by public agencies or by private organizations.
    See also **aftercare (corrections); delinquency; juvenile.**

juvenile parole see **aftercare (corrections).**

K

kerosene [Energy Information Administration] Kerosene is a petroleum middle distillate having burning properties suitable for use as an illuminant when burned in wick lamps. Included are No. 1-K and No. 2-K recognized in ASTM specification D3699 and grades of kerosene called range oil having properties similar to No. 1 fuel oil. Kerosene is used primarily in space heaters, cooking stoves, and water heaters.

kilowatt (kW) [Energy Information Administration] One kilowatt equals one thousand watts.
　　See also **watt (W)**.

kilowatthour (kWh) [Energy Information Administration] One kilowatthour equals one thousand watthours.
　　See also **watthour (Wh)**.

kW see **kilowatt (kW)**.

kWh see **kilowatthour (kWh)**.

L

L see **money stock measures.**

labor force [Department of Labor-Bureau of Labor Statistics] The labor force consists of all persons 16 years of age or over in the United States who are either employed or unemployed. The largest subset of the labor force is the *civilian labor force (CLF)*, which excludes members of the armed forces. The main source of labor force data is the Current Population Survey (CPS), conducted by the Bureau of the Census. The CPS is a monthly household survey that covers the civilian noninstitutional population. Hence, most labor force data reported excludes two groups, members of the armed forces, and the institutional population.

In reporting labor force data, the Bureau of Labor Statistics (BLS) classifies all civilians 16 years of age and over as to their labor force status. All those who are not classified as either employed persons or unemployed persons are, by definition, not in the labor force. Because there are persons who are not in the labor force, the labor force is not equal to the resident population of the United States 16 years old and over. Non-members of the labor force are further classified as *engaged in housework, in school, unable to work* (because of long term physical or mental illness), *retired*, and *other*. The *other* group includes: the voluntarily idle; seasonal workers for whom the CPS survey week fell in an off season and who were not reported as looking for work; persons who did not look for work because they believed that no jobs were available because of the prevailing job market situation or personal factors such as age, lack of education or training; and students with no current interest in labor force activity.

It should be noted that the category, *not in labor force—in school* includes persons attending school during the survey week who did have new jobs to which they were scheduled to report within thirty days. It also includes students looking for jobs for some period in the future, such as the summer months.

All persons, whether or not attending school, who have new jobs not scheduled to begin until thirty days after the survey week and who are not looking for work are also classified as *not in the labor force.*

In addition to labor force status, the BLS sometimes uses the concept of the *experienced civilian labor force* which is comprised of all experienced workers. Experienced workers are all employed CLF members along with those unemployed CLF members who have worked at any time in the past.

Most BLS labor force data comes from the CPS, but data for the total labor force includes information on the resident armed forces obtained from the Department of Defense.

Although the CPS concept of the labor force and the resulting CLF data are broadly used, some federal government survey programs use different definitions. For example, the Survey of Income and Program Participation (SIPP) uses a different definition of the employed, and the concept of an earner as used in the Consumer Expenditure Survey (CEX) is different.

See also **Consumer Expenditure Survey (CEX); Current Population Survey (CPS); earner; employed persons; employment; labor force participation rate; Survey of Income and Program Participation (SIPP); unemployed person; unemployment.**

labor force participation rate [Department of Labor-Bureau of Labor Statistics] The labor force participation rate is the number of labor force members divided by the civilian non-institutional population, expressed as a percent. Labor force participation rates are sometimes computed and presented by age, race, sex, and marital status. In such cases the rate would have the same constraints, i.e., the labor force participation rate for married men would be the number of married men in the labor force divided by the number of married men in the civilian non-institutional population.

See also **labor force.**

labor force status see **labor force.**

labor market area (LMA) [Department of Labor-Bureau of Labor Statistics] A labor market area (LMA) is a geographic area consisting of a central community and contiguous areas which are economically integrated into that community. Within a labor market area, workers can generally change jobs without relocating. The Bureau of Labor Statistics defines LMA's in terms of entire counties, except in New England where cities and towns are used.

LMA's are categorized as either major, which are usually coterminous with a Metropolitan Statistical Area (MSA), or as small. A small LMA is defined as a county or group of counties with a central community of at least 5,000 population and which meets certain commuting requirements. Generally, LMA's do not cross State boundaries.

Counties which are not included in LMA's are designated as estimating areas. In New England, estimating areas are made up of cities or towns, or groups of cities or towns. The LMA concept should not be confused with metropolitan area concepts such as the Metropolitan Statistical Area (MSA).

See also **Metropolitan Statistical Area (MSA).**

land capability [Department of Agriculture-Office of Governmental and Public Affairs] Land capability is a measure of the suitability of land for use without physical damage. In the United States, it usually expresses the effect of physical land conditions, including climate, on the total suitability for agricultural use without damage. Arable soils are grouped according to their limitations for sustained production of the common cultivated crops without soil deterioration. Non-arable soils are grouped according to their limitations for the production of permanent vegetation and their risks of soil damage if mismanaged.

larceny-theft [Department of Justice-Bureau of Justice Statistics] Under the Uniform Crime Reports (UCR), larceny-theft is defined as the unlawful taking, carrying, leading, or riding away by stealth of property other than a motor vehicle from the possession or constructive possession of another, including attempts. Motor vehicle theft is classified separately. Larceny-theft differs from both fraud, which requires deceit, and robbery, which requires violence or the threat of violence.

Larceny-theft is one of the eight Part I offenses, classified UCR 6, and an index crime.

See also **crime; fraud; index crime; Part I offenses; robbery; Uniform Crime Reports (UCR)**.

large denomination time deposit see **time deposits**.

late fetal death rate [Department of Health and Human Services-Public Health Service; National Center for Health Statistics] Late fetal death rate is the number of fetal deaths with stated or presumed gestation of 28 weeks or more per 1,000 live births plus late fetal deaths.

See also **fetal death rate; infant mortality; live birth; neonatal mortality rate; perinatal mortality rate; perinatal mortality ratio; postneonatal mortality rate**.

law enforcement agency [Department of Justice-Bureau of Justice Statistics] A law enforcement agency is a federal, State, or local criminal justice agency, or identifiable subunit, of which the principal functions are the prevention, detection, and investigation of crime, and the apprehension of alleged offenders.

law enforcement officer [Department of Justice-Bureau of Justice Statistics] A law enforcement officer is any government employee who is an officer sworn to carry out law enforcement duties, whether or not employed by an agency or identifiable subunit which primarily performs law enforcement functions.

Sworn personnel are a reporting category for the Uniform Crime Reports (UCR) and are persons formally authorized to make arrests while acting within the scope of explicit legal authority. This term includes agents of the Federal Bureau of Investigation, the Bureau of Alcohol, Firearms and Tobacco, state police officers, state highway patrol officers, state park police, sheriffs, deputy sheriffs, chiefs of police, and police officers, among others.

lease and plant fuel [Energy Information Administration] Lease and plant fuel is natural gas used in lease operations, as gas processing plant fuel, and as net used for gas lift.

lease condensate [Energy Information Administration] Lease condensate is a natural gas liquid recovered from associated and non-associated gas-well gas in lease separators or natural gas field facilities. Lease condensate consists primarily of pentanes and heavier hydrocarbons. It is often blended with crude oil for refining.

legal abortion see **abortion.**

length of stay (hospital) [Department of Health and Human Services-Public Health Service; Alcohol, Drug Abuse, and Mental Health Administration] Length of stay is defined as the number of days a person remains in a hospital between the date of admission and the discharge date. Persons admitted and discharged on the same day are counted as having a one-day stay. The concept of length of stay for hospital inpatients differs from that used for nursing home residents.

See also **average length of stay; length of stay (nursing home); National Health Interview Survey (NHIS).**

length of stay (nursing home) [Department of Health and Human Services-Public Health Service; National Center for Health Statistics] As measured in the National Nursing Home Survey (NNHS), length of stay for residents is the time from their admission until the reporting time, while the length of stay for discharges is the time between the date of admission and the date of discharge. The concept of length of stay for nursing home residents differs from that used for hospital inpatients.

See also **length of stay (hospital); National Nursing Home Survey (NNHS).**

license taxes [Department of Commerce-Bureau of the Census] License taxes are taxes enacted by a government as a condition to the exercise of a business or non-business privilege. Such taxes are at a flat rate or measured by such bases as capital stock, capital surplus, number of business units, or capacity.

Except those to which only nominal rates apply, license taxes exclude taxes measured directly by transactions, gross or net income, or value of property. Licenses based on these latter measures are classified according to the measure concerned and include fees related to licensing activities such as automobile inspection, or professional examinations.

See also **sales and gross receipts taxes; taxes.**

life expectancy [Department of Health and Human Services-Public Health Service; National Center for Health Statistics] Life expectancy is the average number of years of life remaining to a person at a particular age. Life expectancy is based on a given set of age-specific death rates. Life expectancy may be determined by race, sex, or other characteristics using age-specific death rates for the population with that characteristic.

LIFO [Department of Commerce-Bureau of the Census] LIFO (last in, first out) is a system of inventory accounting widely used in industry and is the inventory accounting method favored by the Census Bureau for the economic censuses. Under this method of accounting for inventory, items that are received last are regarded as being used first for a specific accounting period. This results in valuing production based on the most recent purchase costs. This is based on the belief that a business must always keep some stock on hand, therefore as inventory is used up it must be replaced. As such, value equals replacement cost as opposed to the actual cost. To some extent, in times of rising prices this results in undervaluing inventory and minimizing reported profit.

light oil [Energy Information Administration] Light oil is No. 1 and No. 2 fuel oils, kerosene, and jet fuel used as fuel at electric utility plants for the generation of electricity. The term light oil as used by the Energy Information Administration is applied only to fuel consumed in the electric utility sector.
See also **end use sector.**

lignite [Energy Information Administration] Lignite is a brownish-black coal of low rank with high internal moisture and low volatile matter. It is also referred to as brown coal. It conforms to ASTM specification D388 for lignite and is used almost exclusively for electric power generation.
See also **coal.**

limitation of activity [Department of Health and Human Services-Public Health Service; National Center for Health Statistics] In the National Health Interview Survey (NHIS), each person identified as having a chronic condition is classified into one of four groups according to the extent to which his or her activities are limited because of that chronic condition.
The first category is persons unable to carry on a major activity, the principal activity of a person of his or her age-sex group. For persons 1-5 years of age, the principal activity refers to ordinary play with other children. For persons 6-16 years of age, it refers to school attendance. For persons 17 years of age and over, it usually refers to a job, housework, or school attendance.
The second category is persons limited in the amount or kind of major activity performed.
The third category is persons not limited in major activity, but otherwise limited.
The fourth category is those persons who are not limited in activity due to their chronic condition.
See also **condition (health); disability; National Health Interview Survey (NHIS).**

line miles of seismic exploration [Energy Information Administration] Line miles of seismic exploration is the distance along the earth's surface that is covered by seismic surveying.

linter [Department of Agriculture-Office of Governmental and Public Affairs] A linter is a short fiber remaining on cottonseed after ginning. Linters are too short for textile use and are most commonly used for batting and mattress stuffing and as a source for cellulose.

liquified petroleum gases (LPG) [Energy Information Administration] Liquified petroleum gases (LPG) is a term which includes ethane, ethylene, propane, propylene, normal butane, butylene, ethane-propane mixtures, propane-butane mixtures, and isobutane. The Energy Information Administration measures liquified petroleum gases produced at refineries or natural gas processing plants including plants that fractionate raw natural gas plant liquids.

live birth [Department of Health and Human Services-Public Health Service; National Center for Health Statistics] The live birth of an infant is defined as the complete expulsion or extraction from its mother of a product of conception, irrespective of the duration of the pregnancy. After such separation, a live birth breathes or shows evidence of life such as heartbeat, umbilical cord pulsation, or definite movement of voluntary muscles, whether or not the umbilical cord has been cut or the placenta is attached. This definition is used by the World Health Organization, and the United Nations as well as the National Center for Health Statistics.

live-birth order [Department of Health and Human Services-Public Health Service; National Center for Health Statistics] As used in the National Vital Statistics System, the live-birth order pertains to the number of live-born children a women has had previous to and including the birth being counted. For statistical reporting purposes, this information is obtained from birth certificates.
See also live birth.

living quarters [Department of Commerce-Bureau of the Census] Living quarters are places where persons regularly reside. Living quarters include housing units and group quarters. Living quarters may also be in structures intended for non-residential use such as the rooms in a warehouse where a watchman lives, as well as in tents, caves, and old railroad cars.
See also housing unit; group quarters.

LMA see labor market area.

loan rate (agriculture) [Department of Agriculture-Office of Governmental and Public Affairs] The loan rate is the price per unit such as bushel, bale, or pound at which the federal government will provide loans to farmers to enable them to hold their crops for later sale.

local basic administrative unit see **school district.**

local education agency see **school district.**

location [Department of Commerce-Bureau of the Census] A location is minor civil division (MCD) in New Hampshire.
    See also **minor civil division (MCD).**

long-term debt see **debt (government).**

long term hospital see **hospital.**

lost workday case [Department of Labor-Bureau of Labor Statistics] A lost workday case is a case which involves days away from work, days of restricted activity, or both.
    Lost workdays involving days away from work are the number of workdays consecutive or not on which the employee would have worked but could not because of occupational injury or illness.
    Lost workdays, restricted work activity days, are the number of workdays on which because of injury or illness one of the following occurred: The employee was assigned to another job on a temporary basis; or the employee worked at a permanent job less than full time; or the employee worked at a permanently assigned job but could not perform all duties normally connected with it.
    Lost workdays may or may not be consecutive, do not include the day of onset of illness or injury, and do not include any days on which the employee would not have worked even though able to work.
    The Bureau of Labor Statistics tracks lost workdays in its Annual Survey of Occupational Injuries and Illnesses.

low birth weight [Department of Health and Human Services-Public Health Service; National Center for Health Statistics] A low birth weight infant is one that weighs less than 2,500 grams at birth.

LPG see **liquified petroleum gases.**

lubricant [Energy Information Administration] A lubricant is a substance used to reduce friction between bearing surfaces. Petroleum lubricants may be produced either from distillates or residues. Other substances may be added to impart or improve certain required properties.

Lubricants are grouped in three categories: bright stock lubricants; neutral lubricants; and other lubricants. For statistical reporting purposes, lubricants include all grades of lubricating oils from spindle oil to cylinder oil, and those used in greases.

M

M1, M2, M3 see **money stock measures.**

MA see **Metropolitan Area (MA).**

magazine advertising cost [Department of Commerce-Bureau of Economic Analysis] Magazine advertising cost is an aggregate representing the amount of advertising revenue of general magazines and national farm magazines. It excludes advertising in nationally distributed newspaper supplements and sections. Space cost is based on the one-time rate; special rates are used where applicable. The data is presented divided by industry class, with retail and direct mail included in the all other class. Data is from Leading National Advertisers (LNA) and is published monthly in Survey of Current Business.
See also **newspaper advertising expenditures.**

major activity see **limitation of activity.**

major retail center (MRC) [Department of Commerce-Bureau of the Census] A major retail center (MRC) is a unit of census geography frequently used in economic censuses prior to 1987, specifically the Census of Retail Trade. In the 1987 economic census, the MRC concept was eliminated.
An MRC is a concentration of retail stores located in a Metropolitan Statistical Area (MSA) but outside the central business district (CBD). For the 1982 economic censuses 1,545 MRC's were delineated by local officials for areas with at least 25 retail establishments. An MRC has at least one retail establishment which is a department or general-merchandise store, (Standard Industrial Classification Code, SIC 53), with a minimum of 100,000 square feet of floor space.
MRC's include planned shopping centers, unplanned centers and older "string streets" (continuous businesses along a thoroughfare with few cross streets containing any business establishments), neighborhood commercial developments, and combinations of planned and unplanned centers. Where an MRC is a planned center, the boundaries encompass all retail stores in the center. Where an MRC is unplanned, each block within the boundaries must have at least one general merchandise store (SIC 53), apparel and accessory store (SIC 56), furniture, home furnishings and equipment store (SIC 57), or miscellaneous shopping goods store (SIC 594).
See also **census geography; central business district (CBD); Metropolitan Statistical Area (MSA); Standard Industrial Classification (SIC) program.**

malicious mischief see **criminal mischief.**

manslaughter see **murder and nonnegligent manslaughter.**

manufacturers' sales branches and offices see **wholesale trade.**

margin credit [Board of Governors, Federal Reserve System] Margin credit, or margin credit at brokers, is all credit extended by brokers to customers for the purpose of purchasing or carrying stocks or related instruments subject to margin requirements and secured by restricted collateral.

marital status [Department of Commerce-Bureau of the Census] For purposes of the decennial census of population, all persons 15 years of age and older are classified by the Census Bureau by marital status. Marital status is also a subject of inquiry in many intercensal surveys, and household relationships are often based on marital status.

For both censuses and surveys, the Bureau looks at two broad categories of marital status: *single or never married,* which includes all those persons who have never been married including persons whose marriage has been annulled; and, *ever married,* which is composed of the now married, the widowed, and the divorced.

Now married persons are those who are legally married and whose marriage has not ended by widowhood or divorce, some persons who have common law marriages, and some unmarried couples who live together and report their marital status as married. The now married are sometimes further subdivided into "spouse present," "spouse absent," or separated. *Separated* includes those persons legally separated or otherwise absent from their spouse because of marital discord, including both persons who have been deserted, and those who have parted because they no longer want to live together but who have not obtained a divorce.

The remainder of the category ever married include the widowed and divorced. The *widowed* include widows and widowers who have not remarried. The *divorced* are persons who are legally divorced and have not remarried.

The most detailed information on marital status comes from the decennial censuses.

See also **family; family type; household.**

marketable petroleum coke [Energy Information Administration] Marketable petroleum coke is those grades of coke produced in delayed or fluid cokers that may be recovered as relatively pure carbon. This "green" coke may be sold as is or further purified by calcining.

marketing orders and agreements see **federal marketing orders and agreements (agriculture).**

marketing spread (agriculture) [Department of Agriculture-Office of Governmental and Public Affairs] In agricultural terminology, the marketing spread is the difference between the retail price of a product and the farm value of the ingredients in the product. This farm-retail spread includes charges made by marketing firms for assembling, storing, processing, transporting, and distributing products.

marketing year (agriculture) [Department of Agriculture-Office of Governmental and Public Affairs] The marketing year for agricultural crops and commodities begins at harvest time and ends at the beginning of the harvest of the following year.

See also **carryover (agriculture)**.

married couple see **family type**.

married persons see **marital status**.

master's degree [Department of Education-Center for Education Statistics] A master's degree is awarded for the successful completion of a program of study generally requiring one or two years of full-time college-level study beyond the bachelor's degree.

One type of master's degree, including the Master of Arts degree (M.A.), and the Master of Science degree (M.S.), is awarded in the liberal arts and sciences for advanced scholarship in a subject field or discipline and demonstrated ability to perform scholarly research.

A second type of master's degree is awarded for the completion of a professionally oriented program, for example, an M.Ed. in education, an M.B.A. in business administration, an M.F.A. in fine arts, an M.M. in music, an M.S.W. in social work, and an M.P.A. in public administration.

A third type of master's degree is awarded in professional fields for study beyond the first professional degree, for example, the Master of Laws (LL.M.) and Master of Science in various medical specializations.

maximum dependable capacity, net (nuclear power) [Energy Information Administration] The net maximum dependable capacity is a measure which represents the dependable main-unit net capacity of domestic nuclear power plant reactors. Maximum dependable capacity generally varies throughout the year because unit efficiency varies with seasonal cooling water temperature variations. Usually maximum dependable capacity is the highest net dependable output of the turbine generator during the most restrictive seasonal conditions, usually summer.

MCD see **minor civil division**.

mean [Department of Commerce-Bureau of the Census] The mean represents an arithmetic average of a set of values. It is calculated by dividing the sum of a group of numerical items by the total number of items. For example, mean family income is obtained by dividing the sum of all income reported by persons in families by the total number of families.

See also **median.**

mean income see **income.**

mean test score [Department of Education-Center for Education Statistics] The mean test score is obtained by dividing the sum of scores of all individuals in a group by the number of individuals in that group.

measured capacity see **institutional capacity (corrections).**

median [Department of Commerce-Bureau of the Census] The median represents the middle value in a distribution. The median divides the total frequency into two equal parts: one-half of the cases fall below the median and one-half of the cases exceed the median.

See also **mean; quartile.**

median income see **income.**

Medicaid [Department of Health and Human Services-Public Health Service; National Center for Health Statistics] Medicaid is a federally funded but State administered and operated program which provides medical benefits to certain low income persons in need of medical care. The program, authorized in 1965 by Title XIX of the Social Security Act, categorically covers participants in the Aid to Families with Dependent Children (AFDC) program, some participants in the Supplemental Security Income (SSI) program, and those other people deemed medically needy in each participating State. Each State determines the benefits covered, rates of payment to providers, and methods of administering the program.

See also **Medicare; nursing home certification.**

medical specialties see **physician specialty.**

medically needy see **categorically needy.**

Medicare [Department of Health and Human Services-Public Health Service; National Center for Health Statistics] Medicare is a federally funded nationwide health insurance program providing health insurance protection to: people 65 years of age and over; people eligible for social security disability payments for more than two years; and, people with end-state renal disease, regardless of income. The program was enacted July 30, 1965, as title XVIII, Health Insurance for the Aged, of the Social Security Act and became effective on July 1, 1966. It consists of two separate but coordinated programs: hospital insurance (Part A), and supplementary medical insurance (Part B).

See also **Medicaid; nursing home certification.**

megawatt (MW) [Energy Information Administration] One megawatt (MW) equals one million watts.

See also **watt (W).**

megawatthour (MWh) [Energy Information Administration] One megawatthour (MWh) equals one million watthours.

See also **watthour (Wh).**

membership [Department of Education-National Center for Education Statistics] Membership is defined as the number of pupils on the current roll of a class or school, as of a given date. A pupil is a member of a class or school from the date he presents him/herself at school and is placed on the current roll, until he/she permanently leaves the class or school for one of the causes recognized as sufficient by the State. The date of permanent withdrawal is the date on which it is officially known that the pupil has left school, and not necessarily the first day after the date of last attendance.

Membership is obtained by adding the total number of original entries and the total reentries for a school or class and subtracting the withdrawals; it may also be obtained by adding the total number present and the total number absent. Membership is also known as the number belonging.

See also **day of membership.**

mental disorder [Department of Health and Human Services-Public Health Service; Alcohol, Drug Abuse, and Mental Health Administration] A mental disorder is any of the diagnoses classified by the American Psychiatric Association in Diagnostic and Statistical Manual of Mental Disorders, 3rd edition, or in International Classification of Diseases, Ninth Revision, Clinical Modification (ICD-9-CM), as classified under the following numbers: 290-300.16; 300.19; 300.2-300.3; 300.5-300.81; 301.11; 305.1-305.9; 307.4 (except 307.46); 307.8; 308; 309.81; 310; 312.3; 327; and 328.

See also **International Classification of Diseases, Ninth Revision, Clinical Modification (ICD-9-CM).**

mental health organization [Department of Health and Human Services-Public Health Service; National Center for Health Statistics] A mental health organization is an administratively distinct public or private agency or institution whose primary concern is the provision of direct mental health services to the mentally ill or emotionally disturbed. Facilities include public and private psychiatric hospitals, psychiatric units of general hospitals, residential treatment centers for emotionally disturbed children, federally funded community mental health centers, freestanding outpatient psychiatric clinics, multi-service mental health facilities, and halfway houses.

See also **federally funded community mental health center (CMHC); free standing psychiatric outpatient clinic; free standing psychiatric partial care organization; general hospital with separate psychiatric service(s); halfway house (mental health); multi-service mental health organization; psychiatric hospital; residential treatment center for emotionally disturbed children (RTC).**

ental health partial care organization see **freestanding psychiatric partial care organization.**

entally retarded see **handicapped.**

erchant wholesalers see **wholesale trade.**

etallurgical coal [Energy Information Administration] Metallurgical coal is a high-quality bituminous coal suitable for making coal coke.

etropolitan Area (MA) [Department of Commerce-Bureau of the Census] A Metropolitan Area (MA) is a geographic area consisting of a large population nucleus, together with adjacent communities that have a high degree of economic and social integration with that nucleus. MA's are designated in accordance with a detailed 16 section criteria established by the federal Office of Management and Budget (OMB). In general, MA's are a county based concept which must include a place with a minimum population of 50,000; or, a Bureau of the Census defined urbanized area and a total MA population of at least 100,000 (75,000 in New England).

An MA comprises one or more central counties. Adjacent outlying counties are consolidated into a single MA if certain conditions relating to commuting to work, size, and population density, etc. are met. In New England, MA's are composed of cities and towns rather than whole counties.

In MA's with a population of one million or more, Primary Metropolitan Statistical Areas (PMSA's) may be identified. Each such area consists of a large urbanized county or cluster of counties that demonstrates very strong internal economic and social links, in addition to close ties to neighboring areas. When PMSA's are defined, the MA of which they are a component part is redesignated a Consolidated Metropolitan Statistical Area (CMSA).

See also **census geography; central city; Consolidated Metropolitan Statistical Area (CMSA); Metropolitan Statistical Area (MSA); New England County**

Metropolitan Area (NECMA); Primary Metropolitan Statistical Area (PMSA); urbanized area.

Metropolitan Statistical Area (MSA) [Department of Commerce-Bureau of the Census] A Metropolitan Statistical Area (MSA) is a unit of census geography. MSA's are relatively freestanding Metropolitan Areas (MA's) and are not closely associated with other MA's. These areas typically are surrounded by non-metropolitan counties. The concept of the MSA was introduced in June, 1984, to replace the Standard Metropolitan Statistical Area (SMSA) metropolitan area concept.

See also **census geography; central city; Consolidated Metropolitan Statistical Area (CMSA); Metropolitan Area (MA); New England County Metropolitan Area (NECMA); Primary Metropolitan Statistical Area (PMSA); urbanized area.**

microdata [Department of Commerce-Bureau of the Census] Microdata are the un-aggregated records for individual respondents or other reporting units in a census or survey. Because the Census Bureau is required by law to maintain the confidentiality of information which could be associated with a specific respondent, the original census microdata is available only to sworn census employees. In some situations identifiers such as names and addresses are stripped away from microdata to create microdata available for public use. Such public use microdata allows users to manipulate data in order to prepare tabulations of their own design. Such customized tabulations are less reliable than published data, however, since only a small sample of microdata is prepared for public use.

MINS see **PINS/CHINS/JINS/MINS.**

minor civil division (MCD) [Department of Commerce-Bureau of the Census] In census geography, minor civil divisions (MCD's) are the primary political and administrative subdivisions of a county. MCD's are most frequently known as townships, but in some states they are known as towns, magisterial districts, and similar areas. In some States, all or some incorporated places are not located in any MCD and thus serve as MCD's in their own right. In other States, incorporated places are subordinate to the MCD's in which they are located, or the pattern is mixed.

MCD's are used for census purposes in 28 States. In 21 of the remaining states, census county divisions (CCD's) are used in lieu of MCD's; in Alaska, census subareas are used; and in the District of Columbia, the entire area is considered equivalent to an MCD.

See also **census county divisions (CCD's); census subarea; unorganized territory.**

misdemeanor [Department of Justice-Bureau of Justice Statistics] A misdemeanor is an offense punishable by incarceration, usually in a local confinement facility, for a period of time. The upper limit for this time period is prescribed by statute in a given jurisdiction, and is typically limited to one year or less. In most jurisdictions there are two classes of crimes, misdemeanors and felonies.

See also **crime, felony.**

mitigating circumstance [Department of Justice-Bureau of Justice Statistics] Mitigating circumstances are those surrounding the commission of a crime which in law do not justify or excuse the act, but which in fairness may be considered as reducing the blameworthiness of the defendant. Mitigating circumstances may be taken into account when setting bail, deciding what crime the defendant will be charged with in court, or in determining a penalty. Examples of mitigating circumstances are extreme youth or old age, lack of a prior record, willingness to pay restitution, voluntary confession, and provocation. Mitigating circumstances are the opposite of aggravating circumstances.

See also **aggravating circumstance.**

MMDA see **money market deposit account (MMDA).**

MMMF see **money market mutual fund (MMMF).**

mobile home [Department of Commerce-Bureau of the Census] A mobile home is a moveable dwelling eight or more feet wide and 40 or more feet long, designed to be towed on its own chassis. The transportation gear is integral to the dwelling when it leaves the factory. There is no need for a permanent foundation.

Mobile homes are classified as single wide (i.e., any unit so designated by a dealer with only one section and one HUD label number), or double-wide (i.e. any unit so designated by a dealer and consisting of more than one section and more than one HUD label number). Mobile homes or trailers used only for business purposes or for extra sleeping space and mobile homes or trailers for sale on a dealer's lot, at the factory, or in storage are not counted in the housing inventory.

See also **housing unit.**

mobile home credit see **consumer installment credit.**

monetary aggregates see **money stock measures.**

money income [Department of Commerce-Bureau of Economic Analysis] Money income is a type of personal income. Money income is equal to the sum of the amounts received from wages and salaries, self-employment income including losses, Social Security, Supplemental Security Income, public assistance, interest, dividends, rents, royalties, estate or trust income, veterans payments, unemployment and workers' compensation payments, private and government retirement and disability pensions, alimony, child support, and any other source of money income which is regularly received. Capital gains or losses and lump-sum or one-time payments, such as life insurance settlements, are excluded from money income. Also excluded are non-cash benefits such as food stamps, health benefits, housing subsidies, rent-free housing, and the goods produced and consumed on farms.

Money income as collected by the Current Population Survey (CPS) is reported for households and various household types as well as for unrelated individuals. Only the amount received by all family members 15 years old and over is counted, excluding income received by household members not related to the householder.

Money income is used for determining the poverty status of families and unrelated individuals.

Like other income measures, money income may be reported in aggregate, median, mean, and per capita amounts, and as with other definition differences regarding income as a whole, data users should be aware of the specific methodology of how these measures are computed for each program.

See also **disposable income; income; income after taxes; income before taxes; personal income.**

money market deposit account (MMDA) [Department of Agriculture-Agricultural Research Service] A money market deposit account (MMDA) is a type of account at a bank or thrift institution which typically pays a higher rate of interest than a normal savings account. MMDA's offer limited transaction privileges such as check writing and are governed by the rules of the bank.

MMDA's were created to allow banks and thrifts to compete with money market mutual funds (MMMF), and, unlike most MMMF's, MMDA's are insured. Like MMMF's, MMDA balances are a component on the money stock measure, M2.

See also **money market mutual fund (MMMF); money stock measures.**

money market mutual fund (MMMF) [Department of Agriculture-Agricultural Research Service] A money market mutual fund (MMMF) is a type of mutual fund that typically invests in short term securities, such as treasury bills, large denomination certificates of deposit, and commercial paper. Dividends/interest from the fund are paid to investors frequently, and shares are usually held at a constant price, commonly one dollar. Typically money market mutual funds (MMMF's) are not insured. Like money market deposit accounts (MMDA's), MMMF's are a component of the money stock measure, M2.

See also **money market deposit account (MMDA); money stock measures.**

money stock measures [Board of Governors, Federal Reserve System] The Board of Governors of the Federal Reserve System publishes four money stock measures: three monetary aggregates (M1, M2, M3) and one very broad measure of liquid assets (L).

M1 consist of currency outside the Treasury, Federal Reserve Banks, and the vaults of commercial banks; travelers checks of non-bank issuers; demand deposits at commercial banks other than those due to domestic banks, the federal government, and foreign banks and institutions less cash items in the process of collection and Federal Reserve float; and other checkable deposits consisting of NOW accounts and automatic transfer service accounts at depository institutions, credit union share draft accounts, and demand deposits at thrift institutions. The currency and demand deposit components exclude the estimated amount of vault cash and demand deposits held by thrift institutions to service their other checkable deposits liabilities.

M2 consist of M1 plus overnight and continuing contract repurchase agreements (RP's) issued by all commercial banks and overnight eurodollars issued to U.S. residents by foreign branches of U.S. banks worldwide; money market deposit accounts (MMDA's); savings and small denomination (less than $100,000) time deposits; and, balances in both taxable and tax-exempt general purpose and broker/dealer money market mutual funds (MMMF). Keogh and individual Retirement account (IRA) balances at depository institutions and in MMMF's are excluded. Also excluded are all balances held by U.S. commercial banks, money market funds (general purpose and broker/dealer), foreign governments and commercial banks, and the federal government. Also subtracted is a consolidation adjustment that represents the estimated amount of demand deposits and vault case held by thrift institutions to serve their time and savings deposits.

M3 consist of M2 plus large denomination time deposits ($100,000 or more) and term RP liabilities issued by commercial banks and thrift institutions, term eurodollars held by U.S. residents at foreign branches of U.S. Banks worldwide and at all banking offices in the United Kingdom and Canada; and balances in both taxable and tax-exempt institution-only MMMF's. Excluded are amounts held by depository institutions, the federal government, money market funds, and foreign banks and official institutions. Also subtracted is a consolidation adjustment that represents the estimated amount of overnight RP's and eurodollars held by institution-only MMMF's.

L is a broad measure of liquid assets that equals M3 plus non-bank public holdings of U.S. savings bonds, short term Treasury obligations, bankers acceptances and commercial paper, net of MMMF holdings of these assets.

See also **banker's acceptance; commercial paper; eurodollar; money market deposit account (MMDA); money market mutual fund (MMMF); repurchase agreement; time deposit; Treasury securities.**

motor vehicle theft [Department of Justice-Bureau of Justice Statistics] According to the Uniform Crime Reports (UCR) definition, motor vehicle theft is the unlawful taking or attempted taking of a self propelled road vehicle owned by another with the intent to deprive him/her of it permanently or temporarily. As such, motor vehicle theft excludes thefts of trains, farm equipment, bulldozer and construction equipment, airplanes, and boats. Thefts of such items are classified as larceny-theft. Motor vehicle theft is one of the eight Part I offenses, classified UCR 7, and is an index crime.

See also **crime; index crime; larceny-theft; Part I offenses; robbery; Uniform Crime Reports (UCR).**

MRC see **major retail center (MRC).**

MSA see **Metropolitan Statistical Area (MSA).**

multi-handicapped see **handicapped.**

multi-service mental health organization [Department of Health and Human Services-Public Health Service; Alcohol, Drug Abuse, and Mental Health Administration] A multi-service mental health organization is an administratively distinct organization that provides inpatient or residential treatment and any combination of outpatient and day treatment in settings that are under the organization's direct and total control.

See also **mental health organization.**

municipio [Department of Commerce-Bureau of the Census] A municipio is a county equivalent in Puerto Rico.

See also **county.**

murder see **murder and nonnegligent manslaughter; criminal homicide.**

murder and nonnegligent manslaughter [Department of Justice-Bureau of Justice Statistics] In Uniform Crime Reports (UCR) terminology, murder and nonnegligent manslaughter are the intentional causing of the death of another without legal justification or excuse or the causing of the death of another while committing or attempting to commit another crime. Murder and nonnegligent manslaughter differ from negligent manslaughter, which is the causing of the death of another by recklessness or gross negligence.

Murder and nonnegligent manslaughter (UCR 1a) and negligent manslaughter (UCR 1b) together make up the UCR Part I offense category, criminal homicide, UCR

See also **crime; criminal homicide; index crime; negligent manslaughter; Part I offenses; Uniform Crime Reports (UCR).**

144

mutual savings bank see savings institutions.

MW see megawatt (MW).

MWh see megawatthour (MWh).

N

NAMCS see **National Ambulatory Medical Care Survey (NAMCS).**

National Ambulatory Medical Care Survey (NAMCS) [Department of Health and Human Services-Public Health Service; National Center for Health Statistics] The National Ambulatory Medical Care Survey (NAMCS) is a continuing national probability sample survey of ambulatory medical encounters. The scope of the survey covers physician-patient encounters in the offices of non-federally employed physicians classified by the American Medical Association (AMA) or the American Osteopathic Association (AOA) as office based patient care physicians. Excluded are visits to physicians who are primarily engaged in teaching, research, or administration. Telephone contacts and non-office visits are also excluded.

The NAMCS definition of an office differs from that used in the National Health Interview Survey (NHIS). In NAMCS an office is any location for a physician's ambulatory practice other than hospitals, nursing homes, other extended care facilities, patients' homes, and industrial clinics. Private offices in hospitals are included.

The survey employs a multi-stage probability design. For the 1985 survey, a sample of 5,032 non-federal office based physicians was selected from the master files of the AMA and AOA. The physician response rate was 70.2% providing data concerning a random sample of about 71,594 patient visits. Data from NAMCS are published in the National Center for Health Statistics (NCHS) monograph series <u>Vital and Health Statistics.</u>

See also **office (physician's); physician visit.**

National Crime Survey (NCS) [Department of Justice-Bureau of Justice Statistics] Along with the Uniform Crime Reports (UCR), the NCS is one of two major programs which provide national crime statistics. Both programs represent differing statistical approaches to providing information on crime. UCR data are based on crimes known to police, while NCS data results from household questionnaires. The definitions of specific crimes vary between the two surveys as well. The UCR is based on eight index crimes while NCS data is based on the concepts of a criminal incident and victimizations. The overall results of the respective surveys also differ substantially. As might be expected, NCS estimates of crime are substantially higher than UCR data.

The NCS is based on a representative sample of approximately 49,000 households inhabited by about 102,000 persons 12 years old and over. The survey asks about two different types of crimes, household crimes (household burglary, household larceny, and motor vehicle theft) and personal crimes (assault, personal larceny, personal robbery, and rape). Although the definitions of these crimes are similar to UCR definitions, there are some significant differences. In addition, the NCS differs from the UCR in that only crimes whose victims can be interviewed are included and only victims who are 12 years old and over are counted. Hence there are no homicide statistics.

The National Crime Survey (NCS) is a household survey program instituted in 1972. Currently, the NCS is administered by the Bureau of Justice Statistics and data is collected by the Bureau of the Census.

See also **crime; criminal incident; household crime; personal crime; Uniform Crime Reports (UCR); victimization.**

National Health and Nutrition Examination Survey (NHANES) [Department of Health and Human Services-Public Health Service; National Center for Health Statistics] The National Health Examination and Nutrition Survey (NHANES) is a continuing nationwide sample survey conducted by the National Center for Health Statistics (NCHS) in which data for determining the health status of the population are collected through direct standardized physical examinations, clinical and laboratory tests, and measurements. The content of the NHANES program is revised periodically, and selected components are added or deleted to meet current needs for health data of this type.

NHANES supersedes The National Health Examination Survey (NHES) which began in 1960-62. NHANES I, conducted from 1971 through 1974, focused on measuring and monitoring indicators of the nutritional status of the American people. In NHANES II, conducted from 1976 through 1980, the nutritional component remained and primary emphasis was placed on diabetes, kidney and liver functions, allergy, and speech pathology.

Data from NHANES and NHES have been published in the National Center for Health Statistics (NCHS) monograph series Vital and Health Statistics.

National Health Examination Survey (NHES) see **National Health and Nutrition Examination Survey (NHANES).**

National Health Interview Survey (NHIS) [Department of Health and Human Services-Public Health Service; National Center for Health Statistics] The National Health Interview Survey (NHIS) is a continuing nationwide sample survey in which information on personal and demographic characteristics, illness, injuries, impairments, chronic conditions, utilization of health resources, and other health topics is obtained through personal household interviews. The household questionnaire is reviewed each year, and supplemental topics are added or deleted.

The sample design plan of the NHIS follows a multi-stage probability design that permits a continuous sampling of the civilian non-institutional population residing in the United States. For most topics, data are collected over an entire calendar year. The survey is designed in such a way that the sample scheduled for each week is representative of the target population and the weekly samples are additive over time. The response rate for the survey has been between 96 and 98% over the years.

NHIS data is frequently published in the National Center for Health Statistics (NCHS) series of monographs Vital and Health Statistics.

See also **day (hospital); physician visit.**

National Hospital Discharge Survey (NHDS) [Department of Health and Human Services-Public Health Service; National Center for Health Statistics] The National Hospital Discharge Survey (NHDS) is a continuing nationwide sample survey of short stay hospitals in the United States. The scope of the NHDS encompasses patients discharged from non-institutional hospitals, exclusive of military and Veterans Administration hospitals, located in the 50 States and the District of Columbia. Only hospitals having six or more beds for patient use and those of which the average length of stay for all patients is less than thirty days are included in the survey. Discharges of newborn infants from all hospitals are excluded from this report as well as discharges of all patients from federal hospitals.

The sample is selected from a frame of short-stay hospitals listed in the National Master Facility Inventory (NMFI). In 1985, 414 hospitals participated in the study and data was abstracted from approximately 194,800 medical records.

The NHDS provides information about surgical as well as diagnostic and non-surgical procedures, length of stay, and data used to compute hospital utilization rates. NHDS material is published in the National Center for Health Statistics (NCHS) series of monographs Vital and Health Statistics.

See also **day (hospital); discharge (hospital); first listed diagnosis; hospital; National Master Facility Inventory (NMFI).**

National Household Surveys on Drug Abuse [Department of Health and Human Services-Public Health Service; National Center for Health Statistics] The National Household Surveys on Drug Abuse is a series of surveys which began in 1971, and since 1974 have been sponsored by the National Institute of Drug Abuse. The most recent survey in 1985 supplied data on the use of marijuana, cigarettes and alcohol among youth 12 to 17 years of age. It was based on home personal interviews of 8,038 randomly selected Americans 12 years of age and over.

national income [Department of Commerce-Bureau of Economic Analysis] National income is the income that originates in the production of goods and services attributable to labor and property supplied by residents of the U.S. Thus it measures the factor costs of the goods and services produced. It consists of the compensation of employees, proprietor's income with inventory valuation and capital consumption adjustments, rental income of persons with capital consumption adjustment, corporate profits with inventory valuation and capital consumption adjustments, and net interest.

In national economic accounting, national income is an income-side component of the National Income and Product Account (NIP) which, in combination with other income-side components, combine to measure the Gross National Product (GNP).

See also **compensation of employees; corporate profits with inventory valuation and capital consumption adjustments; Gross National Product (GNP); National Income Product Accounts (NIPA); net interest; proprietor's income with inventory valuation and capital consumption adjustments; rental income of persons with capital consumption adjustment.**

National Income and Product Accounts (NIPA) [Department of Commerce-Bureau of Economic Analysis] In the United States, the National Income and Product Accounts (NIPA) has become the most prominent system of national economic accounting. There are five parts to the National Income and Product Accounts: The *National Income and Product Account* itself (NIP) is a consolidation of the sector production accounts and the business appropriation account. It should be noted that the most prominent of the NIPA's is NIP, which shows Gross National Product (GNP). The *personal income and outlay account* is the household appropriation account. The *government receipts and expenditures account* is the government appropriation account. The *foreign transactions account* is a consolidation of the foreign appropriation and savings-investment accounts. The *gross savings and investment account* is a consolidation of the savings-investment accounts of the three domestic sectors. Individual accounts within the system are referred to as NIPA's.

The origin of the NIPA system's configuration of accounts is pragmatic. The information presented was selected because of its importance for economic analysis. The NIP account preserves the detail of the business appropriation account, but suppresses detail on sector production accounts because production outside the business sector is limited.

The household appropriation account and the government appropriation account are shown separately because the behavior of these sectors is important in economic analysis. The former presents information on the income, expenditures, and savings of consumers; and the latter provides a government budget integrated with the rest of the national accounts.

Because of the interest which attaches to foreign transactions, a separate foreign account is presented, but no important information is lost by the consolidation of the foreign appropriation and savings-investment accounts.

In order to present a simple and easily understood system centered on an unduplicated measure of production, the NIPA's do not show some information that is useful in more specialized analyses. This information can be found in other sets of accounts that compliment the NIPA's: the capital finance accounts and the input-output accounts.

See also **capital finance accounts, Gross National Product (GNP); input-output accounts (GNP)**.

National Master Facility Inventory (NMFI) [Department of Health and Human Services-Public Health Service; National Center for Health Statistics] The National Master Facility Inventory (NMFI) is a comprehensive file of inpatient health facilities in the United States. The three broad categories of facilities in the NMFI are hospitals, nursing and related care homes, and other custodial or remedial care facilities. To be included in the NMFI, hospitals must have at least six inpatient beds; nursing and related care homes and other facilities must have at least three beds.

The NMFI is kept current by periodic addition of names and addresses obtained from State licensing and other agencies for all newly established inpatient facilities. In addition, annual surveys of hospitals and periodic surveys of nursing homes and other related facilities are conducted to update name and location, type of business, number of beds, and number of residents or patients in the facilities, and to identify those facilities that have gone out of business.

Since 1976, all hospital data has been collected by the American Hospital Association (AHA). The nursing home and other facilities survey has been conducted by the National Center for Health Statistics (NCHS) in even number years since 1976, except 1984. Up until 1986 nursing and related care homes were covered. In 1986 this coverage was expanded to include facilities for the mentally retarded and the survey was called the Inventory of Long-Term Care Places.

See also **bed; day (hospital); discharge (hospital); hospital**.

National Morbidity Reporting System [Department of Health and Human Services-Public Health Service; National Center for Health Statistics] The National Morbidity Reporting System is a system for collecting demographic, clinical, and laboratory data to provide national surveillance for conditions such as rabies, aseptic meningitis, diphtheria, tetanus, encephalitis, food borne outbreaks, and similar conditions. Depending on the disease, data are collected weekly or monthly and are analyzed to detect epidemiologic trends or to locate cases requiring control efforts. The data comes primarily from State and territorial health agencies. Completeness of reporting varies greatly since not all cases receive medical care and not all treated conditions are reported. Additionally, although State laws and regulations mandate disease reporting, reporting to the Centers for Disease Control (CDC) by States and territories is voluntary. Data are published weekly in Morbidity and Mortality Weekly Report (MMWR) and are summarized annually.

National Nursing Home Study (NNHS) [Department of Health and Human Services-Public Health Service; National Center for Health Statistics] The National Nursing Home Study (NNHS) is a set of three sample surveys conducted by the National Center for Health Statistics (NCHS) to obtain information on nursing homes. The first survey was conducted in 1973-1974, the second in 1977, and the third in 1985-1986. The 1977 and 1985-86 surveys included all types of nursing homes, including personal care and domiciliary care homes. The most recent survey obtained information from 1,079 facilities, 2,763 registered nurses, 5,243 current residents, and 6,023 discharges.

See also **length of stay; primary diagnosis.**

National Prisoner Statistics Program (NPS) [Department of Justice-Bureau of Justice Statistics] The National Prisoner Statistics program (NPS) is a national data program which collects and publishes statistical information on federal and state prisons and prisoners. The program was established in 1926 and is currently sponsored by the Bureau of Justice Statistics (BJS), with data collected by the Bureau of the Census.

There are two annual NPS publications. Prisoners in Federal and State Institutions contains summary counts for each State and the federal government of year-end prison system populations and of additions to and subtractions from these populations. These are categorized by type of movement. Capital Punishment contains statistics on persons under sentence of death, persons executed, and descriptions of changes in capital punishment statutes.

NPS also collects and makes available additional information of State and federal prisoners. The coverage of these supplemental reports and studies includes data on the personal and social characteristics of prisoners and their criminal histories.

national program acreage [Department of Agriculture-Office of Governmental and Public Affairs] The national program acreage is the number of harvested acres of feed grains, wheat, cotton, and rice needed on a national level to meet domestic and export use and to accomplish any desired increase or decrease in carryover levels. Program acreage for an individual farm is based on the producer's share of the national farm program acreage, except when an acreage reduction program has been announced.

See also **carryover (agriculture).**

National Survey of Professional, Administrative, Technical, and Clerical Pay (PATC) [Department of Labor-Bureau of Labor Statistics] The National Survey of Professional, Administrative, Technical, and Clerical Pay (PATC) is a survey which provides broadly based information on white collar salary levels and distribution in private employment as of March of each year. Approximately 110 occupational work levels are studied from the following fields: accounting, legal services, personnel management, engineering and chemistry, purchasing, photography, drafting, computer science, and clerical. Definitions for these occupations provide for classification of employees into appropriate work levels. Reflecting duties and responsibilities in private industry, the definitions are designed to be translatable to specific pay grades of federal white-collar employees. As a result, this survey provides information suitable for use in comparing pay of salaried employees in the federal civil service with pay of their counterparts in private industry.

Monthly and annual average salaries are reported by occupation work level. Data relate to the straight-time salary corresponding to the employees normal work schedule, excluding overtime hours. Salary averages are presented for all establishments covered by the survey, establishments employing 2,500 workers or more, and for metropolitan areas as a group. Industry divisions in this survey are: mining; construction; manufacturing; transportation, communication, electric, gas, and sanitary services; wholesale trade; retail trade; finance, insurance and real estate; and services.

Survey results are published in BLS Bulletins, reports, news releases, and in Monthly Labor Review.

See also **wages**.

National System of Interstate and Defense Highways see **federal-aid highway system; functional systems (highways)**.

natural gas [Energy Information Administration] Natural gas is a mixture of hydrocarbons and small quantities of various non-hydrocarbons existing in gaseous phase or in solution with crude oil in underground reservoirs. Natural gas production measures include: wet natural gas after lease separation; dry production; and marketed production.

Consumption statistics are compiled from a survey of natural gas production, transmission, and distribution companies and electric utility companies. Consumption by end-use sector from these surveys is compiled on a national and individual State basis and then balanced with national and individual State supply data.

See also **end-use sector; natural gas, dry production; natural gas marketed production**.

natural gas, dry production [Energy Information Administration] The dry production of natural gas is a measure of natural gas production derived by subtracting extraction losses from marketed production. It represents the amount of domestic gas production that is available to be marketed and consumed as a gas.

natural gas liquids [Energy Information Administration] Natural gas liquids are those hydrocarbons in natural gas that are separated as a liquid from the gas at lease separators, field facilities, and natural gas processing plants. Natural gas liquids include natural gas plant liquids and lease condensate.

natural gas, marketed production [Energy Information Administration] The marketed production of natural gas is a measure which is derived by taking gross natural gas withdrawals from production reservoirs and subtracting: gas used for reservoir repressuring; quantities vented and flared; and, non-hydrocarbon gasses removed in treating and processing operations.

natural gas plant liquids [Energy Information Administration] Natural gas plant liquids are ethane, propane, normal butane, isobutane, pentanes plus, and products meeting the standards for finished petroleum products produced at natural gas processing plants such as, finished motor gasoline, finished aviation gasoline, special naphthas kerosene, distillate fuel oil, and other miscellaneous products. They are natural gas liquids recovered from natural gas processing plants and, in some situations, from natural gas field facilities. Also included are natural gas liquids extracted by fractionators.

natural gas, wet [Energy Information Administration] Wet natural gas is natural gas prior to the extraction of liquids and other miscellaneous products.

NCS see **National Crime Survey (NCS).**

n.e.c. [Department of Commerce-Bureau of the Census] n.e.c. (not elsewhere classified) is a frequently used organizational category in Census reporting meant to be an inclusive miscellaneous or "other" subcategory. n.e.c. encompasses all entities under a general heading that have not been specifically enumerated, defined, or listed in previous subcategories. It is often used in classification coding systems such as the Standard Industrial Classification system (SIC) and in Census Bureau financial reporting.

NECMA see **New England County Metropolitan Area (NECMA).**

negligence [Department of Justice-Bureau of Justice Statistics] In legal usage, negligence is a state of mind accompanying a person's conduct such that he or she is not aware, though a reasonable person should be, that there is a risk that their conduct might cause a particular harmful result. There are distinctions made between criminal and lesser types of negligence in the definitions of some crimes, most notably, arson and negligent manslaughter.

negligent manslaughter [Department of Justice-Bureau of Justice Statistics] In Uniform Crime Reports (UCR) terminology, negligent manslaughter is causing the death of another by recklessness or gross negligence. Vehicular negligent manslaughter is excluded from this category in reported crime data; however, in reporting and publishing UCR data on arrests, arrests for vehicular manslaughters are placed in this category along with other negligent manslaughter arrests.

Negligent manslaughter is categorized as UCR 1b, and together with murder and nonnegligent homicide, UCR 1a, they make up category UCR 1, criminal homicide. However, only UCR 1a is a crime index offense.

See also **crime; criminal homicide; index crime; murder and nonnegligent manslaughter; Part I offenses; Uniform Crime Reports (UCR).**

neonatal mortality rate [Department of Health and Human Services-Public Health Service; National Center for Health Statistics] The neonatal mortality rate is the number of deaths of infants under 28 days old per 1,000 live births.

See also **fetal death rate; infant mortality; late fetal death rate; live birth; perinatal mortality rate; perinatal mortality ratio; postneonatal mortality rate.**

net electricity generation see **electricity generation.**

net export of goods and services [Department of Commerce-Bureau of Economic Analysis] The net export of goods and services are exports less imports of goods and services. Exports are goods and services provided by U.S. residents to foreigners. Imports are goods and services provided by foreigners to U.S. residents. For both exports and imports, services include services of labor and capital for which factor incomes are paid. Imports are deducted because, although they are included in the expenditure and inventory change components of Gross National Product (GNP), they are not part of national production. Net export of goods and services is a product-side component of the National Income Product Account (NIP) which, in combination with other product-side components, combine to measure the Gross National Product (GNP).

See also **Gross National Product (GNP); National Income Product Accounts (NIPA).**

net farm income see **farm income.**

net interest [Department of Commerce-Bureau of Economic Analysis] Net interest is the interest paid by business less interest received by business, plus interest received from foreigners less interest paid to foreigners. Interest payments on mortgage and home improvement loans are counted as interest paid by business because homeowners are treated as businesses in the National Income and Product Accounts (NIPA's). In addition to monetary interest, net interest includes imputed interest. The imputed interest payments by financial institutions other than life insurance carriers and private non-insured pension plans to persons, governments, and foreigners have imputed service charges as counter-entities in GNP. They are included in personal consumption expenditures, in government purchases, and in exports. Net interest is an income-side component of the National Income Product Account (NIP) which, in combination with other income-side components, combine to measure the Gross National Product (GNP).

See also **Gross National Product (GNP); National Income Product Accounts (NIPA).**

net interstate sales of electricity [Energy Information Administration] Net interstate sales of electricity is a measure which represents the difference between the sum of electricity sales and losses within a State and the total amount of electricity generated within that State. A positive number indicates that more electricity including associated losses came into a State than went out of the State during a given period.

net summer capability [Energy Information Administration] Net summer capability is the steady hourly output that electric generating equipment is expected to supply to system load, exclusive of auxiliary power, as demonstrated by test at the time of peak summer demand.

new and used capital expenditures (manufacturing) [Department of Commerce-Bureau of the Census] New and used capital expenditures are those capital expenditures by manufacturing establishments for permanent additions and major alterations to the establishment, and for machinery and equipment used for both replacement purposes and as additions to plant capacity. Data is included from both manufacturing establishments in operation and those under construction but not yet in operation.

Totals reported for new expenditures exclude that portion of expenditures for facilities and equipment leased from non-manufacturing concerns, new facilities owned by the federal government but operated under contract by private companies, and plant and equipment furnished to the manufacturer by communities and organizations. Expenditures for used plant and equipment, land, and the cost of maintenance and repairs charged as current operating expenses are also omitted. Manufacturers report the full value of all used buildings and equipment purchased during a reporting period at the purchase price. For any equipment or structure transferred to the use of the reporting establishment by the parent company or one of its subsidiaries, the value at which it was transferred to the establishment is reported. If the establishment changed ownership during the reporting period, the cost of the fixed assets (buildings and equipment) is reported under used capital expenditures.

new business incorporations [Department of Commerce-Bureau of Economic Analysis] Total new business incorporations represent the number of stock corporations issued charters under the general business corporation laws of the various States and the District of Columbia. The statistics include completely new businesses that are incorporated, existing businesses that have changed from the non-corporate to corporate form of organization, existing corporations that have been given certificates of authority to operate in another State, and existing corporations transferred to a new State. Data reported for new business incorporations in federal publications comes from data compiled and originally published by the firm, Dun & Bradstreet, Inc.

new construction [Department of Commerce-Bureau of the Census] New construction covers the complete original erection of structures; mechanical installations such as plumbing, heating, and elevators to new or existing structures; additions, alterations, and major replacements to an existing building; the conversion of space to other uses requiring structural changes; and, outside construction of fixed structures such as highways and streets, railroad tracks, air fields, piers, sewers, electric power and distribution lines, and similar facilities built into or fixed to the land.

Value-put-in-place estimates for new construction represent the value of construction installed or erected at the site during a given period. For an individual project, this includes the cost of materials installed or erected; cost of labor by both contractors and force account and a proportionate share of the cost of construction equipment rental; contractor's profit and project owner's overhead costs; architectural and engineering fees; interest and taxes paid during construction; and miscellaneous costs charged to the project on the owner's books.

The *total value-in-place* of new construction for a given period is the sum of the value-put-in-place on all projects underway during this period, regardless of when work on each individual project was started or when payment was made to contractors. For some categories, published estimates represent payments made during a period rather than the value of work actually done during that period. For other categories, estimates are derived by distributing the total construction cost of the project by means of historic construction progress patterns.

The distinction between private and public construction is made on the basis of ownership during the construction period, not the source of funds.

See also **housing start**.

new construction planning index see **Engineering News-Record** (ENR) indexes.

New England County Metropolitan Area (NECMA) [Department of Commerce-Bureau of the Census] A New England County Metropolitan Area (NECMA) is a unit of census geography developed for the New England States (Massachusetts, Connecticut, Rhode Island, Maine, New Hampshire, Vermont) to present data that is only available on a county-level basis. Unlike the rest of the country, Metropolitan Areas (MA's) in the New England states are officially defined in

terms of cities and towns instead of counties. As a result New England MA data may not be directly comparable to MA data in the rest of the country.
See also **census geography; Metropolitan Area (MA)**.

new housing see **housing start.**

new entrants (labor force) see **reason for unemployment.**

newly qualified teacher [Department of Education-Center for Education Statistics] Newly qualified teachers are persons who both, a) first became eligible for a teaching license during the period of the study referenced or who were teaching at the time of the survey but were not certified or eligible for a teaching license, and b) had never held full-time, regular, non-substitute, teaching positions prior to completing the requirements for the degree which brought them into the survey.

newspaper advertising expenditures [Department of Commerce-Bureau of Economic Analysis] Data on newspaper advertising expenditures are compiled by the Newspaper Advertising Bureau (NAB) using lineage data, a standard measure of newspaper advertising, and newspaper advertising rates for approximately 700 daily and 500 Sunday newspapers. The data is presented for three sub-categories: classified advertising, national advertising, and retail advertising.
The advertising of retail merchants is classified as retail while the advertising of products is included under the national category. The retail advertiser is a merchant whose customers are consumers. The national advertiser is the manufacturer who distributes to these merchants.
Newspaper advertising expenditures are published monthly in Survey of Current Business.

NHANES see **National Health and Nutrition Examination Survey (NHANES).**

NHDS see **National Hospital Discharge Survey (NHDS).**

NHES see **National Health and Nutrition Examination Survey (NHANES).**

NHIS see **National Health Interview Survey (NHIS).**

NIP see **National Income and Product Accounts (NIPA).**

NIPA see **National Income and Product Accounts (NIPA).**

NMFI see **National Master Facility Inventory (NMFI).**

NNHS see **National Nursing Home Study (NNHS).**

noncommunity hospital see **hospital.**

non-defense capital goods industry see **capital goods industry.**

non-durable goods 1. [Department of Commerce-Bureau of the Census] Non-durable goods are manufactured products with an expected lifetime of less than three years.

See also **durable goods.**

2. [Department of Commerce-Bureau of Economic Analysis] Non-durable goods include: food and kindred products; tobacco products; textile mill products; paper and allied products; chemicals and allied products; petroleum and coal products; and rubber and plastic products.

See also **durable goods.**

non-federal general hospital with separate psychiatric services [Department of Health and Human Services-Public Health Service; Alcohol, Drug Abuse, and Mental Health Administration] A non-federal general hospital with separate psychiatric services is a short stay non-federal hospital providing services in any combination of separate psychiatric inpatient care, outpatient service, or partial hospitalization.

See also **general hospital with separate psychiatric service(s); hospital; mental health organization.**

non-federal government hospital see **hospital.**

non-federal physician see **physician.**

non-guaranteed debt see **full faith and credit.**

non-recourse loan (agriculture) [Department of Agriculture-Office of Governmental and Public Affairs] A non-recourse loan is a price-support loan to a farmer to enable the farmer to hold crops for later sale. Farmers may redeem such loans by paying them off with interest. The loans are non-recourse loans because if a farmer cannot profitably sell the commodity and repay the loan when it matures, the pledged or mortgaged collateral can be delivered to the federal government for settlement of the loan.

non-response error see **non-sampling error.**

non-sampling error [Department of Labor-Bureau of Labor Statistics] A non-sampling error is an error in a survey estimate due to the process of the survey itself, rather than the fact that only a sample (subset) of the whole was used. The most general categories of non-sampling error are coverage error, non-response error, response error, processing error, and estimation error.

A *coverage error* in an estimate results from the omission of part of the target population (undercoverage) or the inclusion of units from outside the target population (overcoverage).

A *non-response error* results when data are not collected for some sampled units because of the failure to interview respondents. Such failure can occur when selected respondents cannot be contacted or refuse to participate in the survey.

A *response error* results from the collection and use in estimation of incorrect, inconsistent, or incomplete data. Response error may arise because of the collection of data from inappropriate respondents, respondent memory or recall errors, deliberate distortion of responses, interviewer effects, misrecording of responses, misunderstanding or misapplication of data collection procedures, misunderstanding of the survey needs, or lack of cooperation from respondents.

A *processing error* arises from incorrect editing, coding and data-transfer, such as miskeying of data when converted to machine readable form, and in software problems arising from computer processing.

An *estimation error* results when the survey processed does not adequately measure what is intended. Such errors may be conceptual or procedural in nature, arising from a misunderstanding of the underlying survey measurement concepts or a misapplication of rules and procedures.

See also **sampling error.**

non-supervisory employee hours [Department of Labor-Bureau of Labor Statistics] Non-supervisory employee hours is defined as the total number of hours worked by non-supervisory employees paid for by an employer. It is the sum of all hours worked including overtime hours; hours paid for stand-by or reporting time; and hours not worked but paid for which pay was received directly from the firm including holidays, vacations, sick leave, and other paid leave. Overtime or other premium time hours are not converted to straight-time equivalent hours. Non-supervisory employee hours is a concept used in the Current Employment Statistics (CES) program.

See also **Current Employment Statistics program (CES).**

non-supervisory employee payroll [Department of Labor-Bureau of Labor Statistics] The non-supervisory employee payroll is the total amount of pay earned during a given pay period by all non-supervisory employees, before deductions for Social Security, unemployment insurance, health insurance, pensions, 401K plans, federal, State and local income taxes, bonds, and union dues. It includes holiday, overtime, vacation, sick leave and other paid leave; but excludes tips, commissions, lump sum payments, retroactive pay, pay advances, payments in kind, bonuses (unless paid regularly) and travel expenses. Non-supervisory employee payroll is a concept used in the Current Employment Statistics (CES) program. See also **Current Employment Statistics program (CES).**

non-supervisory employees [Department of Labor-Bureau of Labor Statistics] Non-supervisory employees are a subgroup of all employees as defined for the Current Employment Statistics (CES) program. In general non-supervisory employees includes every employee except those whose major responsibility is to supervise, plan, or direct the work of others. Thus it excludes officers of corporations, executives, department heads and managers. Working supervisors and group leaders who may be in charge of a group of employees but whose supervisory functions are incidental to their regular work are included.
See also **employed person.**

non-supervisory instructional staff [Department of Education-Center for Education Statistics] Non-supervisory instructional staff include persons such as curriculum specialists, counselors, librarians, remedial specialists, and others possessing education certification but not responsible for day-to-day teaching of the same group of pupils.
See also **instructional staff.**

notifiable disease [Department of Health and Human Services-Public Health Service; National Center for Health Statistics] A notifiable disease is one that health providers are required, usually by law, to report to federal, State, or local public health officials when diagnosed. Notifiable diseases are those of public interest by reason of their contagiousness, severity, or frequency.

not in labor force see **labor force.**

NPS see **National Prisoner Statistics Program (NPS).**

nuclear power plant [Energy Information Administration] A nuclear power plant produces electrical energy in which the prime mover is a steam turbine. The steam used to turn the turbine is produced by a heat transfer from a nuclear reactor vessel during the period when the nuclear fuel is undergoing fission.

nursing care [Department of Health and Human Services-Public Health Service; National Center for Health Statistics] Nursing care as provided in nursing homes is characterized by the provision of any of the following services: application of dressing or bandages; bowel and bladder retraining; catheterization; enema; full bed bath; hypodermic, intramuscular, or intravenous injection; irrigation; nasal feeding; oxygen therapy; and temperature-pulse-respiration or blood pressure measurement.

See also **nursing home**.

nursing home [Department of Health and Human Services-Public Health Service; National Center for Health Statistics] A nursing home is an establishment with three or more beds that provides nursing or personal care to the aged, infirm, or chronically ill. Nursing homes may be grouped in three types:

A *nursing care home* must employ one or more full-time registered or licensed practical nurses and must provide nursing care to at least half the residents.

A *personal care home with nursing* has some, but fewer than half, the residents receiving nursing care. Such homes must employ one or more registered or licensed practical nurses, or must provide administration of medications and treatments in accordance with physicians' orders, supervision of self-administered medications, or three or more personal services.

A *domiciliary care home* primarily provides supervisory care but also provides one or two personal services.

See also **nursing care; nursing home certification**.

nursing home certification [Department of Health and Human Services-Public Health Service; National Center for Health Statistics] The Medicare and Medicaid programs certify nursing homes as either a skilled nursing facility or an intermediate care facility.

A *skilled nursing facility* provides the most intensive nursing care available outside of a hospital. Such facilities certified by Medicare provide post-hospital care to eligible Medicare enrollees. Facilities certified by Medicaid as skilled nursing facilities provide skilled nursing services on a daily basis to individuals eligible for Medicaid benefits.

An *intermediate care facility* is certified by the Medicaid program to provide health-related services on a regular basis to Medicaid eligible persons who do not require hospital or skilled nursing facility care but do require institutional care above the level of room and board.

Not certified facility is a third category which includes all facilities uncertified under either category by either program.

See also **Medicaid; Medicare; nursing care; nursing home**.

O

OBSCIS see **Offender-Based State Corrections Information System (OBSCIS).**

occasion of service see **outpatient visit.**

occupancy rate (hospital) [Department of Health and Human Services-Public Health Service; National Center for Health Statistics] The National Master Facility Inventory (NMFI) and the American Hospital Association (AHA) define hospital occupancy rate as the average daily census divided by the number of hospital beds during a reporting period.

See also **average daily census; bed (hospital); National Master Facility Inventory (NMFI).**

occupancy status (housing) [Department of Commerce-Bureau of the Census] The classification of a housing unit as either occupied or vacant is the unit's occupancy status. Occupied housing units are those with a person or persons living in them as a usual residence. A vacant housing unit is one with no one living in it as their usual place of residence, unless the occupants are only temporarily absent, such as on vacation. If all the persons staying in a housing unit have their usual place of residence elsewhere, the unit is classified as vacant.

See also **housing unit; seasonal housing unit; vacancy status (housing).**

occupation [Department of Commerce-Bureau of the Census] A person's occupation is the kind of work he or she was doing during the reference week, or, if the person was not at work during the reference week, the kind of work they were doing at their most recent job. Persons holding more than one job are asked to report their occupation for the job at which they work the most hours. Occupations are classified according to a number of different systems. Data on the occupation of persons is collected for the decennial census of population and by the Current Population Survey (CPS).

See also **Dictionary of Occupational Titles (DOT); Standard Occupational Classification (SOC) system.**

Occupational Employment Statistics (OES) survey [Department of Labor-Bureau of Labor Statistics] The Occupational Employment Statistics (OES) survey is a periodic mail survey conducted by State employment security agencies of a sample of non-farm establishments to obtain wage and salary employment information by occupation. This data is used to estimate total employment by occupation for the nation, each State, and selected areas within States. The survey uses the Standard Industrial Classification (SIC) system for industrial classification and the Dictionary of Occupation Titles (DOT) for occupational classification.

The OES sample is designed to yield reliable industry and occupational estimates for the participating States. A report on each OES survey is published by the cooperating State employment security agencies and national estimates are published annually by the Bureau. The purpose of the survey is to allow for the analysis of the occupational composition of different industries, of different plants in the same industry, or of changes in an industry over time.

See also **Dictionary of Occupational Titles (DOT); Standard Industrial Classification (SIC) program.**

occupational illness [Department of Labor-Bureau of Labor Statistics] An occupational illness is any abnormal condition or disorder, other than one resulting from an occupational injury, caused by exposure to environmental factors associated with employment. It includes acute and chronic illnesses or disease which may be caused by inhalation, absorption, ingestion, or direct contact. The Bureau of Labor Statistics uses this Occupational Safety and Health Act of 1970 definition of occupational illness for its Annual Survey of Occupational Injuries and Illnesses, which is perhaps the most extensive national survey in the field.

See also **Annual Survey of Occupational Injuries and Illnesses; occupational injury.**

occupational injury [Department of Labor-Bureau of Labor Statistics] An occupational injury is an injury such as a cut, fracture, sprain, amputation, etc., which results from a work accident or from exposure involving a single incident in the work environment. The Bureau of Labor Statistics uses this Occupational Safety and Health Act of 1970 definition of occupational injury for its Annual Survey of Occupational Injuries and Illnesses, which is perhaps the most extensive national survey in the field.

See also **Annual Survey of Occupational Injuries and Illnesses; occupational illness.**

occupied housing unit see **occupancy status (housing).**

OES see **Occupational Employment Statistics (OES) survey.**

Offender-Based State Corrections Information System (OBSCIS) [Department of Justice-Bureau of Justice Statistics] The Offender-Based State Corrections Information System (OBSCIS) is a multi-State program for the development of prisoner information systems for State correctional agencies. Data about paroling authority decisions and prison/parole population movement come from this system.

offenses known to police [Department of Justice-Bureau of Justice Statistics] In Uniform Crime Reports (UCR) terminology, offenses known to police are reported occurrences of offenses which have been verified at the police level. Offenses known to police are the basis of UCR data and are usually referred to as reported crimes, a term which is slightly misleading. This is because unfounded reported offenses are subtracted from all reported occurrences of offenses in order to arrive at offenses known to police, which comprise the published data. In the UCR, an *unfounded reported offense* is a reported occurrence of an offense which is found by investigation not to have occurred, or not to constitute an offense, or which must be reclassified as another offense. Unfounding is the general mechanism provided in UCR reporting data for making necessary adjustments to initial compilations of occurrences of offenses.

See also **crime; Uniform Crime Reports (UCR)**.

office (physician's) [Department of Health and Human Services-Public Health Service; National Center for Health Statistics] In the National Health Interview Survey (NHIS), an office refers to the office of any physician in private practice, including physicians connected with prepaid group practices. In the National Ambulatory Medical Care Survey (NAMCS), an office is any location for a physician's ambulatory practice other than hospitals, nursing homes, other extended care facilities, patients' homes, or industrial clinics. However, private offices in hospitals are included.

See also **National Ambulatory Medical Care Survey (NAMCS); National Health Interview Survey (NHIS)**.

office based physician see **physician**.

oil seed crops [Department of Agriculture-Office of Governmental and Public Affairs] Oil seed crops are primarily soybeans, peanuts, cottonseed, sunflower seeds, and flaxseed and are used for the production of edible and/or inedible oils and high protein meals.

Lesser oil seed crops are rape seed, safflower, castor beans, and sesame.

operable electric utility [Energy Information Administration] An electrical generating unit is operable when it is available to provide power to the grid. For a nuclear powered unit, this is when it receives its full power amendment to its operating license from the Nuclear Regulatory Commission.

operable refinery [Energy Information Administration] An operable refinery is one that was in one of the following categories in a given year: a) in operation; b) not in operation and not under active repair but capable of being placed into operation within 30 days; and, c) not in operation but under active repair that can be completed within 90 days.

See also **operable refinery capacity**.

operable refinery capacity [Energy Information Administration] Operable refinery capacity is defined and measured in two ways. *Barrels per stream day* represents the maximum number of barrels of input that can be processed in an atmospheric distillation facility running at full capacity under optimal crude and product slate conditions with no allowance for downtime.

Barrels per calendar day represents the maximum number of barrels of input that can be processed in an atmospheric distillation facility during a 24 hour period after making allowances for six types of limitations. These limitations are: the capacity of downstream facilities to absorb the output of crude oil processing facilities of a given refinery; the types and grades of inputs to be processed; the types and grades of products expected to be manufactured; the environmental constraints associated with refinery operations; the reduction in capacity for scheduled downtime such as routine inspection, mechanical problems, maintenance, repairs, and turnaround; and the reduction of capacity for unscheduled downtime such as mechanical problems, repairs, and slowdowns.

operational capacity see **institutional capacity (corrections).**

organized care setting (mental health) [Department of Health and Human Services-Public Health Service; Alcohol, Drug Abuse, and Mental Health Administration] An organized care setting is hospital outpatient departments, emergency rooms, community mental health centers and clinics where ambulatory medical care is provided.

orthopedically impaired see **handicapped.**

other health impaired see **handicapped.**

other hydrocarbons [Energy Information Administration] Other hydrocarbons are other materials processed at petroleum refineries including coal tar derivatives, hydrogen, gilsonite, and natural gas received by the refinery for reforming into hydrogen.

other labor income see **wages and salaries.**

outlying areas [Department of Commerce-Bureau of the Census] The outlying areas of the United States are American Samoa, Guam, the Northern Mariana Islands, Palau, Puerto Rico, and the Virgin Islands of the United States. The outlying areas are treated as the statistical equivalents of States.

See also **census geography; State.**

outpatient mental health clinic [Department of Health and Human Services-Public Health Service; Alcohol, Drug Abuse, and Mental Health Administration] An

outpatient mental health clinic is an organization that provides only ambulatory mental health services. The medical responsibility for all patients/clients and direction of the mental health program is generally assumed by a psychiatrist.

outpatient treatment (mental health) [Department of Health and Human Services-Public Health Service; Alcohol, Drug Abuse, and Mental Health Administration] Mental health outpatient treatment is the provision of mental health services on an ambulatory basis to persons who do not require either 24 hour or partial hospitalization.

outpatient visit [American Hospital Association] An outpatient visit is defined as a visit to a hospital by a patient not lodged at the hospital for medical, dental or other services. Each appearance of an outpatient to each unit of the hospital counts as one outpatient visit. A visit may consist of one or more occasions of service. Each test, examination, treatment, or procedure rendered to an outpatient counts as an occasion of service.

output [Department of Labor-Bureau of Labor Statistics] Output is the constant-dollar market value of final goods and services produced in a given period. Indexes of output per hour of all persons measure changes in the volume of goods and services produced per paid hour of labor output.

overtime hours [Department of Labor-Bureau of Labor Statistics] Overtime hours are hours worked for which premiums were paid because the hours were in excess of the number of hours of either the straight-time workday or workweek. Overtime hours is one of a group of hours-related measures computed for employees in non-agricultural establishments. It is based on data from the Current Employment Statistics (CES) program.

In CES methods, Saturday and Sunday hours (or 6th and 7th day hours) are included as overtime only if overtime premiums were paid. Holiday hours worked as overtime are not included unless they were paid at more than the straight time rate. Hours for which only shift differential, hazard, incentive, or similar types of premiums were paid are excluded from overtime hours. Overtime hours data are collected only from establishments in manufacturing industries.

See also **Current Employment Statistics (CES) program; total hours.**

owned dwelling (expense) [Department of Labor-Bureau of Labor Statistics] The expense for an owned dwelling is a type of consumer unit expenditure detailed in the Consumer Expenditure Survey (CEX). It includes interest on mortgages, property taxes, insurance, refinancing and prepayment charges, ground rent, expenses for property management and security, landscaping expenses for repairs and maintenance contracted out including periodic maintenance and service contracts, and expenses for materials for owner-performed repairs and maintenance of dwellings used or maintained by the consumer unit. Expenses for dwellings maintained for business or rent are excluded.

This concept of owned dwelling expense is unique to the CEX, and should not be confused with housing or home ownership expenses in other surveys.

See also **Consumer Expenditure Survey (CEX)**.

owner-built house [Department of Commerce-Bureau of the Census] An owner-built house is one built for owner occupancy on the owner's land under the supervision of the owner acting as his/her own general contractor. Such houses may be built either by the owner alone, with the owner and some paid help, or entirely with paid help.

See also **American Housing Survey (AHS); contractor-built house.**

owner-occupied housing unit see **tenure (housing).**

P

Pacific Islander see **race.**

parish [Department of Commerce-Bureau of the Census] A parish is a county equivalent in Louisiana.
See also **county.**

parity index [Department of Agriculture-National Agricultural Statistics Service] The parity index is an index of prices paid by farmers for commodities and services including interest, taxes, and wages. 1910-1914 = 100 in this index.
See also **index of prices paid by farmers; index of prices received by farmers; parity price; parity ratio.**

parity price [Department of Agriculture-National Agricultural Statistics Service] The parity price is the price a farmer would have to have received today for a unit of a farm commodity to obtain the same purchasing power, or exchange value, in terms of farm and household goods and services that the farm commodity would have had in the 1910-1914 base period.

Parity prices were first defined by Congress in the Agricultural Adjustment Act of 1933. Congress choose the 1910-1914 base period because price relationships in the agricultural and other sectors of the economy were reasonably well balanced during that period.

Parity prices are computed in terms of prices received at the point of first sale. Prices received by farmers usually relate to the average of all classes and grades of a commodity sold by farmers; the same is true of parity prices. Parity is a national concept; parity prices are not computed by States or for specific markets.

Parity prices are not adjusted for seasonal variation. The data used for calculating parity prices are average prices received by farmers during the last ten years; therefore, seasonal elements are largely averaged out. For commodities that have strong seasonal variation the monthly prices received by farmers are seasonally adjusted for comparison with the parity price.

There are a number of limitations to the concept of parity prices. The parity price is based on price relationships. It does not measure cost of production efficiencies, standard of living, or income parity. It is not a comprehensive measure of the economic well-being of farmers, as prices are only one component in the cost of production and income. Since the base period for comparison specified by law is 1910-1914, ratio-to-parity comparisons do not take into account the many technological developments that have affected the size and efficiency of farm operations since that time.

See also **index of prices paid by farmers; index of prices received by farmers; parity index; parity ratio.**

168

parity ratio [Department of Agriculture-National Agricultural Statistics Service] The parity ratio is the ratio of the index of prices received by farmers to the parity index, with both indexes using 1910-1914 as the base. The parity ratio measures whether the purchasing power of farm products are, on the average, greater or less than the purchasing power of farm commodities during the base period.

See also **index of prices paid by farmers; index of prices received by farmers; parity index; parity price.**

parole [Department of Justice-Bureau of Justice Statistics] Parole is the status of an offender released from prison by discretion of a paroling authority prior to the expiration of sentence. A person paroled is required to observe the conditions of parole and is placed under the supervision of a parole agency. Parole differs from probation in that parole status is determined by an executive authority and follows a period of confinement while probation status is determined by judicial authority and is usually an alternative to confinement.

Part I offenses [Department of Justice-Bureau of Justice Statistics] In Uniform Crime Reports (UCR) terminology, Part I offenses are a group of eight serious crimes which meet the five following criteria: a) the crimes most likely to be reported to police; b) whether a crime has occurred is easily established by police investigation; c) occur in all geographic areas; d) occur with sufficient frequency to provide an adequate basis for comparison; and e) serious crimes by nature and or volume. Part I offenses are also sometimes referred to as serious crimes.

The eight Part I offenses are:
UCR 1 criminal homicide
  1a. murder and non-negligent (voluntary) manslaughter
  1b. negligent (involuntary) manslaughter
UCR 2 forcible rape
  2a. rape by force
  2b. attempted forcible rape
UCR 3 robbery
  3a. firearm
  3b. knife or cutting instrument
  3c. other dangerous weapon
  3d. strongarm
UCR 4 aggravated assault
  4a. firearm
  4b. knife or cutting instrument
  4c. other dangerous weapon
  4d. hands, fist, feet, etc. - aggravated injury

UCR 5 burglary
   5a. forcible entry
   5b. unlawful entry-no force
   5c. attempted forcible entry
UCR 6 larceny-theft
UCR 7 motor vehicle theft
   7a. autos
   7b. trucks and busses
   7c. other vehicles
UCR 8 arson

The lower the UCR number, the more serious is the offense. The UCR index crimes include all Part I offenses except negligent manslaughter (UCR 1b).

For statistical reporting purposes, where two or more Part I offenses are committed as part of a single criminal episode, only the most serious of the offenses is counted and tabulated. However, when arson is one of the Part I offenses which are part of a single criminal episode, the arson is counted and tabulated along with the most serious of the other offenses. Thus in criminal episodes involving arson a total of two reported offenses may be reported.

The UCR publishes annual counts of offenses known to police, as well as arrests, for all Part I offenses in <u>Crime in the United States.</u>

See also **aggravated assault; arson; burglary; crime index; criminal homicide; forcible rape; larceny-theft; motor vehicle theft; Part II offenses; robbery; Uniform Crime Reports (UCR).**

part-time enrollment (higher education) [Department of Education-Center for Education Statistics] Part-time enrollment is the number of students enrolled in higher education courses with a total credit load of less than 75% of the normal full-time credit load.

part-time staff (mental health) [Department of Health and Human Services-Public Health Service; Alcohol, Drug Abuse, and Mental Health Administration] Part-time staff consists of persons employed less than 35 hours per week in a particular mental health setting. Trainees are excluded.

part-time worker see **hours of work.**

Part II offenses [Department of Justice-Bureau of Justice Statistics] In Uniform Crime Reports (UCR) terminology, Part II offenses are a set of offense categories used in UCR arrest data. UCR publishes crime and arrest data for Part I offenses, but only arrest data for Part II offenses. In multiple offense situations for Part II offenses, the published arrest data indicate only the most serious charge at the time of arrest. Categories numbered UCR 27, 28, and 29 do not represent criminal offenses but they are reasons for taking persons into custody. The 21 Part II offenses are as follows:

UCR 9 simple assault
UCR 10 forgery and counterfeiting
UCR 11 fraud
UCR 12 embezzlement
UCR 13 stolen property (buying, receiving, possessing)
UCR 14 vandalism
UCR 15 weapons (carrying, possessing, etc.)
UCR 16 prostitution and commercialized vice
UCR 17 sex offenses (except UCR 2 and UCR 16)
UCR 18 drug abuse violations
UCR 19 gambling
UCR 20 offenses against family and children
UCR 21 driving under the influence
UCR 22 liquor laws
UCR 23 drunkenness
UCR 24 disorderly conduct
UCR 25 vagrancy
UCR 26 all other violations (except traffic)
UCR 27 suspicion
UCR 28 curfew and loitering laws - juveniles
UCR 29 runaway - juveniles

See also **Part I offenses; Uniform Crime Reports (UCR).**

partial care (mental health) [Department of Health and Human Services-Public Health Service; Alcohol, Drug Abuse, and Mental Health Administration] Partial care is a planned program of mental health treatment services generally provided in sessions of three or more hours to groups of patients or clients.

particulate matter [Department of Health and Human Services-Public Health Service; National Center for Health Statistics] Particulate matter is particles of solid or liquid matter in the air including both nontoxic materials such as soot, dust, and dirt and toxic materials such as lead, asbestos, suspended sulfates and nitrates.

PATC see **National Survey of Professional, Administrative, Technical, and Clerical Pay (PATC).**

patient [Department of Health and Human Services-Public Health Service; National Center for Health Statistics] In the National Hospital Discharge Survey (NHDS), a patient is a person who is formally admitted to the inpatient service of a hospital for observation, care, diagnosis, or treatment.

See also **hospital**.

patient care episode (mental health) [Department of Health and Human Services-Public Health Service; Alcohol, Drug Abuse, and Mental Health Administration] A patient care episode is one admission of a patient to treatment in a mental health organization. The total number of patient care episodes is measured by taking the number of residents in inpatient organizations at the beginning of the survey period or the number of persons on the rolls of non-inpatient organizations, and adding the total additions to these organizations during the survey period. Total admissions during the survey period include new admissions and readmissions; it is therefore a duplicated count of persons.

Two types of duplication may be introduced. First, the same person may be admitted more than once to a particular organization during the period or the same person may be admitted to two or more different organizations during the year. In both such cases, each admission is counted as a patient care episode. Second, a person may be admitted to different types of organizations during the year. For example a person who is an inpatient in a hospital, released to a day care program, and then followed as an outpatient, would be counted as having three patient care episodes in the survey period.

patient care staff (mental health) [Department of Health and Human Services-Public Health Services; Alcohol, Drug Abuse, and Mental Health Administration] The patient care staff includes all employees of mental health care organizations except administrative and maintenance employees. *Professional patient care staff* includes psychiatrists, non-psychiatric physicians, psychologists, social workers, registered nurses, other mental health professionals such as occupational therapists, vocational rehabilitation counselors, and physical health professionals such as dieticians, dentists, and pharmacists. *Other patient care staff* includes licensed practical and vocational nurses, and other mental health workers with less than a bachelor's degree.

See also **professional personnel**.

pay see **wages**.

payrolls [Department of Commerce-Bureau of the Census] Payrolls is a measure which represents the total dollar amount of gross earnings paid to all employees on the payrolls of surveyed establishments for a given reporting period. The Bureau uses the same definition of payroll as used by employers for federal withholding tax purposes. Payrolls include all forms of compensation, such as salaries and wages, commissions, dismissal pay, all bonuses, vacation and sick leave pay, and compensation in kind, prior to such deductions as employees' Social Security contributions, withholding taxes, group insurance, union dues, and savings bonds.

Total payrolls includes salaries of officers of corporations but excludes payments to proprietors or partners of unincorporated concerns. Also excluded are payments to members of the armed forces and pensioners carried on the active payroll of surveyed establishments.

pentanes plus [Energy Information Administration] Pentanes plus is a mixture of hydrocarbons, mostly pentanes and heavier, extracted from natural gas. This product includes isopentane, natural gasoline, and plant condensate.

per capita income see **income.**

perinatal mortality rate [Department of Health and Human Services-Public Health Service; National Center for Health Statistics] The perinatal mortality rate is the number of late fetal deaths plus infant deaths within seven days of birth per 1,000 live births plus late fetal deaths.

See also **fetal death rate; infant mortality; late fetal death rate; live birth; neonatal mortality rate; perinatal mortality ratio; postneonatal mortality rate.**

perinatal mortality ratio [Department of Health and Human Services-Public Health Service; National Center for Health Statistics] The perinatal mortality ratio is the number of late fetal deaths plus infant deaths within seven days of birth per 1,000 live births.

See also **fetal death rate; infant mortality; late fetal death rate; live birth; neonatal mortality rate; perinatal mortality rate; postneonatal mortality rate.**

person 1. [Department of Justice-Bureau of Justice Statistics] In legal usage, a person is a human being, or group of human beings considered as a legal unit, having the lawful capacity to defend rights, incur obligations, prosecute claims, or be prosecuted or adjudicated. Examples of legal units include States, territories, governments, counties, partnerships, and corporations.

2. [Department of Commerce-Bureau of Economic Analysis] For purposes of national economic accounting, a person is an individual, a non-profit institution serving individuals, a private non-insured welfare fund, or a private trust fund.

personal consumption expenditures [Department of Commerce-Bureau of Economic Analysis] Personal consumption expenditures are goods and services purchased by individuals, operating expenses of non-profit institutions serving individuals, and the value of food, fuel, clothing, housing and financial services received in-kind by individuals. Net purchases of used goods are also included. Personal consumption expenditures are a product-side component of the National Income

Product Account (NIP) which, in combination with other product-side components, combine to measure the Gross National Product (GNP).

See also **Gross National Product (GNP); gross private domestic investment; National Income Product Accounts (NIPA).**

personal crimes [Department of Justice-Bureau of Justice Statistics] In the National Crime Survey (NCS), personal crimes, along with household crimes, define the two broad categories on NCS crime. Personal crimes include the *personal crimes of violence* (rape, personal robbery, assault) and the *personal crimes of theft* (larceny).

NCS criminal incidence data is based on a household survey, and differs substantially from that of the Uniform Crime Reports (UCR), which is based on crimes known to police. Definitions of specific crimes for both programs are somewhat different as well.

See also **assault; crime; criminal incident; household crimes; National Crime Survey (NCS); personal larceny with contact; personal larceny without contact; personal robbery; rape; Uniform Crime Reports (UCR); victimization.**

personal crimes of theft see **personal crimes; personal larceny with contact; personal larceny without contact.**

personal crimes of violence see **assault; personal crimes; personal robbery; rape.**

personal income [Department of Commerce-Bureau of Economic Analysis] In national economic accounting, personal income is the income received by persons: i.e., individuals, owners of unincorporated businesses (including partnerships), non-profit institutions, private trust funds, and private non-insured welfare funds. Personal income is the sum of wage and salary disbursements, other labor income, proprietors' income, rental income of persons, dividends, and personal interest income and transfer payments, less personal contributions for social insurance.

See also **disposable personal income; Gross National Product (GNP); income; money income; National Income Product Accounts (NIPA).**

personal larceny with contact [Department of Justice-Bureau of Justice Statistics] In the National Crime Survey (NCS), personal larceny with contact is the theft or attempted theft by stealth of money or property from the immediate possession of a person without the use or threat of force. A theft from a person committed or attempted by use of force or threat of force is classified as a personal robbery. Personal larceny with contact is classified by the NCS as a personal crime of theft.

See also **crime; criminal incident; National Crime Survey (NCS); personal crimes; personal larceny without contact; personal robbery; Uniform Crime Reports (UCR); victimization.**

personal larceny without contact [Department of Justice-Bureau of Justice Statistics] In the National Crime Survey (NCS), personal larceny without contact is the theft or attempted theft by stealth of money or property of a person without direct contact between the victim and the offender. Personal larceny without contact is classified by the NCS as a personal crime of theft. Theft without contact occurring in a residence or its immediate vicinity is not classified as a personal crime since a household rather than any individual person(s) is considered to be the victim of the theft. Such incidents are classified as household larcenies, a type of household crime. Thefts of motor vehicles are also classified as household crimes by NCS, as by NCS convention a household rather than any individual person(s) is considered to be the victim.

See also **crime; criminal incident; household crimes; National Crime Survey (NCS); personal crimes; personal larceny with contact; Uniform Crime Reports (UCR); victimization.**

personal outlays [Department of Commerce-Bureau of Economic Analysis] In national economic accounting, personal outlays is the sum of personal consumption expenditures, interest paid by consumers to business, and personal transfer payments to foreigners, net personal remittances in cash and in-kind to abroad, less such remittances from abroad.

See also **personal consumption expenditures.**

personal robbery [Department of Justice-Bureau of Justice Statistics] Personal robbery is the theft or attempted theft of money or property from the immediate possession of a person by force or threat of force, with or without a weapon. In the National Crime Survey (NCS), personal robbery is classified as a personal crime of violence and is categorized according to whether or not the victim(s) suffered physical injury and according to whether the injury resulted from a serious assault or minor assault.

Robbery with injuries is theft or attempted theft from a person accompanied by an attack, either with or without a weapon, resulting in injury. An injury is classified as resulting from a *serious assault* if: a) a weapon was used in the commission of the crime, or, b) the extent of the injury was either serious (e.g., broken bones, loss of teeth, internal injuries, loss of consciousness) or undetermined but requiring two or more days of hospitalization. An injury is classified as resulting from a *minor assault* when the extent of the injury was minor (e.g., bruises, black eye, cuts, scratches, swelling) or undetermined but requiring less than two days of hospitalization.

Personal robbery as defined in the NCS differs somewhat from the Uniform Crime Reports (UCR) Part I crime of robbery, UCR 3.

See also **crime; criminal incident; National Crime Survey (NCS); Part I offense; personal crimes; robbery; Uniform Crime Reports (UCR); victimization.**

personal saving [Department of Commerce-Bureau of Economic Analysis] In national economic accounting, personal saving is personal income less the sum of personal outlays and personal tax and non-tax payments. It is the current savings of individuals including proprietors, non-profit institutions serving individuals, private non-insured welfare funds, and private trust funds.

Personal saving may also be viewed as the sum of net acquisition of financial assets and physical assets, less the sum of net borrowing and of capital consumption allowances.

See also **personal outlays; personal tax and non-tax payments.**

personal tax and non-tax payments [Department of Commerce-Bureau of Economic Analysis] In national economic accounting, personal tax and non-tax payments are tax payments by persons that are not chargeable to business expenses, along with certain other personal payments to government agencies that are convenient to treat like taxes.

Personal taxes include income, estate and gift, and personal property taxes. Personal contributions for social insurance are excluded. Non-tax payments include tuition and fees paid to schools and hospitals mainly operated by the government, passport fees, fines and penalties, and donations. Payments to government enterprises are excluded.

persons in family see **family.**

persons in household see **household.**

petrochemical feedstocks [Energy Information Administration] Petrochemical feedstocks are chemical feedstocks derived from petroleum, principally for the manufacture of chemicals, synthetic rubber, and a variety of plastics. The categories reported by the Energy Information Administration are naphthas less than 400 degrees fahrenheit end-point, and other oils over 400 degrees fahrenheit end-point.

petrolatum [Energy Information Administration] Petrolatum is a semisolid, unctuous product ranging from white to yellow in color produced during the refining of residual stocks or the dewaxing of neutral or bright lubricating oil stocks. It consists of microcrystalline wax associated with relatively high proportions of oil.

petroleum [Energy Information Administration] Petroleum is a generic term applied to oil and oil products in all forms such as crude oil, lease condensate, unfinished oils, petroleum products, natural gas plant liquids, and non-hydrocarbon compounds blended into finished petroleum products.

See also **petroleum products.**

petroleum coke [Energy Information Administration] Petroleum coke is a solid residue that is the final product of the condensation process in cracking. It consists of aromatic hydrocarbons very poor in hydrogen. Calcination of petroleum coke can yield almost pure carbon or artificial graphite suitable for production of carbon or graphite electrodes, structural graphite, motor brushes, dry cells, and similar products. This product is reported as marketable or catalyst coke.
See also **marketable petroleum coke; catalyst petroleum coke.**

petroleum products [Energy Information Administration] A petroleum product is obtained from the processing of crude oil, lease condensate, natural gas, and other hydrocarbon compounds. Petroleum products include unfinished oils, liquified petroleum gases, pentanes plus, aviation gasoline, motor gasoline, naphtha-type jet fuel, kerosene-type jet fuel, kerosene, distillate fuel oil, residual fuel oil, naphtha-less than 400 degrees fahrenheit end-point, other oils over 400 degrees fahrenheit end-point, special naphthas, lubricants, wax, petroleum coke, asphalt, road oil, and still gas.
See also **petroleum.**

petroleum stocks, primary [Energy Information Administration] Primary petroleum stocks is a measure which consists of stocks of crude oil or petroleum products held in storage in leases, refineries, natural gas processing plants, pipelines, tank farms, and bulk terminals that can store at least 50,000 barrels of petroleum products or that can receive petroleum products by tanker, barge, or pipeline. Crude oil that is in transit from Alaska or that is stored in federal leases or in the Strategic Petroleum Reserve is included. Excluded are stocks of foreign origin that are held in bonded warehouse storage.

physical plant assets [Department of Education-Center for Education Statistics] Physical plant assets is a measure which includes the values of land, building and equipment owned, rented, or utilized by colleges. It does not include those plant values which are part of endowment or other capital fund investments in real estate. The measure excludes construction in progress.

physician [Department of Health and Human Services-Public Health Service; National Center for Health Statistics] A physician is a licensed doctor of medicine or osteopathy who is licensed to practice medicine in one of the States or territories of the United States. The American Medical Association classifies physicians through self-reporting as either active physicians or inactive physicians.
An *active physician* or *professionally active physician* currently practices medicine regardless of the number of hours worked per week.
A *federal physician* is an active physician employed by the federal government. A *non-federal physician or civilian physician* is not employed by the federal government.

177

An *office based physician* is a non-federal physician who spends most of his/her time working in a practice based in a private office. A *hospital physician* is a non-federal physician who spends the majority of his/her time as a salaried physician in a hospital.

See also **office (physician's); physician masterfile; physician specialty; physician visit.**

physician masterfile [Department of Health and Human Services-Public Health Service; National Center for Health Statistics] The physician masterfile is maintained by the American Medical Association and currently contains information on almost every physician in the United States and on those graduates of American medical schools temporarily practicing overseas. The file also includes graduates of foreign medical schools who are in the United States and meet education standards for primary recognition as physicians.

Data are obtained from over 2,100 organizations and institutions and are collected and processed on an ongoing basis for the maintenance and updating of over 550,000 individual physician records. A file is initiated on each individual upon entry into medical school or in the case of foreign graduates, upon entry to the United States. A census of physicians is conducted every four years to update file information on professional activities, specialization, and present employment status.

The masterfile is used for a variety of AMA purposes, and provides total counts of physicians that appear in federal publications. The file contains both members and non-members of the AMA.

physician specialty [Department of Health and Human Services-Public Health Service; National Center for Health Statistics] A physician specialty is any specific branch of medicine in which a physician may concentrate. The specialty classifications used by the Bureau of Health Professions (BHP) and National Ambulatory Medical Care Survey (NAMCS) follow the American Medical Association categories, grouping specialties into four classifications.

Primary care specialties are those which include general or family practice, internal medicine, and pediatrics.

Medical specialties include internal medicine, pediatrics, allergy specialties, cardiovascular disease, dermatology, gastroenterology, pediatric allergy and cardiology, and pulmonary diseases.

Surgical specialties include general surgery, neurological surgery; obstetrics and gynecology, ophthalmology, orthopedic surgery, otolaryngology, plastic surgery, colon and rectal surgery, thoracic surgery, and urology.

Other specialties covered by NAMCS are geriatrics, neurology, preventive medicine, psychiatry, and public health. Other specialties covered by the BHP are aerospace medicine, anesthesiology, child psychiatry, neurology, occupational

medicine, pathology, physical medicine and rehabilitation, psychiatry, public health, and radiology.
See also **National Ambulatory Medical Care Survey (NAMCS).**

physician visit [Department of Health and Human Services-Public Health Service; National Center for Health Statistics] The National Health Interview Survey (NHIS) counts as a physician visit any visit either in person or by telephone to a doctor of medicine or doctor of osteopathy for the purpose of examination, diagnosis, treatment, or advice. The service on the occasion of the visit may be provided directly by the physician, a nurse, or another person acting under the physician's supervision. Contacts involving services provided on a mass basis are not counted as physician visits, nor are contacts for hospital inpatients.

Physician visits are generally classified by the type of place of visit. In NHIS, this includes the office, hospital outpatient clinic or emergency room, telephone (advice given by a physician in a telephone call), company or industrial clinic, home, as well as other places.

In the National Ambulatory Medical Care Survey (NAMCS), an office visit is any direct personal exchange between an ambulatory patient and a physician or member of the physician's staff for the purpose of seeking care and rendering health services.
See also **National Ambulatory Medical Care Survey (NAMCS); National Health Interview Survey (NHIS).**

PINS see **PINS/CHINS/JINS/MINS.**

PINS/CHINS/JINS/MINS [Department of Justice-Bureau of Justice Statistics] PINS/CHINS/JINS/MINS (person/child/juvenile/minor in need of supervision) are acronyms used to name a class of juvenile. PINS/CHINS/JINS/MINS often consist of status offenders but the term is defined differently in different jurisdictions.
See also **delinquency; juvenile.**

place [Department of Commerce-Bureau of the Census] A place is a unit of census geography. A place is a concentration of population which may or may not have legally prescribed limits, powers, or functions.

Places are further classified by the Census Bureau into incorporated places and census designated places (CDP's). Most of the places identified in the 1980 and 1990 decennial Censuses are incorporated as cities, towns, villages or boroughs. However, other additional places, CDP's (often referred to as unincorporated places) have been identified, for which data is reported as well.
See also **census county division (CCD); census designated place (CDP); census geography; incorporated place; minor civil division (MCD).**

plant condensate [Energy Information Administration] Plant condensate is one of the natural gas plant liquids, mostly pentanes and heavier hydrocarbons, recovered and separated as liquids at gas inlet separators or scrubbers in processing plants. Plant condensate is not suitable for blending into finished motor gasoline. It is usually blended with crude oil for distilling or processing at other refineries.

plantation [Department of Commerce-Bureau of the Census] A plantation is a minor civil division (MCD) in Maine.
See also **minor civil division (MCD).**

PMSA see **Primary Metropolitan Statistical Area.**

pollutant [Department of Health and Human Services-Public Health Service; National Center for Health Statistics] A pollutant is defined as any substance that renders the atmosphere or water foul or noxious to health.

population [Department of Commerce-Bureau of the Census] The population is the number of inhabitants of an area, or, a group of persons, housing units, or other entities included in a census or survey.

For persons, there are four commonly used measures of the population of the United States.

The *total population of the United States* is the sum of all persons living within the United States plus all members of the Armed Forces living in foreign countries, Puerto Rico, Guam, and the U.S. Virgin Islands. Other Americans living abroad such as civilian federal employees and dependents of members of the Armed Forces or other federal employees are not included in the total population of the United States.

The *resident population of the United States* is the population living within the geographic United States. This includes members of the Armed Forces stationed in the United States, their families, and foreigners working or studying here. It excludes Americans living abroad, foreign military, naval, and diplomatic personnel and their families located here and residing in embassies or similar quarters. Resident population is often the denominator when calculating birth and death rates, incidence of disease, and other rates.

The *civilian population* is the resident population excluding members of the Armed Forces; however, families of members of the Armed Forces are included.

The *civilian non-institutional population* is the civilian population not residing in institutions. Institutions include: correctional institutions; detention homes and training schools for juvenile delinquents; homes for the aged and dependent such as nursing homes and convalescent homes; homes for dependent and neglected children; homes and schools for the mentally and physically handicapped; homes for unwed mothers; psychiatric, tuberculosis, and chronic disease hospitals; and residential treatment centers.

population density [Department of Commerce-Bureau of the Census] The population density is the number of persons per unit of area, usually persons per square mile.

post-baccalaureate enrollment [Department of Education-Center for Education Statistics] The post-baccalaureate enrollment is the number of graduate and first-professional students working toward advanced degrees plus students enrolled in graduate-level classes but not enrolled in degree programs.

See also **first professional enrollment; graduate enrollment.**

postneonatal mortality rate [Department of Health and Human Services-Public Health Service; National Center for Health Statistics] The postneonatal mortality rate is the number of infant deaths that occur from 28 days of age to 365 days of age per 1,000 live births.

See also **fetal death rate; infant mortality; late fetal death rate; live birth; neonatal mortality rate; perinatal mortality rate; perinatal mortality ratio.**

poverty [Department of Commerce-Bureau of the Census] Although the term poverty connotes a complex set of economic, social, and psychological conditions, the standard federal statistical definition provides for only estimates of economic poverty. The Census definition of poverty is based on the receipt of money income before taxes and excludes the value of: government payments and transfers such as food stamps or Medicare; private transfers such as health insurance premiums paid by employers; gifts; the depletion of assets; and borrowed money. For reporting purposes the term poverty is used to classify persons and families in relation to being above or below a specified income level, or poverty threshold. Those below this threshold are said to be in poverty, or more accurately, as being below the poverty level. The poverty threshold is based on the Department of Agriculture's Economy Food Plan and is revised each year according to a formula based on the Consumer Price Index (CPI). In 1980, the poverty threshold for a family of four was $7,356; in 1989 it was $12,675.

Data on the poverty status is gathered in the decennial censuses as well as through intercensal surveys such as the Current Population Survey (CPS). As such, poverty is a concept used in relation to households. The poverty threshold varies by size of family, number of children, and age of the householder. Poverty status is determined not only for families, but also for unrelated individuals living in households. Poverty status is not determined for those living in group quarters, nor for persons in the Armed Forces.

PPI see **Producer Price Index (PPI).**

pre-arraignment lockup [Department of Justice-Bureau of Justice Statistics] Pre-arraignment lockup is a confinement facility for arrested adults awaiting arraignment or consideration for pretrial release. In pre-arraignment lockups, the duration of stay is usually limited by statute to two days or until the next session of the appropriate court. In some jurisdictions, this function is also performed by jails.
See also **jail.**

precinct (election) [Department of Commerce-Bureau of the Census] An election precinct is a minor civil dision (MCD) in Illinois and Nebraska.
See also **minor civil division (MCD).**

prekindergarten class [Department of Education-National Center for Education Statistics] A prekindergarten class is a group or class organized to provide educational experiences for children during the year or years preceding kindergarten, which are part of the elementary school program, and are under the direction of a professionally qualified teacher. A prekindergarten class may be organized as a grade of an elementary school or as part of a separate nursery school.
See also **preschool program.**

preschool program [Department of Education-National Center for Education Statistics] A preschool program is a beginning group or class enrolling children younger than 5 years of age and organized to provide educational experiences under professionally qualified teachers in cooperation with parents during the year or years immediately preceding kindergarten or prior to entry into elementary school when there is no kindergarten.
See also **prekindergarten class.**

prevalence (health) [Department of Health and Human Services-Public Health Service; National Center for Health Statistics] Prevalence is the number of cases of disease, infected persons, or persons with some other attribute, present during a particular period of time. Prevalence is often expressed as a rate.

prevalence of disease see **prevalence (health).**

price [Department of Labor-Bureau of Labor Statistics] For the Producer Price Index (PPI) program, price is defined as the net revenue accruing to a specified producing establishment from a specific kind of buyer for a specified product shipped under specified transaction terms on a specified day of the month.
See also **Producer Price Index (PPI)**

prices (farm) see **index of prices received by farmers; index of prices paid by farmers.**

primary care specialty see **physician specialty.**

primary consumption expenditures (energy) [Energy Information Administration] Primary energy consumption expenditures are expenditures for energy consumed in each of the four major end-use sectors (residential, commercial, industrial, transportation), excluding energy in the form of electricity, plus expenditures by the electric utilities sector for energy used to generate electricity. There are no fuel associated expenditures for hydroelectric power, geothermal energy, photovoltaic and solar energy, or wind energy. Also excluded are quantifiable consumption expenditures that are an integral part of process fuel consumption.
See also **end-use sector; process fuel.**

primary diagnosis [Department of Health and Human Services-Public Health Service; National Center for Health Statistics] In the National Nursing Home Survey (NNHS) the primary diagnosis is the primary condition of a nursing home resident at the last examination as extracted from the resident's medical record.
See also **National Nursing Home Survey (NNHS).**

Primary Metropolitan Statistical Area (PMSA) [Department of Commerce-Bureau of the Census] A Primary Metropolitan Statistical Area (PMSA) is a unit of census geography introduced in June, 1984, which, in combination with the Metropolitan Statistical Area (MSA) and Consolidated Metropolitan Statistical Area (CMSA), replace the Standard Metropolitan Statistical Area (SMSA) and related concepts. PMSA's are designated according to criteria established by the federal Office of Management and Budget.
In the 1990 Census, PMSA's may be defined within a Metropolitan Area (MA) which has more than one million persons. PMSA's consist of a large urbanized county or cluster of counties that demonstrate very strong internal economic and social links, in addition to close ties to other portions of the larger area.
In the 1980 Census, PMSA's are those MSA's which are a county or counties with populations of at least 100,000 (60% of which must be urban), in which less than 50% of resident workers commute to jobs outside the county. In both the 1980 and 1990 Censuses, when PMSA's are defined, the larger area of which they are component parts is redesignated a CMSA.
See also **census geography; Consolidated Metropolitan Statistical Areas (CMSA); Metropolitan Area (MA); Metropolitan Statistical Area (MSA).**

primary school [Department of Education-National Center for Education Statistics] A primary school is a separately organized and administered elementary school for pupils at the primary level, usually including grade 1 through grade 3 or the equivalent, and sometimes including pre-primary years.
See also **elementary school.**

prime mover (electric utilities) [Energy Information Administration] The prime mover is the engine, turbine, water wheel, or similar machine that drives an electric generator.

prime rate [Board of Governors of the Federal Reserve System] The prime rate is the interest rate banks charge their most credit worthy business customers for short-term loans. It is the base used to scale upward the rates charged on most loans to other business customers.

   Monthly prime rate data that is reported by the Federal Reserve is computed by multiplying each predominant prime rate, the rate charged by the majority of 30 large money market banks, by the number of days it was in effect during the month, summing these products, and dividing by the number of days in the month. The annual data are unweighted averages of the monthly averages.

   The prime rate is not as sensitive as money market instrument rates, which fluctuate daily in response to short-term changes in supply and demand. Rather, its movements tend to be infrequent, changing only by increments of one quarter of a percentage point. Major banks tend to change their prime rate in response to increasing differentials with selected open market money rates.

prison [Department of Justice-Bureau of Justice Statistics] A prison is a State or federal confinement facility having custodial authority over adults sentenced to confinement. Generally, prisons hold persons committed after adjudication, usually those committed on sentences of one year or more. In this respect prisons differ from jails, which hold persons detained pending adjudication or those committed on sentences of less than one year. In addition, prisons are different from jails in that they are usually administered by States or the federal government. In five States - Delaware, Connecticut, Hawaii, Rhode Island, and Vermont - all adult confinement facilities are administered at the State level.

   See also **confinement facility; correctional facility (adult); jail**.

prisoner [Department of Justice-Bureau of Justice Statistics] A prisoner is a person in physical custody in a confinement facility or in the personal physical custody of a criminal justice official while being transported to or between confinement facilities. Prisoners differ from inmates, who are persons in physical custody in a local jail.

private industry agreement [Department of Labor-Bureau of Labor Statistics] A private industry agreement is a negotiated wage and benefit change or collective bargaining settlement in the private sector. As an ongoing program, the Bureau of Labor Statistics (BLS) prepares information and reports on current changes in wages and supplementary benefits agreed to both in the private sector and in State and local government agreements. BLS reporting includes a monthly listing of companies and employer associations in which such changes have occurred, the unions involved, and the nature of the change.

The BLS's private industry agreement series summarizes wage rate changes in major collective bargaining settlements covering 1,000 workers or more for production and related workers in manufacturing and non-supervisory workers in non-manufacturing. BLS also prepares quarterly and annual statistical summaries of negotiated wage changes in all major collective bargaining situations in private industry. The Bureau currently follows about 1,350 bargaining situations for virtually complete coverage of major agreements. Changes in total compensation are measured for agreements covering 5,000 workers or more in all industries and 1,000 workers or more in construction. Contracts covering multi-plant firms are included if the agreement as a whole covers 1,000 workers even though each plant employs fewer workers. Also included are contracts with trade associations or with groups of firms that bargain jointly with a union or unions even though the firms are not associated formally and each has fewer than the minimum number of workers within the scope of the series. When two or more unions, together representing at least 1,000 workers but individually representing fewer than 1,000, negotiate essentially identical contracts with one or more firms, the workers involved are considered to constitute one bargaining unit.

The listing of current changes in wages and benefits with summaries grouped by industry is published monthly in Current Wage Developments. The listings include the name of the employer and the union, the number of workers involved, the amount and effective date of the change, details of complex changes, and the reason for the change.

private school or institution [Department of Education-Center for Education Statistics] A private school or institution is controlled by an individual or agency other than a State, a subdivision of a State, or the Federal government. Private schools and institutions are usually supported by other than public funds, and the operation of their program rests with other than publicly elected or appointed officials.

private wage and salary workers see **class of worker**.

process fuel [Energy Information Administration] Process fuel is all energy consumed in the acquisition, processing, and transportation of energy. Quantifiable process fuel includes only four categories: natural gas lease and plant operations (acquisitions and processing); natural gas pipeline operations (transportation); oil refinery operations (processing); and uranium enrichment operations (processing).

processing error see **non-sampling error**

processing gain [Energy Information Administration] In petroleum operations, the processing gain represents the amount by which the total volume of refinery output is greater than the volume of input for a given period of time. This difference is due to the processing of crude oil and other hydrocarbons into products which are less dense than the crude oil processed.

Producer Price Index (PPI) [Department of Labor-Bureau of Labor Statistics] The Producer Price Index (PPI) measures average changes in selling prices received by domestic producers of commodities in all stages of processing for their output. Most of the information used in calculating the PPI is obtained through systematic sampling of virtually every industry in the mining and manufacturing sectors of the economy. The PPI program, also known as the industrial price program, includes some data from other sectors as well - agriculture fishing, forestry, services, gas and electricity. Thus the title, Producer Price Index, actually refers to an entire family or system of indexes.

As of January, 1987, the PPI program included price indexes for nearly 500 mining and manufacturing industries including approximately 8,000 indexes for specific products and product categories; over 3,000 commodity price indexes organized by type of product and end use; and, several major aggregate measures of price change organized by stage of processing. Together, these elements constitute a system of price measures designed to meet the need for both aggregate information and detailed applications such as following price trends in specific industries and products.

There are three primary systems of indexes within the PPI program: a) stage of processing indexes (organizing products by class of buyer and degree of fabrication); b) commodity indexes; and c) indexes for the net output of industries and their products.

For the PPI program, price is defined as the net revenue accruing to a specified producing establishment from a specific kind of buyer for a specified product shipped under specified transaction terms on a specified day of the month. Measures of price changes classified by industry form the basis of the program. These indexes reflect the price trends of a constant set of goods and services which represent the total output of an industry. Industry index codes are based on Standard Industrial Classification (SIC) system and provide comparability with a wide assortment of industry-based data for other economic phenomena, including productivity, production, employment, wages, and earnings.

Movements of price indexes from one month to another are usually expressed as percent changes rather than as changes in index points, because index point changes are affected by the level of the index in relation to the base period, while percent changes are not. Each index measures price changes from a relative reference period which equals 100.0.

Indexes are published in both seasonally adjusted and unadjusted form. The PPI is usually issued in news-release form on the second or third Friday of the month following the month reported on. A monthly publication, Producer Price Indexes, is printed three to four weeks after the news release date.

Until 1978, the PPI was known as the Wholesale Price Index.

See also **seasonal adjustment; stage of processing (SOP); Standard Industrial Classification (SIC) system.**

production worker [Department of Labor-Bureau of Labor Statistics] A production worker is a non-supervisory employee in an establishment engaged in such occupations as fabricating, storage, receiving, warehousing, shipping, trucking, packing, handling, maintenance, repair, processing, assembling, and janitorial. As a group, production workers also include working supervisors and group leaders who may be in charge of a group of employees but whose supervisory functions are only incidental to their regular work. Excluded are employees whose duties concern finance, personnel, technical work, advertising, collection, accounting, legal, sales, purchasing and related activities.

Production worker is a concept used in the Current Employment Statistics (CES) program and in the economic censuses conducted every five years by the Bureau of the Census.

See also **production worker hours; production worker payroll; working supervisor.**

production worker hours [Department of Labor-Bureau of Labor Statistics] Production worker hours is a measure composed of the total number of hours worked by production workers paid for by an employer. It is the sum of all hours worked including overtime hours; hours paid for stand-by or reporting time; and hours not worked but paid for which pay was received directly from the firm including holidays, vacations, sick leave, and other paid leave. Overtime or other premium time hours are not converted to straight-time equivalent hours.

Production worker hours is a concept used in the Current Employment Statistics (CES) program and in the economic censuses conducted every five years by the Bureau of the Census.

See also **production worker; production worker payroll.**

production worker payroll [Department of Labor-Bureau of Labor Statistics] The production worker payroll is the total amount of pay earned during a given pay period by all production workers before deductions for Social Security; unemployment insurance; health insurance; pensions; 401K plans; federal, State and local income taxes; bonds; and union dues. It includes holiday, overtime, vacation, sick leave and other paid leave, but excludes bonuses unless regularly paid, lump sum payments, retroactive pay, pay advances, and payments in kind.

Production worker payroll is a concept used in the Current Employment Statistics (CES) program.

See also **production worker; production worker hours.**

professional personnel [Department of Health and Human Services-Public Health Service; National Center for Health Statistics] In health care, professional personnel is a category which includes chiropractors, dentists, dental hygienists, licensed practical nurses, pharmacists, physical therapists, physicians, podiatrists, and registered nurses, along with some other specialized occupations related to certain aspects of health care which may be covered in certain specific reports.

In the United States, counts of such professionals include only those licensed in the State where they practice. Licensure usually requires the completion of an appropriate degree or certificate program for that profession. In international counts prepared by the World Health Organization (WHO), only those professionals active in their profession are counted.

See also **patient care staff.**

program acreage see **national program acreage.**

propane [Energy Information Administration] A normally gaseous, paraffinic hydrocarbon, propane is extracted from natural gas or refinery streams and includes all products covered by Gas Processors Association specifications for commercial propane and HD-5 propane and ASTM specification D1835.

Propane is used primarily for residential and commercial heating and cooling and as a fuel for transportation. Industrial uses of propane include use as a petrochemical feedstock.

property crime [Department of Justice-Bureau of Justice Statistics] In Uniform Crime Reports (UCR) terminology, property crime refers to four Part I offenses included in the crime index. The four property crimes are burglary (UCR 5), larceny-theft (UCR 6), motor vehicle theft (UCR 7), and arson (UCR 8). Together with the four violent crimes, the eight index crimes are sometimes referred to as serious crimes.

See also **arson; burglary; crime; crime index; larceny-theft; motor vehicle theft; Part I offenses; Uniform Crime Reports (UCR).**

property taxes [Department of Commerce-Bureau of the Census] Property taxes are taxes conditioned on ownership of property and measured by its value. Property taxes include general property taxes relating to property as a whole, real and personal, tangible or intangible, whether taxed at a single rate or at classified rates; and taxes on selected types of property, such as motor vehicles or certain or all intangibles.

See also **taxes.**

proprietary institution [Department of Education-Center for Education Statistics] A proprietary institution is an educational institution that is under private control but whose profits derive from revenues subject to taxation.

proprietary hospital see **hospital.**

proprietors' income with inventory valuation and capital consumption adjustments [Department of Commerce-Bureau of Economic Analysis] Proprietors' income with inventory valuation and capital consumption adjustments is the income, including income in-kind, of sole proprietorships and partnerships and of tax-exempt cooperatives. The imputed net rental income of owner-occupants of farm dwellings is included. Dividends and monetary interest received by proprietors of non-financial business and rental incomes received by persons not primarily engaged in the real estate business are excluded.

The *inventory valuation adjustment* is the difference between the cost of inventory withdrawals as valued in determining profits before tax and the cost of withdrawals valued at current replacement cost.

The *capital consumption adjustment* is the difference between tax-return-based capital consumption allowances and capital consumption based on the use of uniform service lives, straight-line depreciation, and replacement cost.

Proprietors' income with inventory valuation and capital consumption adjustments is an income-side component of the National Income Product Account (NIP) which, in combination with other income-side components, combine to measure the Gross National Product (GNP).

See also **Gross National Product (GNP); National Income Product Accounts (NIPA).**

propylene [Energy Information Administration] Propylene is a normally gaseous olefinic hydrocarbon recovered from refinery processes. For reporting purposes, quantities of propylene are included with propane data.

proved reserves, crude oil [Energy Information Administration] Proved reserves are the estimated quantities of all liquids statistically defined as crude oil that geological and engineering data demonstrate with reasonable certainty to be recoverable in future years from known reservoirs under existing economic and operating conditions.

proved reserves, natural gas [Energy Information Administration] Proved reserves are the estimated quantities of natural gas that analysis of geological and engineering data demonstrate with reasonable certainty to be recoverable in future years from known crude oil and natural gas reservoirs under existing economic and operating conditions.

proved reserves, natural gas liquids [Energy Information Administration] Estimates of proved reserves include: the reserves of liquids that are expected to be recovered from associated and non-associated gas produced from gas wells and processed through lease separators; and reserves of liquids expected to be recovered from associated-dissolved and non-associated gas when processed in field facilities or gas processing plants. Estimates of proved reserves of natural gas liquids are based on proved reserves of natural gas at the time of estimation and rates at which liquids can be recovered from natural gas by using processing equipment of the type currently installed or planned at the time of estimation.

psychiatric hospital [Department of Health and Human Services-Public Health Service; Alcohol, Drug Abuse, and Mental Health Administration] A psychiatric hospital is an entity that is primarily concerned with providing inpatient care to mentally ill persons and either operated by or licensed by a State. Psychiatric hospitals may be either public or private.
    See also **hospital; mental health organization.**

public school or institution [Department of Education-Center for Education Statistics] A public school or institution is controlled and operated by publicly elected and appointed officials and derives its primary support from public funds.

public transportation disability [Department of Commerce-Bureau of the Census] Persons are said to have a public transportation disability if they have a health condition which makes it difficult or impossible to use busses, trains, subways, or other forms of public transportation.
    See also **disability.**

public use microdata see **microdata.**

pueblo [Department of Commerce-Bureau of the Census] A pueblo is an American Indian reservation.
    See also **American Indian reservation.**

pupil see **student.**

pupil-teacher ratio [Department of Education-Center for Education Statistics] The pupil-teacher ratio is the enrollment of pupils at a given period of time, divided by the full-time-equivalent number of classroom teachers serving these pupils during that same period.

purchase [Department of Commerce-Bureau of the Census] A purchase is a minor civil division (MCD) in New Hampshire.
    See also **minor civil division (MCD).**

Q

quarter credit hour see **credit (education).**

quartile [Department of Commerce-Bureau of the Census] A quartile is a measure that divides a distribution into four equal parts. The *first quartile* or *lower quartile* is the value that defines the upper limit of the lowest one-quarter of the cases. The *second quartile* is the median. The *third quartile* or *upper quartile* defines the lower limit of the upper one-quarter of the cases in the distribution. The difference between the upper and lower quartiles is called the *interquartile range.*
See also **median.**

R

race [Department of Commerce-Bureau of the Census] The Bureau of the Census in many of its censuses and surveys asks all persons to identify themselves according to race. The concept of race as used by the Bureau reflects the self-identification of the respondents and is not meant to denote any clear cut scientific definition of biological stock.

For the 1980 Census, persons could choose from the following categories of race: White, Black or Negro, American Indian, Eskimo, Aleut, Japanese, Chinese, Filipino, Korean, Asian Indian, Vietnamese, Hawaiian, Guamanian, Samoan, and Other. The Other category includes Malayan, Polynesian, Thai, and other groups not included in the specific categories listed on the questionnaire.

For the 1990 Census, persons could choose from the following categories of race: White, Black, American Indian, Eskimo, Aleut, Chinese, Filipino, Japanese, Asian Indian, Korean, Vietnamese, Other Asian, Hawaiian, Samoan, Guamanian, Other Pacific Islander, or Other. The Other race category includes write-in entries such as multiracial, multiethnic, mixed, interracial, Wesort, or a Spanish/Hispanic origin group.

The Other Asian and Other Pacific Islander write-in categories were added in the 1990 Census to more accurately reflect those races. For example, persons who identified themselves as Laotian or Thai were tabulated at "Other race" in the 1980 Census, but were tabulated as "Other Asian" in the 1990 Census.

For reporting Census data, these categories are most often consolidated into groupings of White, Black, and Other. Sometimes five groupings are aggregated, White; Black; American Indian, Eskimo and Aleut; Asian and Pacific Islander; and Other.

Although it is often reported in proximity to racial categories, hispanic origin or Spanish origin is not a racial category. Persons may be of any race and of be of hispanic origin. Those who describe themselves as hispanic (or Mexican, Cuban, Chicano, etc) in response to a question about race are usually included by the Bureau in the racial classification, Other, even though most Americans of hispanic origin are white.

See also **hispanic origin.**

rancheria [Department of Commerce-Bureau of the Census] A rancheria is an American Indian reservation.

See also **American Indian reservation.**

rape [Department of Justice-Bureau of Justice Statistics] In the National Crime Survey (NCS), rape is defined as carnal knowledge through the use of force or threat of force, including attempts. Both heterosexual and homosexual rapes are included. Statutory rape (without force) is excluded. For the NCS, rape is classified as a personal crime of violence.

It should be noted that the NCS definition of rape differs from the Uniform Crime Reports (UCR) definition of forcible rape in that the UCR excludes homosexual rapes.

See also **crime; forcible rape; index crime; National Crime Survey (NCS); Part I offense; personal crimes; Uniform Crime Reports (UCR).**

rate of change see **diffusion index/rate of change.**

rated capacity see **institutional capacity (corrections).**

real compensation per hour see **compensation per hour.**

reason for unemployment [Department of Labor-Bureau of Labor Statistics] The Bureau of Labor Statistics reports unemployment by reason for unemployment. Reasons for unemployment are divided into four major groups: *Job losers* are persons whose employment ended involuntarily and immediately began looking for work. This group also includes those on layoff. *Job leavers* are persons who quit or otherwise terminated their employment voluntarily and immediately began looking for work. *Re-entrants* are persons who previously worked at a full-time job lasting two weeks or longer but who were out of the labor force prior to beginning to look for work. *New entrants* are persons who have never worked at a full time job lasting two weeks or longer.

Reason for unemployment information comes from the Current Population Survey (CPS).

See also **labor force; unemployment.**

receipts [Department of Commerce-Bureau of the Census] In the economic censuses conducted by the Census Bureau, receipts of business enterprises include the gross value of all products sold, services rendered, or other receipts from customers during a given period of time, less returns and allowances.

The value of sales and services is provided whether or not payment was actually received during the period and therefore does not indicate cash flow. Generally, no adjustments are made in reporting receipts. Due to the nature of some industries such as banking, real estate, insurance, educational and social services, receipts may not be a good indicator of financial worth or size.

recordable occupational injuries and illnesses see **Annual Survey of Occupational Injuries and Illnesses; occupational illness; occupational injury.**

re-entrants (labor force) see **reason for unemployment.**

reference person [Department of Commerce-Bureau of the Census] In the collection of data in household surveys by the Census Bureau, the reference person is either the householder or the first person listed in response to questions about the regular residents of the housing unit. The status of other household members is defined by their relationship to the reference person.

See also **householder**.

refinery [Energy Information Administration] A refinery is an installation that manufactures finished petroleum products from crude oil, unfinished oils, natural gas liquids, other hydrocarbons, and alcohol.

See also **crude oil; natural gas liquids; operable refinery capacity; petroleum products**.

refinery capacity see **operable refinery capacity**.

refinery gas see **still gas**.

refunding (government finance) [Department of Commerce-Bureau of the Census] Refunding is the issuance of long-term debt in exchange for, or to provide funds for, the retirement of long-term debt already outstanding.

See also **debt (government)**.

region [Department of Commerce-Bureau of the Census] A region is a specific geographical subdivision of the United States. The Bureau of the Census has divided the nation into four regions comprised of individual States and the District of Columbia. This regional division is used as the primary geographic subdivision of the nation for statistical reporting purposes by almost all federal agencies and many private-sector data collectors. *The Northeast* includes Maine, New Hampshire, Vermont, Massachusetts, Rhode Island, Connecticut, New York, New Jersey, and Pennsylvania. *The Midwest* includes Ohio, Indiana, Illinois, Michigan, Wisconsin, Minnesota, Iowa, Missouri, North Dakota, South Dakota, Kansas, and Nebraska. *The South* includes Delaware, Maryland, District of Columbia, Virginia, West Virginia, North Carolina, South Carolina, Georgia, Florida, Kentucky, Tennessee, Alabama, Mississippi, Arkansas, Louisiana, Oklahoma, and Texas. *The West* includes Montana, Idaho, Colorado, Wyoming, New Mexico, Arizona, Utah, Nevada, Washington, Oregon, California, Alaska, and Hawaii.

See also **census geography; division**.

registered hospital see **hospital**

regular school see **school enrollment**.

relative survival rate [Department of Health and Human Services-Public Health Service; National Center for Health Statistics] The relative survival rate is the ratio of the observed survival rate for a specific patient group to the expected survival rate for persons in the general population similar to the patient group with respect to age, sex, race, and calendar year of observation. The relative survival rate is frequently measured for five year periods, especially in reporting the relative survival rate for cancer patients.

The five-year relative survival rate is used to estimate the proportion of cancer patients potentially curable. Because over half of all cancers occur in patients 65 years of age and over, many of these individuals die of other causes with no evidence of the recurrence of their cancer. Thus because the relative survival rate is obtained by adjusting observed survival for the normal life expectancy of the general population of the same age, the relative survival rate is an estimate of the chance of surviving cancer.

remedial education [Department of Education-Center for Education Statistics] Remedial education is instruction for a student lacking those reading, writing, or math skills necessary to perform college-level work at the level required by the institution the student is attending.

rent [Department of Commerce-Bureau of the Census] In the Bureau's censuses and surveys there are two concepts of rent employed, contract rent and gross rent.

Contract rent is the monthly rent agreed to, or contracted for, regardless of any furnishings, utilities, or services that may be included. *Gross rent* is the contract rent plus the estimated average monthly cost of utilities (water, electricity, gas) and fuel (oil, coal, kerosene, wood, etc.) to the extent these are paid for by the renter in addition to the rent. Both contract rents and gross rents are often calculated for specified renter-occupied housing units.

The Bureau also uses the category *no cash rent* for rental units occupied without the payment of cash rent. Such units may be owned by friends or relatives of the occupant who live elsewhere and who allow occupancy without charge, or may by housing provided as compensation to caretakers, ministers, tenant farmers, sharecroppers and others.

See also **housing unit; specified owner-occupied housing units.**

rental income of persons with capital consumption adjustments [Department of Commerce-Bureau of Economic Analysis] Rental income of persons with capital consumption adjustments is the income of persons from the rental of real property; the imputed net rental income of owner-occupants of non-farm dwellings; and the royalties received by persons from patents, copyrights, and the rights to natural resources. The income of persons primarily engaged in the real estate business is excluded.

The capital consumption adjustment is the difference between tax-return-based capital consumption allowances and capital consumption based on the use of uniform service lives, straight-line depreciation, and replacement cost.

Rental income of persons with capital consumption adjustments is an income-side component of the National Income Product Account (NIP) which, in combination with other income-side components, combine to measure the Gross National Product (GNP).

See also **Gross National Product (GNP); National Income Product Accounts (NIPA).**

rental payments (manufacturing industries) [Department of Commerce-Bureau of the Census] In the Annual Survey of Manufactures (ASM), rental payments include all amounts paid for the use of all items for which depreciation reserves would have been maintained if they were owned by the establishment. These items include structures and buildings, and production, office and transportation equipment. Excluded are land rents where separate and royalties and other payments for use for intangibles and depletable assets.

When an establishment of a multi-establishment company is charged a rent by another part of the same company for use of assets owned by the company, such payments are excluded from rental payments. However, the book-value of these company-owned assets are reported as assets at the end of the year. If assets are rented from another company but the rents are paid centrally by the head office of an establishment, such rental payments are counted as if they were paid directly by the establishment.

renter occupied housing unit see **tenure (housing).**

repurchase agreement [Board of Governors, Federal Reserve System] A repurchase agreement is a purchase-sale agreement in which a seller sells a security or securities on a temporary basis, agreeing as part of the initial sale to buy the securities back at a future date at a specified price. In effect, the securities become collateral for the sellers borrowing. Repurchase agreements were originally used by the Federal Reserve to expand credit when credit becomes tight and more recently have been used by commercial banks and thrifts as a product to sell to retail customers. Repurchase agreements are also called RP's or repos.

reservation see **American Indian reservation.**

reserve see **American Indian reservation.**

reserve margin (electric utilities) [Energy Information Administration] The reserve margin is the amount of unused available capability of an electric power system at peak load for a utility system. This figure is calculated by adding running and

quick-start capability to the available but not needed capability and then subtracting the peak load.
See also **capability (electric utilities).**

reserve requirement [Board of Governors, Federal Reserve System] Commercial banks are required to set aside a portion of their deposits as reserves. For Federal Reserve member banks, the amount of the reserve is determined by the commercial bank's size and location and ranges between 3-12% of the bank's deposits. Such reserves are usually kept in the form of deposits at a regional Federal Reserve bank.
Reserves have a two-fold purpose: to provide some measure of protection to the member bank's customers; and to give the Federal Reserve System a means of controlling the money supply.
See also **federal funds (banking).**

resident population see **population.**

residential facility [Department of Justice-Bureau of Justice Statistics] A residential facility is a correctional facility from which residents are regularly permitted to depart, unaccompanied by any official, for the purpose of daily use of community resources such as schools or treatment programs, and seeking or holding employment.
See also **confinement facility; correctional facility (adult); jail; juvenile facility (corrections); prison.**

residential sector see **end-use sector.**

residential treatment center for emotionally disturbed children (RTC) [Department of Health and Human Services-Public Health Service; Alcohol, Drug Abuse, and Mental Health Administration] A residential treatment center for emotionally disturbed children (RTC) is an organization that meets all of the following criteria: a) it is an organization not licensed as a psychiatric hospital and the primary purpose of which is the provision of individually planned programs of mental health treatment services in conjunction with residential care; b) it has a clinical program within the organization that is directed by a psychiatrist, psychologist, social worker, or psychiatric nurse who has a master's or doctorate degree; c) it serves children and youth primarily under the age of 18; and d) the primary reason for the admission of 50% or more of the children and youth is mental illness that has been classified by DSM-II/ICDA-8 or DSM-III/ICD-9-CM codes, other than those codes for mental retardation, drug related disorders, and alcoholism.
See also **International Classification of Diseases, Ninth edition, Clinical Modification (ICD-9-CM); mental health organization.**

residual fuel oil [Energy Information Administration] Residual fuel oil is composed of those oils that remain after distillate fuel oils and lighter hydrocarbons are distilled away in refinery operations. Included are No. 5 and No. 6 fuel oils that conform to ASTM specification D396, Navy Special fuel oil, and Bunker C fuel oil.

Residual fuel oil is used for the production of electric power, space heating vessel bunkering, and various industrial purposes.

Statistics for imports of residual fuel oil include imported crude oil burned as fuel.

residue gas [Energy Information Administration] Residue gas is natural gas from which natural gas processing plant liquid products (and in some cases, non-hydrocarbon components) have been extracted.

response error see **non-sampling error.**

restricted-activity day see **disability day.**

retired person see **labor force**

retirements (capital assets) [Department of Commerce-Bureau of the Census] Retirements are the removal from use of capital assets used by an establishment through either sale or scrapping. In the economic censuses, retirements are the gross value of assets sold, retired, scrapped, destroyed, etc. When a complete operation or establishment changes ownership the value of the assets sold is recorded at the original cost as recorded in the books of the seller. Retirements of assets owned by a parent company but used by a given establishment are reported by that establishment as if it were a tenant.

See also **depreciation charges.**

revenue [Department of Education-Center for Education Statistics] Revenue includes all funds received from external sources, net of refunds, and correcting transactions. Noncash transactions such as receipt of services, commodities, or other receipts in kind are excluded, as are funds received from the issuance of debt, liquidation of investments, and non-routine sale of property.

revenue (government) [Department of Commerce-Bureau of the Census] Government revenue consists of all amounts of money received by a government from external sources net of refunds and other correcting transactions, other than from the issuance of debt, liquidation of investments, and as agency and private trust transactions. Government revenue excludes non-cash transactions such as receipt of services, commodities, or other receipts in kind. Government revenue includes intergovernmental revenue.

See also **general revenue (government); intergovernmental revenue; taxes.**

revenue passenger-load factor [Department of Transportation-Transportation Systems Center] The revenue passenger-load factor is a measure used in commercial air transport. It is a percentage obtained by dividing revenue passenger-miles by the number of available seat miles in revenue passenger service.

See also **revenue passenger-mile.**

revenue passenger-mile [Department of Transportation-Transportation Systems Center] A revenue passenger-mile is a unit of measure representing one revenue-paying passenger transported one mile in revenue service. Revenue passenger-miles are computed by summing the products of the revenue aircraft miles flown on each inter-airport flight multiplied by the number of revenue passengers on that flight. Revenue passengers exclude airline personnel flying for token charges and travel and cargo agents and tour conductors traveling under reduced rate transportation.

revenue ton-mile [Department of Transportation-Transportation Systems Center] A revenue ton-mile is a measure used in commercial air transport. It is a unit of measure representing one ton of revenue traffic transported one statute mile. Ton-miles are the product of aircraft miles flown on each inter-airport flight segment multiplied by the number of tons carried on that flight segment.

revolving credit see **consumer installment credit.**

road oil [Energy Information Administration] Road oil is any heavy petroleum oil including residual asphaltic oil, used as a dust palliative and surface treatment on roads and highways. It is generally produced in six grades from 0, the most liquid, to 5, the most viscous.

robbery [Department of Justice-Bureau of Justice Statistics] Robbery is the unlawful taking or attempted taking of property that is in the immediate possession of another by force or threat of force. In the Uniform Crime Reports (UCR), robbery is classified as UCR 3, a violent crime, a crime index crime, and a Part I offense.

In the National Crime Survey (NCS), robberies are known as personal robberies, a type of personal crime of violence. They are defined and counted differently than in the UCR.

See also **crime; crime index; National Crime Survey (NCS); personal crimes; personal robbery; Uniform Crime Reporting Program (UCR).**

rooms [Department of Commerce-Bureau of the Census] Rooms is a Census Bureau measure of the number of whole rooms intended for living purposes in both occupied and vacant housing units. Rooms includes living rooms, dining rooms, kitchens, bedrooms, finished recreation rooms, enclosed porches suitable for year-round use, and lodger's rooms. Excluded are strip or pullman kitchens, bathrooms, open porches, balconies, foyers, halls, half-rooms, utility rooms, unfinished attics or basements, or other unfinished space used for storage. A partially divided room is a separate room only if there is a partition from floor to ceiling, but not if the partition consists solely of shelves or cabinets.

RP see **repurchase agreement.**

RTC see **residential treatment center for emotionally disturbed children (RTC).**

rural see **urban/rural.**

S

salaries see **wages and salaries.**

salary (education) [Department of Education-Center for Education Statistics] Salary is the total amount regularly paid or stipulated to be paid to an individual, before deductions, for personal services rendered while on the payroll of a business or organization.

sales and gross receipts taxes [Department of Commerce-Bureau of the Census] Sales and gross receipts taxes are taxes based on the volume or value of transfers of goods or services, upon gross receipts therefrom, or upon gross income, and related taxes based on use, storage, production, importation, or consumption of goods. Licenses issued at more than nominal rates are included. Dealer discounts or commissions allowed to merchants for collection of taxes from consumers are excluded. Severance of natural resources are also excluded.

Sales and gross receipts taxes are generally divided into general sales and gross receipts taxes and selective sales and gross receipts taxes.

General sales and gross receipts taxes are sales and gross receipts taxes which are applicable with only specified exceptions to all types of goods and services or all gross income, whether at a single rate or at classified rates.

Selective sales and gross receipts taxes are taxes imposed on sales or gross receipts from selected commodities, services, or businesses, and are reported separately. They include taxes on alcoholic beverages, amusements, insurance, motor fuels, parimutuels, public utilities, and tobacco products.

sales price (housing) [Department of Commerce-Bureau of the Census] For the American Housing Survey, the sales price is the price agreed upon between the purchaser and seller at the time the first sales contract is signed or deposit is made for the house. The sales price does not reflect any subsequent price changes resulting from change orders or from any other factors affecting the price of the house. Furthermore, the sales price does not include the cost of any extras or options paid for in cash by the purchaser or otherwise not included in the original sales price reported by the seller.

The *median sales price* is the middle point in all sales prices reported; the point is chosen so that half the houses were sold with a sales price below the median and half with a sales price above the median. The *average,* or *arithmetic mean, sales price* is obtained by dividing the sum of all the sales prices reported by the number of houses reporting a sales price.

sampling error [Department of Commerce-Bureau of the Census] The sampling error of a survey is that part of the error associated with a statistical estimate that is due to the fact that only a subset or sample of the whole population was observed. Sampling error is distinct from non-sampling error.

See also **non-sampling error**.

SAT see **scholastic aptitude test (SAT)**.

savings [Department of Commerce-Bureau of Economic Analysis] In national economic accounting, savings is the difference between income and expenditures during an accounting period. *Total gross savings* includes personal savings, business savings (mainly undistributed corporate profits and capital consumption allowances), and government surplus or deficit.

See also **Gross National Product (GNP); National Income Product Accounts (NIPA); personal savings**.

savings and loan institution see **savings institutions**.

savings bank see **savings institutions**.

savings deposit [Federal Reserve Bank of New York] A savings deposit is an interest bearing deposit at a bank which does not have a specific maturity. The depository institution may require notice before withdrawal of savings deposits. Savings deposits are one component of the larger category, time deposits.

See also **time deposit**.

savings institutions [Federal Reserve Bank of New York] Savings institutions is a generic term for cooperative banks, savings and loan associations, savings banks, mutual savings banks, and the like. Such institutions differ from each other by their type of charter or method of organization. For example, savings institutions with capital stock are called savings banks, those without capital stock are called mutual savings banks. The primary business of all savings institutions is to receive and place the savings of small depositors, usually individuals, into mortgages and other similar type loans. Their primary source of funds is savings deposits and other consumer-type time deposits.

Savings institutions are a type of depository institution.

scholarships and fellowships [Department of Education-Center for Education Statistics] Scholarships and fellowships is a category of college expenditure which apply only to money given in the form of outright grants and trainee stipends to individuals enrolled in formal course work, either for credit or not. Aid to students in the form of tuition or fee remission is included. College work-study funds are excluded and are reported under the program which the student is working.

scholastic aptitude test (SAT) [Department of Education-Center for Education Statistics] The scholastic aptitude test (SAT) is an examination administered by the Educational Testing Service which is used to predict the facility with which an individual will progress in learning college-level academic subjects.

school [Department of Education-Center for Education Statistics] A school is a division of a school system consisting of one or more grades or other identifiable groups and organized to give instruction of a defined type. One school may share a school building with another school, or one school may be housed in several buildings.

school district [Department of Education-Center for Education Statistics] A school district is an education agency at the local level that exists primarily to operate public schools or to contract for public school services. For statistical reporting purposes, *local basic administrative unit* and *local education agency* are synonymous with school district.

school district government [Department of Commerce-Bureau of the Census] A school district government is a type of sub-State level government which provides public elementary, secondary, and/or higher education which, under State law, has sufficient administration and fiscal autonomy to qualify as a separate government. School district governments are distinct from dependent public school systems of county, municipal, township, or state governments.

school enrollment [Department of Commerce-Bureau of the Census] The Bureau of the Census collects data on school enrollment as part of the decennial census of population and in the October supplement to the Current Population Survey (CPS).

Persons three years old and older are classified as enrolled in school if they are attending regular school or college. Regular school includes nursery schools and kindergartens, elementary schools, and schooling which leads to a high school diploma or college degree. Attendance can be either full-time or part-time. Enrollment in other schools (such as trade or vocational schools, business schools, correspondence courses and the like) is only counted if the course or courses taken would be accepted for credit at a regular elementary school, high school, or college.

See also **school type**.

school-loss day see **disability day**.

school term [Department of Education-National Center for Education Statistics] A school term is a prescribed span of time when school is open and the students are under the guidance and direction of teachers.

See also **school year**.

school type [Department of Commerce-Bureau of the Census] The Bureau of the Census classifies schools for reporting purposes into three types: *Public schools* include any school or college which is controlled and supported primarily by government. *Church related schools* are supported primarily by a religious organization. *Other private schools* are controlled and supported by organizations other than the government or religious organizations.

school year [Department of Education-National Center for Education Statistics] The school year is the 12 month period of time denoting the beginning and ending dates for school accounting purposes, usually from July 1 through June 30. This sometimes is referred to as the school fiscal year.

SDR see **Special Drawing Rights (SDR)**.

seasonal adjustment 1. [Department of Labor-Bureau of Labor Statistics] Many economic statistics reflect a regularly recurring seasonal movement which can be measured on the basis of past experience. Such seasonal movements are frequently due to climatic conditions, model changeovers, vacation practices, holidays, and similar factors. Sometimes it is important to remove such seasonal variations. To seasonally adjust a given economic time series is to eliminate that part of the change in the series which can be ascribed to the normal seasonal variation. Thus it is possible to observe solely the cyclical and other non-seasonal movements in these series.

2. [Department of Commerce-Bureau of Economic Analysis] Seasonal adjustment is a mathematical process whereby the effects of recurring non-economic factors are removed from an economic time series. The process is used to separate each time series into its recurring or seasonal, trend, cyclical, and random or irregular components.

seasonal housing unit [Department of Commerce-Bureau of the Census] A seasonal housing unit is a vacant housing unit which is intended by the owner to be occupied during only certain seasons of the year. A seasonal unit may be used in more than one season (for example, for both summer and winter sports); however, any unit used throughout the year is excluded even if the use is only occasional. Seasonal housing units also include those used for migrant farm workers, herders, and loggers.

As a seasonal housing unit is intended for use only during certain seasons, it is by definition vacant. This is true even if persons are staying there at the time of a census or survey. If, on the other hand, the persons staying in the unit at the time of the census or survey are staying there as their usual residence and have no other residence elsewhere, the unit would be considered a year round occupied housing unit.

In the 1990 Census, the category "seasonal/recreational/occasional use" combined vacant units classified in 1980 as "seasonal or migratory" and "held for occasional use."

See also **housing unit; occupancy status; vacancy status (housing).**

seasonal workers see **labor force.**

secondary instructional level [Department of Education-Center for Education Statistics] The secondary instructional level is the general level of instruction provided for pupils in secondary schools and any instruction of a comparable nature and difficulty provided for adults and youth beyond the age of compulsory school attendance.

See also **secondary school.**

secondary school [Department of Education-Center for Education Statistics] A secondary school comprises any span of grades beginning with the next grade following an elementary or middle school (usually 7, 8, or 9) and ending with or below grade 12. Both junior high schools and senior high schools are included.

self-employed worker see **class of worker.**

self-employment income [Department of Commerce-Bureau of the Census] Self-employment income is a type of money income which comprises the net income received by persons from an unincorporated business, profession, or from the operation of a farm as a farm owner, tenant, or sharecropper. Net income is gross receipts minus operating expenses.

See also **money income.**

semester credit hours see **credit.**

semi-independent municipalities [Department of Commerce-Bureau of the Census] Semi-independent municipalities are a special type of place used for statistical reporting purposes. For the 1982 and 1987 economic censuses, the Bureau recognized five consolidated governments in the United States which included separately incorporated municipalities. If such a semi-independent municipality had a population of 2,500 or more it was treated as a separate tabulation area and excluded from the consolidated government; if it had less than that number it was included as a part of the consolidated government, which was treated as an incorporated place. The cases are as follows:

The Jacksonville, FL, consolidated government contained all of Duval County, but the semi-independent municipalities of Atlantic Beach, Jacksonville Beach, and Neptune Beach were tabulated separately.

The Columbus, GA, consolidated government contained all of Muscogee County, including the semi-independent town of Bibb City, which did not have sufficient population for tabulation.

The Indianapolis, IN, consolidated government included all of Marion County, except four independent municipalities: Beech Grove, Lawrence, Southport, and Speedway. Thirteen of the fourteen semi-independent municipalities did not have sufficient population for separate tabulation, however, Cumberland was tabulated separately.

The Butte-Silver Bow, MT, consolidated government contained the semi-independent city of Walkerville, which did not have sufficient population for separate tabulation.

The Nashville-Davidson, TN, consolidated government covered all of Davidson County, but the semi-independent municipalities of Belle Meade, Forest Hills, Goodlettsville, and Oak Hill were tabulated separately. The other three semi-independent municipalities of Berry Hill, Lakewood, and Ridgetop did not have enough inhabitants for separate tabulation.

See also **consolidated city; consolidated government.**

senior high school [Department of Education-Center for Education Statistics] A senior high school is a secondary school offering the final years of high school work necessary for graduation and invariably preceded by a junior high school.

See also **junior high school.**

separate psychiatric inpatient setting [Department of Health and Human Services-Public Health Service; Alcohol, Drug Abuse, and Mental Health Administration] A separate psychiatric inpatient setting is a part of a general hospital with separate psychiatric service(s) in which beds are specifically set up and staffed exclusively for psychiatric patients. These beds may be in a specific wing, floor, or ward, or they may be a specific group of beds physically separated from regular medical or surgical beds.

See also **general hospital with separate psychiatric service(s), separate psychiatric outpatient setting.**

separate psychiatric outpatient setting [Department of Health and Human Services-Public Health Service; Alcohol, Drug Abuse, and Mental Health Administration] A separate psychiatric outpatient setting is a part of a general hospital with separate psychiatric service(s) in which organized psychiatric services are provided in a separate hospital clinic established exclusively for the care of ambulatory psychiatric patients.

See also **general hospital with separate psychiatric service(s)**, **separate psychiatric inpatient setting**.

seriously emotionally disturbed see **handicapped**.

set aside [Department of Agriculture-Office of Governmental and Public Affairs] A set aside is the acreage a farmer must devote to soil conservation uses in order to be eligible for production adjustment payments and price-support loans.

SEUA see **Special Economic Urban Area (SEUA)**.

severance taxes [Department of Commerce-Bureau of the Census] Severance taxes are taxes imposed distinctively on the removal of natural products from land or water and measured by value of quantity of products removed or sold. These natural products include oil, gas, minerals, timber, and fish.

SHA see **State health agency**.

short stay hospital see **hospital**.

short-term debt (government) see **debt (government)**.

short term hospital see **hospital**.

SIC see **Standard Industrial Classification (SIC) Program**.

SIPP see **Survey of Income and Program Participation (SIPP)**.

skilled nursing facility see **nursing home certification**.

small denomination time deposit see **time deposit**.

SMSA see **Standard Metropolitan Statistical Area (SMSA)**.

SNG see **synthetic natural gas (SNG)**.

SOC see **Standard Occupational Classification (SOC) system**.

soft coal see **bituminous coal**.

SOP see **stage of processing (SOP)**.

Spanish origin see **hispanic origin; race.**

special assessments [Department of Commerce-Bureau of the Census] Special assessments are compulsory contributions collected from owners of property benefited by special public improvements such as street paving, sidewalks, or sewer lines to defray the cost of such improvements. Special assessments may be collected either directly or through payment of debt service on indebtedness incurred to finance the improvements. Special assessments are apportioned according to the assumed benefits to the property affected by the improvements.

See also **taxes.**

Special Drawing Rights (SDR) [Federal Reserve Bank of New York] Special Drawing Rights (SDR) are an international monetary reserve asset created by the International Monetary Fund (IMF) in 1970 to provide an orderly and adequate growth in international liquidity. SDR's are used by governments in official balance of trade transactions.

Initial allocations were made to the United States and other participating nations in 1970-1972 and again in 1979-81. In international transaction accounts, SDR's are shown as a separate credit entry. Changes in holdings of SDR's are included in U.S. official reserve assets.

Reserve holdings of SDR's change not only as a result of allocations, but also through purchase of SDR's from other countries or through sales of SDR's to other countries, and by use of SDR's in transactions with the IMF.

Special Economic Urban Area (SEUA) [Department of Commerce-Bureau of the Census] An SEUA is a geographic area concept. The Bureau of the Census recognizes Special Economic Urban Areas (SEUA's) for reporting purposes for the economic censuses. SEUA's comprised townships in Connecticut, Massachusetts, Rhode Island, Maine, Vermont, New Hampshire, New Jersey and Pennsylvania with a population of more than 10,000 inhabitants.

special education [Department of Education-Center for Education Statistics] Special education encompasses direct instructional activities or special learning experiences designed primarily for students identified as having exceptionalities in one or more aspects of the cognitive process or as being underachievers in relation to the general level or model of their overall abilities. Such services are usually directed at students who are physically handicapped, emotionally handicapped, culturally different, mentally retarded, and those students with learning disabilities. Programs for mentally gifted and talented are also included in some special education programs.

See also **handicapped.**

special naphthas [Energy Information Administration] Special naphthas are all finished petroleum products within the gasoline range specially refined to a specific flash point and boiling range for use as paint thinners, cleaners, and solvents. Commercial hexane conforming with ASTM specification D1836 and cleaning solvent conforming to ASTM specification D484 are included. Excluded are naphthas to be blended or marketed as motor gasoline or aviation gasoline, or to be used as petrochemical and synthetic natural gas feedstock.

specialized district government [Department of Commerce-Bureau of the Census] A specialized district government is an organized local entity other than a county, municipality, township, or school district, authorized by State law to provide only one or a limited number of designated functions, and with sufficient administrative and fiscal autonomy to qualify as a separate government. Specialized district governments are known by a variety of titles including districts, authorities, boards, and commissions.

specialty hospital see **hospital.**

specialty oils [Energy Information Administration] Specialty oils are a class of petroleum products with properties similar to lubricating oils but with primary uses other than lubricants.

specific learning disabled see **handicapped.**

specified owner-occupied housing units [Department of Commerce-Bureau of the Census] Specified owner-occupied housing units are single family homes on less than ten acres which have no commercial enterprise or medical practice on the property. Also excluded from counts of this type of housing unit are owner-occupied condominium housing units, mobile homes, trailers, boats, tents, or vans occupied as a usual residence, or owner-occupied non-condominium units in multi-family buildings.
See also **housing unit.**

speech impaired see **handicapped.**

spot price (energy) [Energy Information Administration] A spot price is a transaction price concluded "on the spot"; that is, on a one-time, prompt basis. Usually a spot price transaction involves only one specific quantity of product. Spot prices contrast with contract sale prices, in which a seller is obligated to deliver a product to a buyer at an agreed frequency and price over an extended period.

spouse see **householder.**

SSI see **Supplemental Security Income program.**

staff capacity see **institutional capacity (corrections).**

staff member (education) [Department of Education-National Center for Education Statistics] A staff member is a person whose relationship with the local education agency meets the following criteria: a) the person performs activities or provides services for the local education agency which are under the direction or control of the agency's governing authority; and b) the person is either compensated for such services by the local education agency and is considered an employee for the purposes of workmen's compensation coverage, the Federal Insurance Contribution Act (FICA), and wage and salary withholdings; or the person performs such services on a volunteer, uncompensated basis.

stage of processing (SOP) [Department of Labor-Bureau of Labor Statistics] Stage of processing (SOP) is a system of looking at products according to the class of buyer and the degree of processing, manufacturing, or assembling to which the products are subjected before they enter the market. The Bureau of Labor Statistics produces SOP indexes in the Producer Price Index (PPI). The SOP price indexes regroup commodities at the sub-product class level according to these criteria.

The *Finished Goods Price Index* roughly measures changes in prices received by producers for finished goods for two portions of the gross national product: personal consumption expenditures on goods and capital investment expenditures on equipment. Finished goods are commodities that are ready for sale to the final demand user, either an individual or a business firm.

Within the Finished Goods Price Index, the *consumer foods* category includes unprocessed foods such as eggs and fresh fruits, as well as processed foods such as bakery products. The *finished energy goods* component includes those types of energy to be sold to households, primarily gasoline home heating oil and natural gas. The category for consumer goods *other than food and energy* includes durables such as passenger cars and household furniture, and non-durables such as apparel and prescription drugs. The other portion of the Finished Goods Price Index, the *capital equipment index,* measures changes in prices received by producers of durable investment goods such as heavy motor trucks, tractors, and machine tools.

Intermediate goods (materials, supplies and components) are commodities that have been processed but require further processing before they become finished goods. Also included are physically complete goods purchased by business firms as inputs for their operations such as diesel fuel, belts and belting, and fertilizers. The *Intermediate Materials Index* measures the changes in prices of these materials.

Crude materials are unprocessed commodities entering the market for the first time which have not been manufactured or fabricated but will be processed before becoming finished goods. Crude materials are not sold directly to consumers. Included are crude foodstuffs and feedstuffs (e.g. grain and livestock), crude energy goods (crude petroleum and coal) and crude non-food materials (raw cotton, construction sand and gravel, and iron and steel scrap). Price changes are measured by the *Crude Materials Index.*

See also **Producer Price Index.**

Standard Industrial Classification (SIC) program [Executive Office of the President-Office of Management and Budget; Statistical Policy Division] The Standard Industrial Classification (SIC) program, embodied in the <u>Standard Industrial Classification Manual</u>, defines industries in accordance with the composition and structure of the economy and covers the entire field of economic activity. Each defined industry is assigned a code number called an SIC code. SIC codes are widely used throughout all levels of government as well as in the private sector.

There were three main purposes in developing the SIC; to classify establishments by type of activity in which they are engaged; to facilitate the collection, tabulation, presentation and analysis of data relating to establishments; and for promoting uniformity and comparability in the presentation of statistical data collected by various agencies of the federal government, State agencies, trade associations, and private research organizations. In large measure, the SIC and its revision have met these goals.

The manual was developed as a classification system for establishments as opposed to enterprises and is based on kind of business as opposed to occupations or commodities.

The SIC is a numeric system with the initial division of economic activities into ten groupings; agriculture, forestry, and fishing, (0100-0971); mining (1000-1499); construction (1500-1799); manufacturing (2000-3999); transportation and public utilities (4000-4971); wholesale trade (5000-5199); retail trade (5200-5999); finance, insurance, and real estate (6000-6799); services (7000-8999); and public administration (9100-9721). Non-classifiable establishments are numbered 99. The first two digits are the general industry classification of the establishment, while the third and fourth digits add specificity. For example, the group beginning with the digits 57 is for furniture and home furnishing stores; 573 is the grouping for radio, television and music stores; and 5733 is the grouping for music stores. Four digits represents the maximum SIC level of detail.

See also **establishment; enterprise.**

Standard Metropolitan Statistical Area (SMSA) [Department of Commerce-Bureau of the Census] A Standard Metropolitan Statistical Area (SMSA) is a unit of census geography and was the basic metropolitan area concept used until 1984. In general, an SMSA is a large population nucleus combined with nearby communities which have a high degree of economic and social integration within that nucleus. Each SMSA consists of one or more entire counties or county equivalents that meet certain criteria of population, commuting ties, and metropolitan character. In New England, towns and cities rather than counties are the basic units and count as county equivalents. An SMSA includes a city and, generally, the entire surrounding urbanized area and the remainder of the county or counties in which the urbanized area is located. An SMSA also includes those additional outlying counties which meet specified criteria relating to metropolitan character and level of commuting ties.

The SMSA concept was developed in 1949 and has been refined for each succeeding decennial census since 1950. In June, 1984, SMSA's were superseded by three new metropolitan area concepts: Metropolitan Statistical Area (MSA), Consolidated Metropolitan Statistical Area (CMSA), and Primary Metropolitan Statistical Area (PMSA). These concepts, in turn, have been refined for the 1990 Census.

See also **census geography; Consolidated Metropolitan Statistical Area (CMSA); Metropolitan Area (MA); Metropolitan Statistical Area (MSA); Primary Metropolitan Statistical Area (PMSA).**

Standard Occupational Classification (SOC) system [Executive Office of the President-Office of Management and Budget] The Standard Occupational Classification (SOC) system provides a mechanism for cross-referencing and aggregating occupation-related data collected by social and economic statistical reporting programs. It covers all occupations in which work is performed for pay or profit including work performed in family-operated enterprises where direct remuneration may not be made to family members. The coding system and nomenclature enable users to identify and classify occupations within a framework suitable for use both in and out of government.

The SOC is structured in four levels: division, major group, minor group and unit group. Each level represents groupings in successively finer detail which let users tabulate or analyze data on different levels of aggregation. In the SOC manual, each group includes a listing of Dictionary of Occupation Titles (DOT) titles which are descriptive of the group. All base DOT titles are included in the SOC classification. A number of other steps have been taken to increase compatibility between SOC and DOT.

The Standard Occupational Classification (SOC) system was conceived as a federal interagency effort to reconcile differing government systems of occupational classification, principally those of the Bureau of the Census and the U.S. Employment service. The first SOC classification manual was published in 1977 and was first used by the Bureau of the Census for occupational classification in the 1980 Census.

See also **Dictionary of Occupation Titles (DOT).**

standby facility (electric utility) [Energy Information Administration] A standby facility is an electricity generation facility that supports a utility system and is generally running under no load. It is available to replace or supplement a facility normally in service.

State [Department of Commerce-Bureau of the Census] A State is the primary governmental division of the United States. The District of Columbia is treated as a statistical equivalent of a State for census purposes. The outlying areas are also treated as State equivalents for the 1990 census.

See also **census geography; outlying areas; United States.**

State and local government agreements [Department of Labor-Bureau of Labor Statistics] State and local government agreements is a term used in negotiated wage and benefit changes for State and local government employees.

The state and local government agreements series summarize wage and benefit changes for workers in State and local government where: a) a labor organization is recognized as the bargaining agent for a group of workers; b) the settlements are embodied in signed, mutually binding contracts; and c) wages are determined by collective bargaining. The Bureau of Labor Statistics collects information on current changes in wages and supplementary benefits agreed to in collective bargaining agreements and prepares monthly listings of governmental units in which such changes have occurred. The listings include the name of the employer, the union, the number of workers involved, the amount and effective date of the change, details of complex changes, and the reason for the change. The Bureau also prepares semiannual summaries for State and local government bargaining units. Data is now gathered and presented for government units of 1,000 workers or more covering 2.3 million workers in 612 bargaining units. About one half of all State and local government employees covered by collective bargaining agreements are included in this series. The listing of current changes in wages and benefits is published monthly in Current Wage Developments.

State health agency (SHA) [Department of Health and Human Services-Public Health Service; National Center for Health Statistics] The State health agency (SHA) is that agency or department, regardless of specific name, which is headed by the State or territorial health official. The SHA is responsible for setting State-wide public health priorities, carrying out national and State mandates, responding to public health hazards, and assuring access to health care for underserved state residents.

status offender see **delinquency.**

status offense see **delinquency.**

still gas [Energy Information Administration] Still gas is any form or mixture of gas produced in refineries by distillation, cracking, reforming, and other processes. The principal constituents of still gas are methane, ethane, ethylene, normal butane, butylene, propane, and propylene. Still gas is used primarily as a refinery fuel and petrochemical feedstock.

stolport [Department of Transportation-Federal Aviation Administration] A stolport is an airport specifically designed for STOL (short takeoff and landing aircraft), separate from conventional airport facilities.

story (housing) [Department of Commerce-Bureau of the Census] A story is that portion of a building between the floor and the ceiling or the roof, or the next floor above in the case of a multi-story house. A basement is not counted as a story even if it is finished as a den or a recreation room. Houses referred to as *bi-levels* or *split-foyers* are classified as two story houses.

A *half story* is a story finished as living accommodations located wholly or partly within the roof frame. For the American Housing Survey (AHS) a house with one and one half stories is counted as a two story house.

A *split level house* is a house having floors on more than one level when the difference in some floor levels is less than one story.

See also **American Housing Survey (AHS); housing unit.**

straight time [Department of Labor-Bureau of Labor Statistics] Straight time is the normal number of hours or days an employee works. Straight time pay is paid to an employee based on the number of hours worked, as opposed to the amount of work accomplished. The straight time wage rate is often used for calculating over-time, premium-time and shift differential rates. Straight time is used by the Bureau of Labor Statistics in its hours and earnings concepts.

See also **hours and earnings.**

strike see **work stoppage.**

structure [Department of Commerce-Bureau of the Census] A structure is a separate building that either has open space on all sides or is separated from other structures by dividing walls that extend from ground to roof.

See also **units in structure (housing).**

student [Department of Education-Center for Education Statistics] A student is an individual for whom instruction is provided in an educational program under the jurisdiction of a school, school system, or other education institution. No distinction is made between students and pupils, though the term student may refer to one receiving instruction at any level, while pupil usually refers only to one attending school at the elementary or secondary level.

A student may receive instruction in a school facility or in another location, such as at home or in a hospital. Instruction may be provided by direct student-teacher interaction or by some other approved medium such as television, radio, telephone, or correspondence.

sub-bituminous coal [Energy Information Administration] Sub-bituminous coal is a dull, black coal of intermediate rank between lignite and bituminous coal. It conforms to ASTM specification D388 for sub-bituminous coal and is used almost exclusively for electric power generation.

See also **coal**.

sub-family [Department of Commerce-Bureau of the Census] A sub-family is a married couple with or without never-married children under 18 years old, or one parent with one or more never-married children under 18 years old, living in a household and related to, but not including, either the householder or the householder's spouse. An example of a sub-family would be a married couple sharing the home of either the husband or wife's parents. In Census Bureau surveys, sub-families are counted as members of the householder's family.

See also **family; household; householder**.

substation (electric utilities) [Energy Information Administration] A substation is facility equipment that switches, changes, or regulates electric voltage.

summary probation see **court probation**.

supervisory staff [Department of Education-Center for Education Statistics] In sub-collegiate schools, supervisory staff includes principals, assistant principals, and supervisors of instruction but does not include superintendents or assistant superintendents of schools.

supplemental air carrier see **air carrier**.

supplemental gaseous fuels [Energy Information Administration] Supplemental gaseous fuels consist primarily of synthetic natural gas, propane-air, and refinery (still) gas. They may also include coke oven gas, biomass gas, manufactured gas, and air injected for Btu stabilization.

Supplemental Security Income (SSI) [Department of Health and Human Services-Social Security Administration] Supplemental Security Income (SSI) is a cash assistance program funded and administered by the Social Security Administration (SSA). The purpose of SSI is to assure a minimum level of income to people who are aged, blind or disabled and who have limited income and resources. The amount of a person's income is used to determine both eligibility for, and amount of, the person's SSI benefit.

For SSI purposes, income is anything an individual receives and can use to meet the individual's needs for food, clothing, or shelter. Income may be in cash or in kind. Certain things of value are excluded from income, such as medical care and services, social services, and income tax refunds.

See also **income**.

supplements to wages and salaries see **wages and salaries**.

surgical specialties see **physician specialty**.

survey [Department of Commerce-Bureau of the Census] A survey is a data collection activity involving observations or questionnaires for a sample of a population. A census is a 100 percent sample survey. Surveys are generally taken more frequently by the Census Bureau than are censuses and provide greater detail than is obtained in a census.

Surveys conducted by the Bureau and most other federal agencies are based on a scientifically selected sample universe in an effort to obtain an authentic cross section of the survey universe. Thus, sample selection is key to a survey's usefulness. Sample selection methodology is usually described in some detail in published results.

An important difference between censuses and surveys is that participation in the Bureau's decennial censuses is mandatory, while participation in surveys is voluntary.

See also **census; economic census**.

Survey of Income and Program Participation (SIPP) [Department of Commerce-Bureau of the Census] The Survey of Income and Program Participation (SIPP) is a continuing household survey with monthly interviews providing information on general demographic characteristics, cash and non-cash income, labor force participation, and government program participation. Its purpose is to measure the effectiveness of existing government transfer programs and to provide data for program planning.

The SIPP contains a core section of questions covering labor force participation, program participation, and income designed to measure the income situation of persons in the United States. These questions expand the data currently available on the distribution of cash and non-cash income and are repeated at each interviewing wave. The survey has also been designed to provide a broader context for analysis by adding questions on a variety of topics not covered in the core section. These additional questions or topical modules have focused on child care arrangements, marital history, pension plan coverage, assets and liabilities, and other similar areas.

SIPP is a continuing series of national panels, each having an average duration of two and one-half years. Panels of approximately 12,500 eligible households are introduced each year in February. Each household is visited three times over this two and one-half year period. Thus, estimates can be based on approximately 25,000 households by combining two concurrent panels. All household members 15 years old and over are interviewed by self-response if possible; proxy response is permitted when household members are not available for interviewing.

Results of the survey are published in the Bureau's P-70 series of the Current Population Reports Household Economic Studies.

survival rate see **relative survival rate.**

swindle [Department of Justice-Bureau of Justice Statistics] A swindle is defined as intentional false representation to obtain money or any other thing of value. Deception is accomplished through the victim's belief in the validity of some statement or object presented by the offender.

See also **confidence game; fraud; Uniform Crime Reports (UCR).**

synthetic natural gas (SNG) [Energy Information Administration] Synthetic natural gas (SNG) is a product resulting from the manufacture, conversion, or reforming of hydrocarbons that may be easily substituted for or interchanged with pipeline-quality natural gas.

system (electric) [Energy Information Administration] An electric power system is composed of physically connected generation, transmission, and distribution facilities operated as an integrated unit under one central management or operating supervision.

T

tall oil [Department of Agriculture-Office of Governmental and Public Affairs] Tall oil is a byproduct from the manufacture of chemical wood pulp and is used in making soaps and various industrial products.

target price (agriculture) [Department of Agriculture-Office of Governmental and Public Affairs] A target price represents a minimum level of price determined by law to provide an economic safety net for farmers. Target prices are sometimes called the guaranteed price level. The target price for a given farm product is based on the cost of production. It becomes the price support level at which the federal government will bolster farm income by making price support payments to qualifying farmers when national average market prices fall below the target.
See also **deficiency payment (agriculture)**.

taxes [Department of Commerce-Bureau of the Census] Taxes are compulsory contributions exacted by a government for public purposes. Employee and employer assessments for retirement and social insurance purposes are classified as insurance trust revenue and are not taxes. All tax revenue is classified as general revenue and comprises amounts received from all taxes imposed by a government, including interest and penalties, but excluding protested amounts and refunds.
See also **license taxes; revenue (Government); sales and gross receipts taxes; severance taxes; special assessments.**

TDSA see **tribal designated statistical area (TDSA).**

technical education [Department of Education-Center for Education Statistics] Technical education is a program of vocational instruction that ordinarily includes the study of the sciences and mathematics underlying a technology as well as the methods, skills, and materials commonly used and the service performed in the technology. Technical education prepares individuals for positions in the occupational area between the skilled craftsman and the professional person.

tenure (housing) [Department of Commerce-Bureau of the Census] Tenure is a Census Bureau concept relating to housing units. All occupied housing units are classified as to their tenure, i.e., whether they are either owner-occupied or renter occupied. A housing unit is owner-occupied if the owner or co-owner lives in the unit, even if the unit is mortgaged or not fully paid for. All other housing units are considered to be renter occupied, regardless of whether or not cash rent is paid for them by a member of the household.
See also **housing unit.**

thrift see **thrift institution.**

thrift institution [Federal Reserve Bank of New York] A thrift institution is a savings and loan association, mutual savings bank, or a credit union. It is a financial institution which deals largely with individuals and provides largely non-business banking-type services. Thrift institutions are sometimes called thrifts.

TIGER [Department of Commerce-Bureau of the Census] TIGER (Topologically Integrated Geographic Encoding and Referencing) is an acronym for the digital, computer readable, geographic data base that automates the mapping and related geographic activities required to support the Census Bureau's census and survey programs.

time deposit [Federal Reserve Bank of New York] A time deposit consists of a certificate of deposit, a time deposit on open account, or a savings deposit. Time deposits are often reported as being in small denominations (less than $100,000) or large denominations (more than $100,000).
　　See also **certificate of deposit (CD); savings deposits; time deposit on open account.**

time deposit on open account [Federal Reserve Bank of New York] A time deposit on open account is a balance of a bank which may be added to or withdrawn from in accordance with a written contract, providing maturity is not less than 14 days after deposit. Time deposits on open account are a component of the overall category time deposits.
　　See also **time deposit.**

time series see **economic time series.**

TJSA see **tribal jurisdiction statistical area (TJSA).**

ton-mile see **revenue ton-mile.**

total hours [Department of Labor-Bureau of Labor Statistics] Total hours is a measure of the total number of hours worked by employees in non-agricultural establishments and is based on data from the Current Employment Statistics (CES) program. Total hours include all hours worked, overtime hours, hours paid for standby or reporting time, and equivalent hours for which employees received pay directly from the employer for sick leave, holidays, vacations, and other leave. Overtime or other premium pay hours are not converted to straight-time equivalent hours.
　　Total hours differ from scheduled hours or hours worked.
　　See also **Current Employment Statistics (CES) program; overtime hours.**

town [Department of Commerce-Bureau of the Census] A town is a minor civil division (MCD) in eight States, and an MCD equivalent in New Jersey, Pennsylvania, and South Dakota. A town is a place in 30 States and the Virgin Islands of the United States.

See also **minor civil division (MCD); place.**

township governments [Department of Commerce-Bureau of the Census] Township governments are organized local governments authorized in State constitutions and statutes and established to provide general government for areas defined without regard to population concentration. Townships include those governments designated as towns in Connecticut, Maine (including organized plantations), Massachusetts, Minnesota, New Hampshire (including organized locations), New York, Rhode Island, Vermont, and Wisconsin, and townships in other States.

Township governments are different from the Census Bureau concept of incorporated place. A township is a minor civil division (MCD) in 16 States.

See also **census geography; incorporated place; minor civil division (MCD).**

tract see **census tract.**

trade and industrial occupation [Department of Education-Center for Education Statistics] Trade and industrial occupation is that branch of vocation education which is concerned with preparing persons for initial employment or with updating or retraining workers in a wide range of trade and industrial occupations. Such occupations are skilled or semi-skilled and are concerned with layout designing, producing, processing, assembling, testing, maintaining, servicing, or repairing any product or commodity.

trade balance see **balance of trade.**

trailer see **housing unit.**

transfer payments [Department of Commerce-Bureau of Economic Analysis] Transfer payments are income payments made for which services are not currently rendered, customarily in monetary form. Government transfer payments to individuals include federal old-age payments, railroad retirement payments, and State unemployment insurance. Business transfer payments to persons include liability payments for personal injury, and corporate gifts to non-profit institutions.

See also **business transfer payment.**

transportation sector see **end-use sector.**

Treasury bill see **Treasury securities.**

Treasury bond see **Treasury securities.**

Treasury note see **Treasury securities.**

Treasury securities [Department of Agriculture-Agricultural Research Service] The U.S. Treasury issues bills, bonds, and notes termed collectively as Treasury securities. Each is sold at a discounted face amount, can be cashed in for full face amount at maturity, and can be traded on the open market.

A *Treasury bill* is a security with a minimum denomination of $10,000 and that matures in one year or less. Treasury bills are a key indicator of what the U.S. Government must pay for money and many other instruments are set to fluctuate in concert with Treasury bill rates.

A *Treasury bond* has a minimum denomination of $1,000 and has a maturity of from ten to thirty years.

A *Treasury note* has a minimum denomination of $1,000 and matures in one to ten years.

trial court [Department of Justice-Bureau of Justice Statistics] A trial court is one in which the primary function is to hear and decide cases.

See also **court.**

tribal designated statistical area (TDSA) [Department of Commerce-Bureau of the Census] A tribal designated statistical area (TDSA) is an area, delineated outside Oklahoma by federally- and State-recognized tribes without a land base or associated trust lands. TDSA's represent areas generally containing the American Indian population over which federally-recognized tribes have jurisdiction and areas in which State tribes provide benefits and services to their members.

See also **American Indian reservation; tribal jurisdiction statistical area (TJSA); trust land.**

tribal jurisdiction statistical area (TJSA) [Department of Commerce-Bureau of the Census] A tribal jurisdiction statistical area (TJSA) is an area, delineated federally-recognized tribes in Oklahoma without a reservation, for which the Census Bureau tabulates data. TJSA's represent areas generally containing the American Indian population over which one or more tribal governments have jurisdiction.

TJSA's replace the "Historic Areas of Oklahoma (excluding urbanized areas)" used in the 1980 census.

See also **American Indian reservation; tribal designated statistical area (TDSA); trust land.**

trust land [Department of Commerce-Bureau of the Census] Trust land is property associated with a particular American Indian reservation or tribe, held in trust by the Federal Government. Trust lands recognized for the 1990 census comprise all tribal trust lands and inhabited individual trust lands located outside of a reservation boundary.

See also **American Indian reservation; tribal designated statistical area (TDSA); tribal jurisdiction statistical area (TJSA).**

type of school see **school type.**

U

UA see **urbanized area (UA).**

UCR see **Uniform Crime Reports (UCR).**

unable to work see **labor force.**

unclassified student [Department of Education-Center for Education Statistics] An unclassified student is one in an institution of higher education who is not a candidate for a degree or other formal award, even though the student is taking higher education courses for credit in regular classes with other students.

undergraduate student [Department of Education-Center for Education Statistics] An undergraduate student is registered in an institution of higher education and is working in a program leading to a baccalaureate degree or other formal award below the baccalaureate level, such as an associate degree.

unemployed person 1. [Department of Labor-Bureau of Labor Statistics] An unemployed person is one who, during a given reference period (a survey week): a) did not work at all; b) was looking for work; and c) was available for work (except for temporary illness). Those who had made specific efforts to find work such as registering at a public or private employment agency, writing letters of application, or canvasing for work within the four week period preceding the survey week are considered to be looking for work. Persons who were waiting to be recalled to a job from which they had been laid off or were waiting to report to a new job within thirty days need not be looking for work to be classified as unemployed. Bureau of Labor Statistics data on unemployed persons comes from the Current Population survey (CPS).

See also **duration of unemployment; reason for unemployment, unemployment.**

2. [Department of Commerce-Bureau of the Census] The Current Population Survey (CPS) is done monthly by the Bureau and is a primary source of unemployment data. However, the Census Bureau began a new, ongoing survey program, the Survey of Income and Program Participation (SIPP) in 1983, which is also a household survey that collects data on employment and unemployment. There is one significant difference in employment and unemployment definitions between CPS and SIPP. For CPS, those who are temporarily absent from a job due to layoff and those who were waiting to begin a new job within 30 days are considered unemployed. Under SIPP methodology, such persons are considered to be employed.

See also **Survey of Income and Program Participation (SIPP).**

unemployment [Department of Labor-Bureau of Labor Statistics] Unemployment is a measure which comprises the total of all unemployed persons. Information on unemployment is gathered through the Current Population Survey (CPS) and is published by the Bureau of Labor Statistics (BLS) as a part of labor force information.

Insured unemployment represents those unemployed persons receiving unemployment compensation.

See also **unemployed person; Current Population Survey (CPS); duration of unemployment; employment; labor force; reason for unemployment.**

unemployment compensation expenditure see **unemployment compensation system.**

unemployment compensation revenue see **unemployment compensation system.**

unemployment compensation system [Department of Commerce-Bureau of the Census] An unemployment compensation system is a State administered plan for compulsory unemployment insurance financed through accumulation of assets. Contributions are collected from employers and employees for use in making cash benefit payments to eligible unemployed persons. Financial data for such systems do not include sickness or disability insurance plans carried out in conjunction with unemployment insurance programs by certain states.

Unemployment insurance contributions collected by a State are deposited in the U.S. Treasury in a trust account maintained for the State. Interest is credited by the U.S. Treasury on balances in State accounts and funds are withdrawn by the State as needed to make unemployment compensation benefit payments.

Amounts reported as *unemployment compensation expenditures* include trust expenditures for benefit payments only. Administration of unemployment compensation is classified as a general expenditure.

Amounts reported as *unemployment compensation revenue* include employer and employee contributions along with interest on trust accounts credited by the U.S. Treasury.

unfinished oil [Energy Information Administration] Unfinished oil is a category of petroleum product which includes all oils requiring further refinery processing except those that require only mechanical blending.

unfounded reported offense see **offenses known to police.**

unfounding see **offenses known to police.**

unfractionated stream [Energy Information Administration] An unfractionated stream is a mixture of unsegregated natural gas liquid components, excluding those in plant condensate. Unfractionated streams are extracted from natural gas.

Uniform Crime Reports (UCR) [Department of Justice-Bureau of Justice Statistics] The Uniform Crime Reports (UCR) are a program administered by the Federal Bureau of Investigation (FBI), the national agency authorized by Congress to act as a national clearinghouse for crime statistics. The FBI receives monthly and annual reports from law enforcement agencies around the country representing approximately 97% of the population. The bulk of information in these reports concerns three areas: *Reported crime* instances of the FBI's crime index offenses are offenses known to police. *Reported arrests* for all crimes include information concerning crimes cleared by arrest, arrests and dispositions of arrested persons, and dispositions of juveniles taken into custody. The third area covers law enforcement agency employee data.

The reported crime and reported arrest data are categorized by geographic area and are presented in relationship to various factors. The FBI publishes its aggregations and analysis of these reports from police agencies in its annual publication Crime in the United States. The UCR program also produces three other major annual publications: Law Enforcement Officers Killed, Assaults of Federal Officers, and Bomb Summary.

Note that the UCR does not publish any data on reported crimes outside the category of Part I offenses, the UCR's grouping of the most serious crimes. Only arrest data is provided for Part II offenses.

See also **arrest; clearance (crime); crime; crime index; offenses known to police; Part I offenses; Part II offenses.**

Uniform Parole Reports (UPR) [Department of Justice-Bureau of Justice Statistics] The Uniform Parole Reports (UPR) are a statistical program sponsored by the Bureau of Justice Statistics and administered by the National Council on Crime and Delinquency. The program publishes statistical information on parolees, parole authority decisions, and parole agency workloads.

United States [Department of Commerce-Bureau of the Census] The United States comprises the 50 States and the District of Columbia. In addition, the outlying areas are treated as statistical equivalents of States for the 1990 census.

See also **outlying areas; State.**

United States Immunization Survey [Department of Health and Human Services-Public Health Service; National Center for Health Statistics] The United States Immunization Survey is used to estimate the immunization level of the nation's child population against vaccine-preventable diseases. From time to time, immunization level data on the adult population are collected as well.

The survey is the result of a contractual agreement between the Center for Preventive Services of the Centers for Disease Control (CDC) and the Bureau of the Census. Estimates for the survey are based on data obtained during the third week of each September for a subsample of households interviewed for the Current Population Survey (CPS). The reporting system contains demographic variables and vaccine history along with disease history when relevant to vaccine history. The scope of the survey covers the fifty States and the District of Columbia. It is published annually by the CDC as <u>United States Immunization Survey</u>.

See also **Current Population Survey (CPS).**

United States population see **population.**

United States Postal Service (USPS) code [Department of Commerce-Bureau of the Census] The United States Postal Service (USPS) codes for States are two-character alphabetic abbreviations.

See also **Federal Information Processing Standards (FIPS) code.**

units in structure (housing) [Department of Commerce-Bureau of the Census] Units in structure refers to the number of housing units in a building. The number of units in a structure includes all the housing units in the structure whether they are occupied or vacant, but the count excludes group quarters and businesses which also may occupy the structure.

See also **structure.**

university [Department of Education-Center for Education Statistics] A university is an institution of higher education consisting of a liberal arts college, a diverse graduate program, and usually two or more professional schools or faculties; and is empowered to confer degrees in various fields of study. In order to maintain trend data, the selection of universities has not been revised by the Center for Education Statistics since 1982.

unmarried-couple household [Department of Commerce-Bureau of the Census] An unmarried-couple household is composed of two unrelated adults of the opposite sex, one of whom is the householder, who share a housing unit with or without the presence of children under 15 years old.

See also **household; unmarried-partner household.**

unmarried-partner household [Department of Commerce-Bureau of the Census] An unmarried-partner household is a household other than a married-couple household that includes a householder and an unmarried partner. An unmarried partner can be of the same sex or of the opposite sex of the householder. An unmarried partner in an unmarried-partner household is an adult who is unrelated to the householder, but shares living quarters and has a close personal relationship with the householder.

See also **household; unmarried-couple household.**

unorg. see **unorganized territory.**

unorganized territory [Department of Commerce-Bureau of the Census] In nine States (Arkansas, Iowa, Kansas, Louisiana, Maine, Minnesota, North Carolina, North Dakota, and South Dakota) some counties contain territory that is not included in a minor civil division (MCD). These areas of unorganized territory are recognized as one or more separate county subdivisions, function as MCD equivalents, and are given a descriptive name, followed by the designation "unorg."

See also **census geography; census subarea; minor civil division (MCD).**

unpaid family worker see **class of worker.**

unrelated individual [Department of Commerce-Bureau of the Census] An unrelated individual is: (1) a householder living alone or with nonrelatives only, (2) a household member who is not related to the householder, or (3) a person living in group quarters who is not an inmate of an institution.

See also **household.**

unsupervised probation see **court probation.**

upland cotton [Department of Agriculture-Office of Governmental and Public Affairs] Upland cotton is a fiber plant developed in the United States from stock native to Mexico and Central America. Upland cotton includes all cotton grown in the continental United States except sea island cotton and American pima cotton.

UPR see **Uniform Parole Reports (UPR).**

urban consumer see **Consumer Price Index (CPI).**

urbanized area (UA) [Department of Commerce-Bureau of the Census] The Census Bureau delineates urbanized areas (UA's) to provide a better separation of urban and rural territory, population, and housing in the vicinity of large places. A UA comprises one or more places, the central place(s); and the adjacent densely settled surrounding territory, the urban fringe. Together the central place(s) and urban fringe have a minimum of 50,000 persons.

The *urban fringe* generally consists of contiguous territory having a density of at least 1,000 persons per square mile. It also includes outlying territory of such density if it was connected to the core of the contiguous area by road and is within 1.5 road miles of that core, or within 5 road miles of the core but separated by water or other undevelopable territory. Other territory with a population density of fewer than 1,000 people per square mile is included in the urban fringe under some circumstances.

See also **census geography; central city; extended city; Metropolitan Area (MA); urban/rural.**

urbanized area central place [Department of Commerce-Bureau of the Census] One or more central places function as the dominant centers of each urbanized area (UA). UA central places include each place entirely within the UA that is a central city of a Metropolitan Area (MA); or each place partially if the place is an extended city. If the UA does not contain an MA central city or is located outside an MA, the UA central place(s) is determined by population size.

See also **census geography; central city; extended city; Metropolitan Area (MA); urbanized area (UA).**

urban/rural [Department of Commerce-Bureau of the Census] Urban and rural are types of area concepts, rather than specific areas outlined on maps. The urban population comprises all persons living in urbanized areas and in places of 2,500 or more inhabitants outside urbanized areas. The rural population consists of everyone else. Therefore, a rural classification need not imply a farm or sparsely settled areas, since a small city or town is rural when it is outside an urbanized area and has fewer than 2,500 inhabitants. The terms urban and rural are independent of metropolitan and non-metropolitan; both urban and rural areas occur inside and outside metropolitan areas.

See also **urbanized area (UA).**

USPS code see **United States Postal Service (USPS) code.**

usual activity see **limitation of activity.**

utility (government) [Department of Commerce-Bureau of the Census] A government owned and operated utility is a water supply system, electric power and light utility, gas supply system or transit system owned and operated by a unit of government.

For purposes of financial reporting by the Census Bureau, government revenues, expenditures and debt relating to government utility facilities leased to other governments or persons are classified as general government activities. As such, *utility expenditures* as reported by the Bureau include only expenditures for the construction of utility facilities, the purchase of facility and related equipment, the production and distribution of commodities or services, and interest on utility debt. Utility expenditures do not include expenditures in connection with administration of utility debt and investments, which are treated as general expenditures. Also excluded is the cost of providing services to the parent government; such costs, when identified, are treated as expenditure for the function served.

Likewise, *utility revenues* include revenues from the sale of utility commodities and services to the public and other governments. Such revenues do not include sales to the parent government, nor from utility fund investments and non-operating property income, both of which are classed as general revenue. Any revenue from taxes, special assessments and intergovernmental aid is classified as general revenues, not utility revenues.

Utility debt covers debt originally issued specifically to finance government owned and operated utilities.

V

vacancy status (housing) [Department of Commerce-Bureau of the Census] The Census Bureau determines the vacancy status of housing units for the decennial census and other intercensal surveys. Vacancy status pertains to both seasonal and year-round vacant housing units.

Seasonal housing units are, by definition, vacant.

Vacant year-round housing units are classified in six categories, according to the reason for their vacancy status: *Vacant, for sale only* re those vacant year-round units offered for sale only. *Vacant, for rent* includes those units for sale or rent at the same time as well as vacant units for rent in a building that is for sale. *Vacant, rented or sold, not occupied* are those vacant units whose renter or owner have not moved in yet. *Vacant, for seasonal, recreational, or occasional use* are those vacant units which are used seasonally on weekends or year-round for other occasional uses, including time sharing units. *Vacant, for migrant workers* are those vacant units intended for occupancy by migratory workers employed in farm work during the crop season. *Other vacant* includes units that do not fall into any of the classifications above, such as those vacant because they are being held for a janitor or caretaker, or those vacant for personal reasons of the owner.

See also **housing unit; occupancy status; seasonal housing unit.**

value (housing) [Department of Commerce-Bureau of the Census] In surveys done by the Bureau of the Census, the value of owner-occupied housing units is the respondent's estimate of the current dollar worth of the property; for vacant units, the value is the price asked for the property.

A property is defined as the house and the land on which it stands. Respondents are asked by the Bureau to estimate the value of the house and land even if they own only the house, or own the house jointly.

Statistics for value are only gathered by the Bureau for owner-occupied condominium units and for specified owner-occupied units.

See also **housing unit; specified owner-occupied housing units.**

value added by manufacturing [Department of Commerce-Bureau of the Census] Value added by manufacturing is a primary measure of manufacturing activity. It is derived by subtracting the cost of materials, supplies, containers, fuel, purchased electricity, and contract work from the value of shipments for products manufactured plus receipts for services rendered. The result of this calculation is then adjusted by the addition of value added by merchandising operations plus the net change in finished goods and work-in-process inventories between the beginning and end of the year.

Value added avoids the duplication in the value of shipments figure which results from the use of products of some establishments as materials for others.

Consequently, it is considered to be the best value measure available for comparing the relative economic importance of manufacturing among industries and geographic areas.

See also **cost of materials; new and used capital expenditures (manufacturing); value of shipments (manufacturing)**.

value-in-place see **new construction**.

value of new construction put in place see **new construction**.

value of shipments (manufacturing) [Department of Commerce-Bureau of the Census] The value of shipments of manufacturing establishments is the amount received or receivable, f.o.b. plant of manufacture, after discounts and allowances, and excluding freight charges and excise taxes. In cases where the products in a given industry are customarily delivered by the manufacturing establishment (e.g., bakery products, fluid milk, soft drinks), the value of shipments is based on the delivered price of the goods rather than the f.o.b. plant of manufacture price.

value-put-in-place see **new construction**.

VFR see **visual flight rules (VFR)**.

victim [Department of Justice-Bureau of Justice Statistics] A victim is a person who has suffered death, physical or mental anguish, or loss of property as the result of an actual or attempted criminal offense committed by another person. In law, a victim can be a single human being or a group of human beings considered as a unit.

See also **victimization**.

victimization [Department of Justice-Bureau of Justice Statistics] In National Crime Survey (NCS) terminology, victimization is the harming of any single victim in a criminal incident. Harm, in this definition, means at minimum physical injury, economic loss, or psychological distress. The NCS offenses cover attempts as well as completed acts, including instances where no physical or economic harm has resulted.

In NCS methodology a critical distinction is made between a victimization and a criminal incident. The procedures by which data relating to these two distinct events are compiled differ significantly. Only one criminal incident is recorded for any continuous sequence of criminal behavior, even though the incident may contain acts which may constitute two or more NCS offenses or involve two or more separate victims. One victimization is recorded for each separate victim harmed as a result of a given criminal incident.

As a result, the number of household victimizations will be equal to the number of criminal incidents of household crimes, since each incident is treated as having a single unique household as victim. However, the number of recorded victimizations of persons can be greater than the number of recorded incidents of personal crimes, because more than one person can be victimized in what is identified as a single incident of a personal crime. For example, where two persons have been robbed in the same event, two victimizations of persons are recorded, and one criminal incident.

The NCS represents a different methodological approach for measuring crime than the Uniform Crime Reports (UCR).

See also **criminal incident; household crimes; National Crime Survey (NCS); personal larceny with contact; personal larceny without contact; Uniform Crime Reports (UCR).**

village [Department of Commerce-Bureau of the Census] A village is a minor civil division (MCD) equivalent in New Jersey, Ohio, South Dakota, and Wisconsin. In 19 States, a village is a place.

See also **minor civil division (MCD); place.**

violent crime [Department of Justice-Bureau of Justice Statistics] In Uniform Crime Reports (UCR) terminology, violent crime refers to the first four Part I offenses included in the crime index. The four UCR violent crimes are: murder and nonnegligent manslaughter (UCR 1a); forcible rape (UCR 2); robbery (UCR 3); and aggravated assault (UCR 4a-d).

See also **aggravated assault; crime index; forcible rape; index crime; murder and nonnegligent manslaughter; Part I offenses; robbery; Uniform Crime Reports (UCR).**

visits to dentists see **dental visit.**

visits to doctors see **physician visit.**

visual flight rules (VFR) [Department of Transportation-Federal Aviation Administration] Visual flight rules (VFR) are rules governing flights where the pilot does not depend upon instruments for takeoff, flight, and landing. The Federal Aviation Administration reports some aviation statistics based on whether the aircraft was operating under VFR.

See also **instrument flight rules (IFR).**

visually handicapped see **handicapped.**

vocational education   [Department of Education-Center for Education Statistics] Vocational education is a program of studies designed to prepare students for employment in one or more semiskilled, skilled, or technical occupations.

See also **technical education; trade and industrial occupation.**

voluntarily idle (labor force) see **labor force.**

voluntary hospital see **hospital.**

voting age population [Department of Commerce-Bureau of the Census] The voting age population consists of all persons over the age of 18, the voting age for federal elections.

Data users should note that the voting age population does include a small number of persons who, although of voting age, are not eligible to vote such as resident aliens, and inmates of institutions.

The voting age population is estimated in even numbered years by the Bureau of the Census, and is reported for various geographic areas.

voting district (VTD) [Department of Commerce-Bureau of the Census] A voting district (VTD) is any of a variety of types of areas established by State and local governments for purposes of elections, such as election districts or precincts. States outline the boundaries of VTD's around groups of whole census blocks on census maps. In the 1980 census, VTD's were referred to as "election precincts."

See also **census block; census geography.**

VTD see **voting district (VTD).**

W

wage rates [Department of Labor-Bureau of Labor Statistics] Wage rates are the stipulated amount of compensation paid to employees for a given unit of work or time.

See also **area wage survey; industry wage surveys; Engineering News-Record (ENR) indexes; wages.**

wage surveys see **area wage survey; industry wage surveys.**

wages [Department of Labor-Bureau of Labor Statistics] In the Bureau of Labor Statistics' occupational and industrial wage surveys, wages are the rate of pay for individual workers, excluding premium pay for overtime and for work on weekends, holidays, and late shifts. Wages also exclude performance bonuses and lump-sum payments of the type negotiated in the auto and aerospace industries. Also excluded are profit sharing payments, attendance bonuses, Christmas or year-end bonuses, and other non-production bonuses. Pay increases under cost-of-living allowances clauses and incentive payments are included.

For workers paid under piece work or other types of production incentive pay plans, an hourly earnings figure serves as a proxy for the wage rate; it is computed by dividing straight-time earnings over a time period by corresponding hours worked.

Unless stated otherwise, wage rates reported do not include tips or allowances for the value of meals, room, uniforms, etc. The earnings figure thus represented by wages is cash wages, prior to deductions for Social Security and income taxes, savings bonds, premium payments for group insurance, meals, room or uniform, and after the exclusion of premium pay for overtime, weekend, holiday, or late shift work.

Hours shown for salaried occupations relate to standard weekly hours for which the employee receives regular straight-time salary.

This concept of wages is used in all of the Bureau's occupational and industrial wage surveys, which include area wage surveys, industry wage surveys, and the National Survey of Professional, Administrative, Technical, and Clerical Pay.

See also **Engineering News-Record** (ENR) indexes.

wages and salaries [Department of Commerce-Bureau of Economic Analysis] Wages and salaries are the monetary remuneration of employees, including the compensation of corporate officers; commissions, tips, and bonuses; and receipts in-kind which represent income to the recipients.

Supplements to wages and salaries consist of employer contributions for social insurance and other labor income, primarily employer contributions to private pension and private welfare funds, including privately administered workers' compensation funds.

Wages and salaries and supplements to wages and salaries combine to form compensation of employees, an income-side component of the National Income Product Account (NIP). Compensation of employees, along with other income-side components of NIP, are summed to measure the Gross National Product (GNP).

See also **compensation of employees; Gross National Product (GNP); National Income Product Accounts (NIPA).**

water area [Department of Commerce-Bureau of the Census] Water area is the size, in square kilometers or square miles, of the water in a geographic entity. Water includes inland, coastal, Great Lakes, and territorial water.

Inland water includes lakes, reservoirs, ponds, rivers, creeks, canals, and streams.

Coastal and *territorial water* includes the portions of the oceans and related large embayments, the Gulf of Mexico, and the Caribbean Sea that belong to the United States and its possessions.

For the 1980 census, water area included inland water area only.

watt (W) [Energy Information Administration] A watt is an electrical unit of power. A watt is the rate of energy transfer equivalent to one ampere flowing under a pressure of one volt at unity power factor.

watthour (Wh) [Energy Information Administration] A watthour is an electrical energy unit of measure equal to one watt of power supplied to, or taken from, an electric circuit steadily for one hour.

wax [Energy Information Administration] Wax is a solid or semi-solid material derived from petroleum distillates or residues. Wax is a light-colored, more or less translucent crystalline mass, slightly greasy to the touch, consisting of a mixture of hydrocarbons in which the paraffin series predominates.

As a category, wax includes all marketable wax whether crude scale or fully refined. Wax is used primarily as an industrial coating for surface protection.

well [Energy Information Administration] A well is a hole drilled for the purpose of finding or producing crude oil or natural gas or providing services related to the production of crude oil or natural gas. Wells are classified as oil wells, gas wells, dry holes, stratigraphic or core tests, or service wells.

wet natural gas see **natural gas; natural gas, wet.**

Wh see **watthour (Wh).**

wheeling charge (electric utilities) [Energy Information Administration] A wheeling charge is an amount charged by one electrical system to transmit the energy of, and for, another system or systems.

See also **wheeling service (electric utilities)**.

wheeling service (electric utilities) [Energy Information Administration] Wheeling service is the movement of electricity from one system to another over transmission facilities of intervening systems. Wheeling service contracts can be established between two or more systems.

white-collar crime [Department of Justice-Bureau of Justice Statistics] White-collar crime is non-violent crime for financial gain committed by means of deception by persons utilizing their special occupational skills and opportunities and whose occupational status is entrepreneurial, professional, or semi-professional. Non-violent crime also includes crimes committed for financial gain utilizing deception which are committed by anyone having special technical and/or professional knowledge of business and/or government, but irrespective of the person's occupation. Actual instances of while collar crime are prosecuted as specific offenses defined in statutes, typically under headings such as theft, fraud, and embezzlement.

wholesale price index see **Producer Price Index (PPI)**.

wholesale trade [Department of Commerce-Bureau of the Census] The Census Bureau classifies establishments engaged in wholesale trade by type of operation, ownership of the business, ownership of the goods sold, or character of the principal transactions. Such distinctions are used in reporting data collected from the quinquennial economic censuses. There are three major categories of wholesale establishment.

Merchant wholesalers are those establishments primarily engaged in buying and selling merchandise on their own account. These include wholesale merchants or jobbers, industrial distributors, voluntary group wholesalers, retail cooperative warehouses, terminal and country grain elevators, farm products assemblers, wholesale cooperative associations, and petroleum bulk plants and terminals operated by non-refining companies.

Manufacturers' sales branches and offices are those establishments maintained by manufacturing, refining, and mining companies apart from their own plants or mines for marketing their products at wholesale. Branch stores selling to household consumers and individuals are classified in retail trade. Sales branches and sales offices located at plants and at administrative offices are included when separate records are available.

Agents, brokers, and commission merchants are those establishments whose operators are in business for themselves and are primarily engaged in selling or buying goods for others. Included are auction companies, import agents, export agents, selling agents, merchandise brokers, and commission merchants.

See also **economic censuses; establishment.**

willful homicide see **criminal homicide.**

work disability [Department of Commerce-Bureau of the Census] Persons who have a health condition which limits the kind or amount of work they can do are said to have a work disability.

A person is limited in the kind of work he or she can do if the person has a health condition which restricts his or her choice of jobs. A person is limited in the amount of work if he or she is not able to work at a full-time (35 hours per week or more) job or business.

See also **disability.**

work in process [Department of Commerce-Bureau of Economic Analysis] Work in process represents the partially finished products of a manufacturing or processing concern.

work-loss day see **disability day.**

work stoppage [Department of Labor-Bureau of Labor Statistics] For statistical reporting purposes, a work stoppage is a strike or lockout involving 1,000 workers or more which lasts one full shift or longer.

worker see **class of worker; hours of work.**

working gas (energy) [Energy Information Administration] Working gas is the total volume of gas in a storage reservoir that is in excess of the base gas.

working supervisor [Department of Labor-Bureau of Labor Statistics] A working supervisor is an employee of an establishment who spends 20% or more of their time at work similar to that performed by workers under their supervision.

workmen's compensation expenditure see **workmen's compensation system.**

workmen's compensation revenue see **workmen's compensation system.**

workmen's compensation system [Department of Commerce-Bureau of the Census] A workmen's compensation system is a State administered plan for compulsory accident and injury insurance for workers. It is funded through the accumulation of assets from contributions collected from employers for financing cash benefits to eligible injured workers.

Amounts reported as expenditures for such systems consist of cash benefit payments to covered injured workers, and excludes State contributions to the system on behalf of State employees and expenditures for administration of the system.

Amounts reported as revenues for such systems include employer premiums, assessments and other contributions, excluding contributions for State government for State employees covered by the system.

X

Y

year-round housing unit see **housing unit.**

years of potential life lost [Department of Health and Human Services-Public Health Service; National Center for Health Statistics] Years of potential life lost is a measure which is calculated over the age range from birth to 65 years. The number of deaths for each age group is multiplied by the years of life lost (the difference between 65 and the midpoint of the age group) and then years of potential life lost are summed for all age groups.

Years of potential life lost is calculated as a part of mortality statistics.

yield (agriculture) see **economic maximum yield (agriculture).**

youthful offender [Department of Justice-Bureau of Justice Statistics] A youthful offender is a person adjudicated in criminal court who may be above the statutory age limit for juveniles but is below a specified upper limit, and for whom special correctional commitments and special record sealing procedures are made available by statute.

Z

ZIP code [Department of Commerce-Bureau of the Census] A ZIP code is an administrative unit established by the United States Postal Service (USPS) for the distribution of mail. ZIP codes serve addresses for the most efficient delivery of mail, and therefore generally do not respect political or census statistical area boundaries. ZIP codes usually do not have clearly identifiable boundaries, often service a continually changing area, and change periodically to meet postal requirements, and do not cover all the land area of the United States.

Some 1990 census products are tabulated by ZIP code.

See also **United States Postal Service (USPS) code.**

zona urbana [Department of Commerce-Bureau of the Census] A zona urbana is a census designated place in Puerto Rico.

See also **census designated place.**

BIBLIOGRAPHY

<u>1980 Census of Population and Housing: Users Guide</u>, (PHC80-R1-A). Washington, DC: U.S. Department of Commerce, Bureau of the Census, 1982.

<u>1980 Supplement to Economic Indicators: Historical and Descriptive Background</u>. Washington, DC: U.S. Congress, Joint Economic Committee, Council of Economic Advisors, 1980.

<u>1987 Factbook of Agriculture</u> (Miscellaneous Publication # 1063). Washington, DC: U.S. Department of Agriculture, Office of Government and Public Affairs, 1987.

"A User's Guide to BEA Information: Publications, Computer Tapes, Diskettes, and Other Information Services." <u>Survey of Current Business</u>. Washington, DC: U.S. Department of Commerce, Bureau of Economic Analysis, February, 1987.

<u>Annual Energy Review, 1985</u>. Washington, DC: U.S. Energy Information Administration, 1985.

<u>Annual Housing Survey, 1984</u>. Washington, DC: U.S. Department of Commerce, Bureau of the Census, 1987.

<u>Annual Survey of Manufactures, 1986</u>. Washington, DC: U.S. Department of Commerce, Bureau of the Census, 1987.

"Appendix A: Area Classifications." <u>Summary Population and Housing Characteristics, CPH1</u>. Washington, DC: U.S. Department of Commerce, Bureau of the Census, 1991.

"Appendix B: Definitions of Subject Characteristics." <u>Summary Population and Housing Characteristics, CPH1</u>. Washington, DC: U.S. Department of Commerce, Bureau of the Census, 1991.

<u>BLS Handbook of Methods</u> (Bulletin # 2285). Washington, DC: U.S. Department of Labor, Bureau of Labor Statistics, 1988.

<u>Business Conditions Digest</u>. Washington, DC: U.S. Department of Commerce, Bureau of Economic Analysis, (monthly).

<u>Business Statistics 1986: A Supplement to the "Survey of Current Business"</u>. Washington, DC: U.S. Department of Commerce, Bureau of Economic Analysis, 1987.

Census of Wholesale Trade, 1982. Washington, DC: U.S. Department of Commerce, Bureau of the Census, 1984.

Consumer Expenditure Survey, 1984. Washington, DC: U.S. Department of Labor, Bureau of Labor Statistics, 1986.

CPI Detailed Report. Washington, DC: U.S. Department of Labor, Bureau of Labor Statistics, (monthly).

Current Construction Reports—C20. Washington, DC: U.S. Department of Commerce, Bureau of the Census, (monthly).

Current Construction Reports—C21. Washington, DC: U.S. Department of Commerce, Bureau of the Census, (monthly).

Current Construction Reports—C25. Washington, DC: U.S. Department of Commerce, Bureau of the Census, (monthly).

Current Construction Reports—C30. Washington, DC: U.S. Department of Commerce, Bureau of the Census, (monthly).

Data Dictionary, STF1A File. Washington, DC: U.S. Department of Commerce, Bureau of the Census, 1991.

Demographic Surveys Division Project Descriptions. Washington, DC: U.S. Department of Commerce, Bureau of the Census, 1987.

Dictionary of Criminal Justice Data Terminology. Washington, DC: U.S. Department of Justice, Bureau of Justice Statistics, 1981.

Dictionary of Economic and Statistical Terms. Washington, DC: U.S. Department of Commerce, Social and Economic Statistics Administration, 1972.

Dictionary of Occupational Titles, 1977. Washington, DC: U.S. Department of Labor, 1977.

Digest of Education Statistics, 1987. Washington, DC: U.S. Department of Education, National Center for Education Statistics, 1987.

Economic Indicators. Washington, DC: U.S. Congress, Joint Economic Committee, Council of Economic Advisors, (monthly).

Education Division Combined Glossary: Terms and Definitions from Handbooks of State Educational Records and Reports Series. Washington, DC: U.S. Department of Health, Education, and Welfare, 1975.

Electric Power Annual, 1985. Washington, DC: U.S. Energy Information Administration, 1985.

"Federal Sources of Family Economic Data." Family Economic Review. Washington, DC: U.S. Department of Agriculture, Statistical Research Service, 1986, No. 1.

Government Finances – GF 3, 1985. Washington, DC: U.S. Department of Commerce, Bureau of the Census, 1987.

Government Finances – GF 5, 1985. Washington, DC: U.S. Department of Commerce, Bureau of the Census, 1987.

Guide to the 1982 Economic Censuses and Related Statistics. Washington, DC: U.S. Department of Commerce, Bureau of the Census, 1985.

Handbook of Cyclical Indicators: A Supplement to Business Conditions Digest. Washington, DC: U.S. Department of Commerce, Bureau of Economic Analysis, 1984.

Handbook of Labor Statistics, 1985. Washington, DC: U.S. Department of Labor, Bureau of Labor Statistics, 1986.

Health, United States, 1988. Washington, DC: U.S. Department of Health and Human Services, Public Health Service, 1987 .

Highway Statistics, 1985. Washington, DC: U.S. Department of Transportation, Federal Highway Administration, 1986.

Hospital Statistics. Chicago, IL: American Hospital Association, 1986.

Mental Health, United States, 1987. Washington, DC: U.S. Department of Health and Human Services, Public Health Service, 1987.

Methodology Papers: U.S. National Income and Product Accounts – An Introduction to National Economic Accounting. Washington, DC: U.S. Department of Commerce, Bureau of Economic Analysis, 1987.

Methodology Papers: U.S. National Income and Product Accounts—Corporate Profits. Washington, DC: U.S. Department of Commerce, Bureau of Economic Analysis, 1987.

Methodology Papers: U.S. National Income and Product Accounts—Foreign Transactions. Washington, DC: U.S. Department of Commerce, Bureau of Economic Analysis, 1987.

Methodology Papers: U.S. National Income and Product Accounts—GNP: An Overview of Source Data and Estimating Methods. Washington, DC: U.S. Department of Commerce, Bureau of Economic Analysis, 1987.

Natural Gas Annual, 1985. Washington, DC: U.S. Energy Information Administration, 1985.

Occupational Employment in Manufacturing Industries. Washington, DC: U.S. Department of Labor, Bureau of Labor Statistics, 1985.

Occupational Injuries and Illnesses in the United States by Industry, 1986. Washington, DC: U.S. Department of Labor, Bureau of Labor Statistics, 1988.

Scope and Methods of the Statistical Reporting Service (Miscellaneous Publication #1308). Washington, DC: U.S. Department of Agriculture, Statistical Reporting Service, 1983.

Social Security Handbook, Tenth Edition. Washington, DC: U.S. Department of Health and Human Services, Social Security Administration, 1988.

Standard Industrial Classification Manual. Washington, DC: U.S. Executive Office of the President, Office of Management and Budget, 1972.

Standard Occupational Classification Manual. Washington, DC: U.S. Executive Office of the President, Office of Management and Budget, 1981.

State Energy Data Report, 1960-1985. Washington, DC: U.S. Energy Information Administration, 1985.

Statfacts: Understanding Federal Reserve Statistical Reports. New York: Federal Reserve Bank of New York, 1981.

Statistical Handbook of Aviation, 1985. Washington, DC: U.S. Department of Transportation, Federal Aviation Administration, 1986.

Supplement to Producer Price Indexes Data for 1986. Washington, DC: U.S. Department of Labor, Bureau of Labor Statistics, 1987.

Survey of Current Business. Washington, DC: U.S. Department of Commerce, Bureau of Economic Analysis, (monthly).

"Terms, Concepts, and Acronyms in Family Financial Planning." Family Economic Review. Washington, DC: U.S. Department of Agriculture, Statistical Research Service, 1986, No. 1.

Understanding United States Foreign Trade Data. Washington, DC: U.S. Department of Commerce, International Trade Administration, (undated).